Thank you for great area —

Anne (McMullen) Belliveau

Small Moments in Time
The Story of Alberta's Big West Country

Upper North Saskatchewan River Corridor,
Shunda Basin, Brazeau Collieries, and Nordegg

Anne (McMullen) Belliveau

Detselig Enterprises Ltd.

Calgary, Alberta, Canada

Small Moments in Time
© 1999 Anne Belliveau

Canadian Cataloguing in Publication Data

Belliveau, Anne,
Small moments in time

Includes bibliographical references and index.
ISBN 1-55059-178-9

1. Alberta—History. 2. Nordegg, Martin, 1868-1948—Biography. 3. Nordegg (Alta.)—History. 4. Nordegg (Alta.)—Biography. I. Title.
FC3699.N67B44   1999   971.23'3   C99-910054-8
F1079.5.N67B44   1999

Detselig Enterprises Ltd.
210-1220 Kensington Rd. N.W.
Calgary, Alberta T2N 3P5
Phone: (403) 283-0900/Fax: (403) 283-6947
e-mail: temeron@telusplanet.net
www.temerondetselig.com

Detselig Enterprises Ltd. appreciates the financial support for our 1999 publishing program, provided by Canadian Heritage and other sources.

Detselig Enterprises Ltd. also appreciates the support provided by the Alberta Historic Resources Foundation towards the publication of this book.

All rights reserved. No part of this book may be reproduced in any form or by any means without permission in writing from the publisher.

Printed in Canada
ISBN: 1-55059-178-9
SAN 115-0324

Cover design by Dean Macdonald.

In Memory

*Mom and Dad,
for you, with love.*

*Martha (Fallow) McMullen (d. 1976)
who filled the house with laughter and song, and who taught
her children to reach for the stars*

and

*Arthur "Mac" McMullen (d. 1991)
who shared with his children both his love and his knowledge of this land, and
who taught them to keep their feet firmly planted on the ground*

and for

*Dr. Howard Palmer (d. 1991)
who believed in this project.*

*God Bless;
Requiescat in pace.*

When the world intrudes too much
. . . too often,
I escape . . .
Into my special places,
Bright spaces,
Small moments in time.

You cannot reach me then;
I am no longer here.

                                                A.Mc.B.

Contents

Preface and Acknowledgements . . . . *vii*
Introduction . . . . *xiii*
The Land Before Time 15
As Long as the Sun Shines 27
Native and Immigrant 35
West Country Legend: The "Missing" Fort 45
Through the Shining Mountains 53
Explorers, Prospectors, and Other Visitors 63
Nordegg and the Changing Face of the West 71
An Unusual Alliance – Mackenzie and Mann, and Martin Nordegg . . . 79
Unfolding the Dream 89
Nordegg: A Town is Born 99
Dreams and Reality 113
Nordegg – Its People 127
The Brazeau Collieries Mining Operation 141
Challenge and Change 153
Turning Points 165
Through the Years 179
Bright Spaces, Special Places – The Upper North Saskatchewan River Corridor Today 191
Notes and Additional References 209

Preface and Acknowledgements

*H*istory is people – people who knew love and hate and fear, who laughed and cried, who struggled with the land and the elements and, out of it all, carved lives for themselves and for their children. Each person remembers different things, and even the same things differently. That is why it is so important for history to have many, many stories, so that out of all the memories there arises a picture which tells the complete tale. I have tried to find the total picture of Nordegg and the Upper North Saskatchewan River Corridor by reading everything I could find written about it, and by talking with a great many people who were part of this land, or who contributed in some way to the story of this area. But it is far from complete . . .

*I*n retrospect, I realize that I have been researching this book all my life. Growing up in the Nordegg region, with the entire Upper North Saskatchewan River Corridor as a playground, this country has become more than familiar – it is part of me. I was fortunate that my parents could answer nearly all the questions I asked them and fill in many of the unasked details as well. I always had the desire to know more about this land, and where it fits into the overall scheme of history, and of the world.

Nordegg has been home to a number of members of my extended family. Beginning in 1913, one or more family members resided in Nordegg until the town closed in 1955. In 1912-13, my great-uncle Gilbert McKenzie built trestles for the Canadian Northern Western Railway line to the Brazeau Collieries. In 1913, he was hired by Brazeau Collieries as a timber boss and Nordegg's sawyer. Over the years, some of his children, grandchildren, and now great-grandchildren, remained involved in this region. Gilbert's son Allan McKenzie was one-half of the firm of Baird and McKenzie of Red Deer, the construction firm contracted to build Nordegg's business district and the first houses.

When Nordegg's Bighorn Trading Company opened in 1914, my uncle Duncan Stewart became an accountant there. In 1918, after both Mom's parents had died, she moved to Nordegg to live with the Stewarts and later became stenographer and secretary at the Brazeau Collieries Mine Office. She met Martin Nordegg when he visited there in 1922. Mom was a marvellous story-teller, and from her I heard many stories of the early days in Nordegg. She was able to answer and explain many of the questions I had about people, places, and events.

Dad (Arthur "Mac" McMullen) came to Nordegg from England in 1926, after taking training in mining engineering at the University College of Nottingham and apprenticing at Whitehaven Collieries. When he came to Nordegg, he started work in the mines as a timberman's helper. In 1928 he became Chief Engineer and Surveyor, and over the years he took on a series of jobs. Dad loved learning for its own sake, and he gradually built a commanding and comprehensive knowledge and understanding of all aspects of the Brazeau Collieries complex. For a number of years he continued surveying, drafting, and assaying. Part of his duties included lot selection for house construction, and house assignment to residents. When briquetting was instituted in the late 1930s, he oversaw the operation. After the 1941 mine explosion inquiry was completed, he was appointed Mine Manager of Number 2 Mine and, in 1945, he also became Manager of Surface Operations, thus becoming technical operations manager of Brazeau Collieries. In later years he also became the town Magistrate. In 1950, when the Brazeau Collieries surface complex burned, Dad was given a leave of absence from Brazeau Collieries in order to work as consulting engineer with Riverside Ironworks during planning and preparation of the new surface structures at Brazeau Collieries. These are the briquetting structures which still stand at the mine site and which, on August 25, 1993, were designated an Alberta Provincial Historic Resource.

As a child, during the summer months I often accompanied Dad on trips to the Bighorn and Blackstone areas, where Brazeau Collieries had other coal holdings. From him I learned much about the history of Brazeau Collieries, as well as some of the geology of the country, and how to recognize shale and coal strata. Years later, when I began compiling information on Nordegg and the Brazeau Collieries, he gave me his collection of books, pamphlets, blueprints, diagrams, maps, and pictures. He also helped me understand the massive undertaking of removing coal from beneath the ground and making it into briquettes.

As children, my brother Art and I travelled with Dad from where the coal was mined underground, while he explained each process required until the coal, as briquettes, was loaded into boxcars on the Ottumwa loader. He expected us to listen, and to grasp the concepts of the mining process. I just wish I had paid more attention, and had a greater ability to grasp all the intricacies he showed us. Impressions of these excursions certainly remain vivid, even if technical detail does not.

A number of members of Dad's family also lived in Nordegg. His mother (Mary Ann McMullen) lived with us for a number of years. His sister Mary, her husband Frank (Hap) Wall, and their infant son moved to Nordegg in the late 1940s, and Hap worked for Guido Blasetti as mechanic at the Brazeau Motors service station. Dad's other sister, Sara, spent some time nursing at the Nordegg hospital during the late 1940s. All these family connections to the town helped give me insights into, and understanding of, many areas of Nordegg activities and life.

I got a complete picture of religion. Mom loved to sing. She had had professional voice training and, prior to coming to Nordegg, she attended whatever church had the most active choir. When she moved to Nordegg she became a strong member of the Protestant congregation, teaching Sunday School and singing in the choir. Then she became a Roman Catholic when she and Dad were married. I grew up with one foot in each world, so to speak.

Dad, through active participation in religious activities, had a strong influence in preventing problems between Catholic and Protestant congregations, as often happened in resource-based towns. Except for Dad, all senior management were Protestant. A large number of the labor force were Catholic. Dad became their representative, as needed, to ensure equality in funding, supplies and maintenance.

In recent years I have become much more aware of the high regard and affection a large number of ex-Nordeggers felt for him. Out of it all, there seems to arise a picture of a man whose influence was felt in the lives of many. It is my belief that, through his respect and love for all people, his highly developed sense of fairness and justice, and his strong work ethic, he was one of the people whose influence helped to shape the community of Nordegg into the cohesive unit that it was.

Through Dad and Mom, I grew up steeped in the knowledge of the country, the mining operation, the town, and the people; I couldn't have had a better apprenticeship in researching this book. However, it is with surprise that I realize just how long I have been compiling information for it. I began formal research in the fall of 1971, when the Glenbow Archives still was located in Central Park. My youngest son, a preschooler at the time, accompanied me there.

Outside of the journals of early explorers, little has been published about the Upper North Saskatchewan River Corridor. Research has been long and arduous, covering material in numerous archives, and information gathered from as far away as Berlin, Germany. A special thank-you to Alberta Historic Resources Foundation for funding ($3000) to do research at the National Archives, Ottawa, and other research in Toronto, Montreal, and Halifax during the summer of 1988 and, a decade later, for a grant to assist in publication costs of the book.

In 1986-87, I received a sabbatical leave from the Calgary Board of Education and, during that year at the University of Calgary, I met two excellent historians and extremely helpful individuals – Dr. Howard Palmer and Dr. Don Smith. They were of inestimable help to me in shaping the direction and contents of this book, and in guiding and encouraging me in this project when the going got rough. I deeply regret that Howard Palmer did not live to see its completion.

A thank you also goes to University of Calgary archaeologists (in 1987) Dr. R. Forbis and Dr. B. Reeves; Jim Dolph, petroleum geologist (retired) and a personal friend; to the staff and Directors of the Nordegg Historic Heritage Interest Group (now the Nordegg Historical Society), especially Rita Sehn of Rocky Mountain House, who helped with research at the Public Archives in Edmonton; to the staff at Rocky Mountain House Historic Park for giving me full access to their research materials, and for locating the various papers I needed.

Some information contained herein was first published in the *Rocky Mountaineer* "Nordegg Memories" column, for which I frequently wrote. Thank you to the Mazza family, who publish the *Mountaineer*, for being so understanding when I insisted upon retaining copyright.

Thanks to Bob Bachelder, University of Calgary Library, Maps Division, who knew exactly what I was searching for when I told him the folklore of Martin Nordegg "lifting" the plan of "the C.N.R. township in Montreal" to use for the town of Nordegg. It was he who helped me see that the dates and the partnership information supported joint use of the plan. A 1912 Montreal city map confirmed the similarities in design. A 1988 visit to Mount Royal supported this. Norman Lowe, CNR historian (retired), Montreal, also helped to put this story together, and he supplied copies of maps and information. This small section of the total picture, contained in chapter 10, took over 10 months of research.

Thanks also to Barry Potyondi of Great Plains Research, who simplified my task by turning over to me his research material from the Nordegg Feasibility Study for the Department of Culture and for the Nordegg Historic Heritage Interest Group; and to John and Maria Koch – John has been very generous in giving me access to material he has gathered in his research on Martin Nordegg. In return, I hope I have assisted his research as well.

The large, extended "family" of ex-Nordeggers also have given me a tremendous amount of support and guidance in compiling information, and special thanks go to those who fielded so many of my questions.

Milio Marasco, who helped my understanding of the Native/White relationships in Nordegg and who gave me a great deal of information on the Brazeau Collieries Timber Camps; Zupi D'Amico, who was both Brazeau Collieries' and Kananaskis' last Mine Manager, took over the task of helping me to understand technical detail after Dad's death and also gave me a large amount of the Kananaskis information.

Fred Kidd (now deceased), son of Stuart Kidd, gave me a great deal of information on his father's involvement with the town and with the Stoneys; Virginia Kidd, custodian of the Kidd family papers, was very kind in allowing me to have access to some of Stuart's private papers.

Guido Blasetti helped me to understand the role of the Italian community in Nordegg, and he gave me information on the regions of Italy from which immigrants to Nordegg had come. Rudolf Dibus, who was a briquette plant foreman, answered many questions on briquetting and about the Slavic Society.

Tony Mele is one of a number of ex-Nordeggers who are at home anywhere in the Upper North Saskatchewan River Corridor. He was invaluable in locating and explaining some of the major Indian trails near Nordegg.

Sincere thanks to Nellie Letcher (deceased) for filling in so much of the "human interest" detail of Nordegg's earliest years.

I am very grateful to various other individuals, some of whom now are deceased, who supplied photographs, answered numerous questions, and who spoke with me at length about Nordegg and area topics: Art McMullen Jr., Father Tony Dittrich, Red and Helen Jahelka, Rudolph Dibus, Dennis Morley, John Galloway, Ken and Nita Janigo, Serena and Bob Duncan, Maggie and Alfred Morris, Archie and Vera Pasechnik, Jim Colosimo, Elsie Veenstra, Gino and Kay Poscente, Helen (Letcher) Ross, Guy Blasetti, Joe Baker, Reg Wickens, Charlie Abraham, Clayton Grosso, Ed McKenzie, Martha Slaymaker, Johnny and Olga Janigo. And the list goes on and on. Also thank you to Tom Wilson III for the use of his scrapbooks and materials, and for his patience in the long wait before getting them back.

When the memoirs of Martin Nordegg, edited by Dr. T. D. Regehr, were published in 1971, many ex-Nordeggers could not recognize "their" town as they had known it. Most of them by that time were second or third generation Nordeggers, and the severe social structure and the red-light tent town were two elements almost completely unknown to people who had grown up in Nordegg. Yet these were two items pounced upon by book reviewers of the early 1970s. One must keep in mind that Martin Nordegg left the town in June, 1915, while the town was in its infancy. The town went through numerous, and often fairly rapid, changes over the next two decades.

Martin Nordegg wrote his memoirs during a later period of his life, after he left Canada in 1936 and settled in New York City. While there is no doubt that his memory served him very well as he recorded the events and impressions of his time in the west, a few minor details appear to have become blurred. One specific example is his statement, "Next to the pretty and comfortable officials' cottages we built the hospital, the policeman's cottage, and the official's club . . ." (*Memoirs*, Regehr, p. 195). The hospital actually was the last building to the west on Marcelle Avenue, after which there was a wide ravine cut through by Cabin (Mine) Creek. On the next hill, where the Brazeau Collieries plant was situated, and over a mile away from the hospital, was located the policeman's cottage and the officials' club, which very early in the town's history was converted into another home, and west of the plant site were the remainder of the officials' cottages. It was possible to skirt this divisional ravine by way of the Brazeau's logging road that was south, and above, the hospital and the mine site, but the separating span was still considerable. It is quite understandable that time and distance caused some blurring of detail in Martin Nordegg's memories.

Some journalists and researchers, who wrote about the Brazeau Collieries and Nordegg town after Martin Nordegg's memoirs were published, used material from this book in such a way that it was considered the total and long-term summation of Nordegg. In some cases, material was added from very comprehensive but generalized information on the Alberta coal industry and Alberta coal towns. Of course, in some instances there were strong similarities among Alberta coal areas, but in other cases there were marked differences. An assessment of Nordegg, or of any coal town, based on the generalized picture of Alberta coal towns, is incomplete.

Many ex-Nordeggers feel that this is what has happened with the public understanding of what Nordegg really was. One individual who was more outspoken about it than most was Nellie Letcher, who arrived in Nordegg in the summer of 1914 as a four year old girl. Nellie had an incredible memory for detail, and she had far more stories than any one book could hold.

A very special thank you and God bless to all four of my children, Chuck Jr., Karen, Mike, and Patrick; they have grown up with this project. They may not have lived in the Upper North Saskatchewan River Corridor, but they certainly have lived with it for a very long time. It has been a part of their lives as well as mine, and all of them have helped in one way or another.

Many thanks go to Patrick and Mike, and to Cheryl, Mike's wife. As university students, they all were actively involved in the research process during the summer of 1988, even to the point of falling asleep over the books. They came up with various ingenious methods of tracking down information that was difficult to locate, and all of them have been continuous in their support and help. And to Patrick's significant other, Mohini, thanks for helping me spin my dream castles.

Thanks also go to Chuck Jr., his wife Patricia (both of whom have helped with proofreading), and their son Ryan; they have visited the region frequently, and they have developed a very strong attachment to the area. It adds a special dimension to the memories when they are shared.

Thanks go to my husband, Chuck, to my daughter Karen, and to her husband Graham, all of whom, at different times, have given me the opportunity to write by "taking up the slack" in our busy household. Karen, who also has helped with proofreading, often has unwittingly maintained my focus; she is so much like Mom in so many ways that this alone is enough to keep the memories alive. Special thanks to Chuck, who "went along for the ride," patiently accompanying me throughout the west country and to wherever the research requirements led, and who spent many days tracking down specific photographs I needed.

To my grandchildren, Nicole, Ryan, Michael, and Kristian, you are very special and I love you very much; you have helped by making life a little brighter for us all.

*I*t is ironic, yet fortunate, that this region of the Upper Saskatchewan, once the focus of westward exploration, and a few times the choice to carry the traffic of the nation, is still relatively unchanged in many ways. But the stampede of "civilization" constantly moves closer. I hope that, in some small way, the information contained in this book will help others to understand and to love this country. And, above all else, I hope it will move them to protect this historic corridor for future generations, so they too may see and understand how it used to be.

Introduction

My growing-up world and that of my children are light-years apart. They grew up in a world of art galleries and major performers, of any organized sport they chose and any school they wished to attend. But they've rarely known the freedom of walking without following sidewalks, and they can't comprehend a land with no fences except to pasture horses.

They've listened in fascination to my tales of growing up in the Upper North Saskatchewan River Corridor, the Shunda Basin, and Nordegg. They, surrounded by people and noise, find it hard to imagine a world that consisted of 2500 people with an entire mountain play-ground at the doorstep, and no other settlement of comparable size any closer than 60 miles to the east.

It is now possible to fly from Alberta to Nova Scotia, approximately 3000 miles (5000 km) in under six hours; I remember a six-hour train ride to get to Red Deer, a distance of 120 miles (200 km). My children drove to classes or caught a bus, while I remember the thrill of riding a bob-sled down the south mountain to get to school. (And, with luck, we could find a driver who would hitch the sled to his car's bumper and pull it, and us, back up the hill after school.) My children have never even ridden on a wooden bob-sled.

A. Belliveau collection.

They live in a world of super-highways where broken or patched pavement means a poor road. I remember a dirt road where poor conditions meant so much mud and water lying in a low spot that getting through it became nearly impossible.

In the world where I grew up, horses frequently were the transportation of choice; I never owned a bike but always had a horse to ride. In my children's world, horses are looked upon as a recreational activity. My family drive to stables where horses are already saddled and ready to go; I recall tracking horses through underbrush and muskeg, and then riding bareback to the corral for the saddle. They ride well-marked paths within a fenced-in area; I reminisce about riding over flats and through forests, occasionally coming unexpectedly upon tents of a small group of people from the Wesley band who wandered throughout the region between the Kootenay Plains and Nordegg, pitching camp whenever and wherever they chose.

My family have access to the latest movies and the most recent fashions, but they have never had the chance to watch the mountains as they change with the seasons, and with the time of day. They've never even seen my greatest visual treasure – the sight of snow-covered mountains etched against a sky brightly lit by a full moon.

Yes, my growing-up world and that of my children are light-years apart, and I often wonder which of those two worlds has the most to offer.

The Land Before Time

The heart of the Big West Country is the North Saskatchewan River. From its source, where the icy waters are released from the Columbia Icefields' Saskatchewan Glacier, the river rushes eastward until it passes over the rapids near which the Rocky Mountain House fur trading forts were constructed. Here the Saskatchewan takes an abrupt shift in direction, turning north/northwest beyond the rapids which mark the end of the Upper Saskatchewan Corridor. The river then follows a route which runs at a distance from, but almost parallel to, the mountains before being joined by the waters of the Brazeau River (or North Fork), after which it turns eastward once again. Already a mighty river at this point, it continues past Edmonton on its journey to Hudson Bay and the Atlantic Ocean. From its heart, Big West Country extends to encompass numerous valleys, basins, and rivers which make up the drainage system of the Saskatchewan.

Early travellers who came from the east, following the river's erratic journey upstream toward the mountains, noted the river's change of character at the rapids where Rocky Mountain House was located. The flow altered from a reasonably navigable river highway to a narrower, swiftly-flowing torrent of numerous rapids rushing from the mountains. Fur trader Alexander Henry the Younger describes the first set of rapids west of the river's turning as "the first significant interruption in approaching the mountains."[1] Two centuries ago these rapids, now known as the Brierley Rapids, were much rougher than they now are.[2]

When Dr. James Hector of the Palliser Expedition observed the rapids in 1858 he noted that they included a small, three-foot high waterfall created by ledges of greenish sandstone stretching across the river.[3] But since the days of the fur trade the river has been migrating slowly upstream, wearing away much of this rock. The continuous action of water, wind, and weather keeps this land in a state of constant change.

The mighty Saskatchewan is now harnessed by TransAlta Utilities' Bighorn Dam, located approximately 80 miles (129 km) upstream along the Saskatchewan from the Brierley Rapids. This dam has taken control of the river's flow through the Corridor, taming the raging waters which challenged travellers of centuries ago. However, Big West Country is still a land of swiftly rushing rivers, sub-alpine meadows, rocky gorges, glacial lakes, and towering mountains. Ever-changing, yet eternally the same, this land has guarded and protected, frustrated and baffled mankind since first he attempted to become part of it.

Long before North America's earliest inhabitants became part of this magnificent area, the progression of geological time gradually was burying mineral wealth deep within the ground. Alberta lies upon huge reserves of oil, gas, and coal – a legacy from the past. Alberta has, by far, the largest portion of Canada's total coal resources. The natural formation of these coal deposits took place over many millions of years. The nature of any coal seam is related to the pressure, temperature, and time involved in the formation of the seam.

Coal is formed from plants and trees which lived in swampy areas millions of years ago. The remains of this vegetation gradually accumulated, forming a deep layer of rotting matter. Eventually, many feet of mud and sand lay above this vegetation and gradually compressed into rock, mainly shale and sandstone, and the vegetation layer, subjected to ever-increasing pressure and heat, hardened slowly into coal beds.

Coal is located beneath most of Alberta, and Alberta coal mines developed three separate and distinct coal horizons.[4] The majority of Alberta coal is lignite, or Upper Cretaceous coal, known as the Edmonton formation. It is the youngest of Alberta coals. Classified as domestic, it is too soft to have had any great commercial value. Drumheller coalfields, part of the Edmonton formation, became Alberta's most important domestic coal producer.[5]

In Alberta, the Mid-Upper Cretaceous, or Belly River formation, is extensive but it runs at a considerable depth below the surface. One of the few areas where it reaches the surface, or outcrops, is in the Lethbridge basin, but it is difficult to mine because the faulting does not follow any particular direction. Alberta's major producing mines dealt with the Lower Cretaceous, or Kootenay formation. Coal from these lower formations is older and has been subjected to greater weight, therefore it is harder and of better quality. These formations usually produce good steam coal, but also create more dangerous mining conditions because the mines usually are gaseous and dry. Kootenay formation mines were eventually located along the eastern slopes of the Rockies, at Brazeau/Nordegg in the Upper North Saskatchewan River Corridor, and in the districts of Crowsnest Pass, Banff/Canmore, the Coal Branch, and Jasper. Generally the grade of coal improves the further west the coal seam extends because the movement of mountain-creating forces caused tighter compression to the west.

Fixed carbon is the main chemical component of coal; the harder the coal the greater is the amount of fixed carbon. The heat content of coal, measured in British Thermal Units or BTUs, is what determines its value. Bituminous coal, such as much of that found in the Rocky Mountains, has the important ability to "coke," or carbonize. When coal is baked in large ovens the volatile matter is driven off, leaving hard, porous carbon. Also recovered from this process are by-products, of which the most important is coal tar, which is used for perfumes, dyes, food colors, food flavors, medicines, plastics, lipstick, nylon, gasoline, fuel oil, fertilizers, textiles, and explosives.

In the regions of the Upper Saskatchewan, coal could be seen along the river banks and early explorers commented upon this in their journals.[6] Until oil and gas replaced coal as favored fuels, "availability and use of coal" was the basis of that country becoming powerful.

Records of early European exploration indicated that the Saskatchewan valley was rich in mineral deposits, coal in particular, and there was speculation that gold also would be found.[7] Geologists tell us that there are no gold-bearing formations on the eastern slopes of the Rockies, yet gold dust still is found along the Saskatchewan. One theory about the presence of gold in the Saskatchewan Corridor is that during the last ice age it was picked up by glaciers from a northern mother-lode, ground into fine dust by glacial action, and deposited all over the landscape. Spring run-off then carries the gold into streams and rivers, and eventually alluvial gold deposits build up in a few locations.

In 1870, news spread throughout the west that there really was gold on the Saskatchewan. It had been found along the sand bars, especially at the inner curves of the river's meanders, where particles of heavy gold would drop amongst the gravel. Panners working the river from Rocky Mountain House to east of Edmonton, even as late as the 1950s, were able to make about $5.00 a day in their search for gold, based upon a gold price of approximately $40.00 per troy ounce. This gold often had traces of iron, giving it a reddish cast.[8]

Adding to the speculation about gold along the Saskatchewan, many of the formations to be found in the Crowsnest Pass region of the fabled Lost Lemon gold mine also are found in the Upper Saskatchewan Corridor. At the base of the geological Blairmore group and its equivalents is an ancient river deposit, the Cadomin Conglomerate, which consists of gravel and sand deposited by ancient rivers. Just as the present Saskatchewan River carries flakes of gold dust with it, so an ancient river might have left deposits of gold dust now sealed into the rocks of the Cadomin Conglomerate.

Cadomin Conglomerate can be seen at the eastern edge of Shunda Gap where it has been cut through to make way for the David Thompson Highway. It is distinguished here by green "chert" pebbles seen in outcrop on both sides of the highway. Chert, a solid form of silica, was preferred by early tribes for their projectile points. It can be found within the Upper Saskatchewan River valley and throughout the Rocky Mountains, but flint-quality chert is difficult to locate. The Mississippian (Rundle and Banff)

Both the Cadomin Conglomerate and the Five Mile Bridge train trestle were cut to make way for the new highway. Collection A. Belliveau.

The Red-Gold Cache

Kerry Wood, historian and naturalist of the Red Deer area, learned of the Red-Gold Cache through Gerald Thompson, whose grandfather, Colin Thompson, was an early homesteader west of Bowden in the late 19th century.

One of the stories recorded by Colin took place on a cold winter day of the Thompsons' first year in the area. A trapper was visiting Colin when they saw two young Natives and eight pack-horses appear out of the blizzard. The Natives were both starving and freezing, so Colin stabled their horses, brought the young men inside, and fed them. Colin had learned to speak some First Nations languages, both through his wife and during his years of working with the Hudson's Bay Company, so he was able to understand most of what the Native lads said. They told of their tribe's extreme hardship through lack of game for food, and how they finally had been forced to eat their dogs and some of their horses. Several tribal members had died and, finally, the Band Council had decided to send two of their strongest young men with their remaining horses to buy white men's food.

When Colin asked the two how they were to buy food for their tribe, one of them took out two buckskin bags and poured out coarse flakes of reddish-gold dust. The trapper, who had not understood the conversation, stepped forward and asked where this had come from. Thompson translated the answer that it was from a taboo burial place which the aboriginal people were not able to visit, and that only the Chief and Medicine Man knew where to find the gold. It was taboo for them too, but because of the band's extreme hardship the Councillors felt it was necessary to use the gold to buy food.

Thompson warned the Natives that the trapper might try to follow them, and when they left so did the trapper. He later returned, and told Thompson he had intended to follow until the lads reached their home, which he estimated to be about 100 miles (160 km) distant, west of present day Sundre. He had gotten as far as the Red Deer River, but the blizzard still had been raging and he was unable to follow the tracks further westward.

The following summer Thompson met one of the Native lads who reported that, after picking up supplies, they had made a wide detour to prevent being followed, and their band had made it safely through the winter after having received the supplies.

Rumors of the Red-Gold Cache occasionally surfaced during following years. In the early 20th century a Native lady who lived near Red Deer, Mrs. Bella Johnson, firmly believed the gold had killed her husband. According to Mrs. Johnson, her husband accidentally had discovered the cache, and brought out more than one thousand dollars worth of the gold dust. (Between 1920 and 1933, gold was valued at $20.67 a troy ounce, U.S. funds) He died not long after, and his wife was convinced that his death resulted from violation of the tribal taboo on the Red-Gold Cache.*

*Wood, Kerry. *A Corner of Canada: A Personalized History of the Red Deer River Country.* Calgary: John D. McAra, 1967, pp. 63-65.

The Haven Brothers

The Haven brothers were among the very early Europeans present in the Corridor. They found coarse gold somewhere in the West Country and they used it in trade with the factor at Rocky Mountain House. These brothers lived approximately eight miles (13 km) west of where Nordegg later was built, making their home beside the creek which now bears their name.*

*Wood, Kerry; Wilson, Thomas Edward III. *Scrapbook No. 4,* p.32

Heavy Gold

In central Alberta the first mention of gold is found in fur trader journals. This account is one of the better known tales of gold in the West Country, and it relates the story of a Native man who, about 1850, used to come east to trade at the Rocky Mountain House fort. He had an old muzzle loading musket, fired with nipple and cap, and with powder poured in with a horn, rammed tightly and wadded. It was capable of firing either shot or ball. The Native, however, did not make trade for ball because he had his own, made of gold. He preferred them because they were heavier.*

*Rocky Mountaineer, Anniversary Edition, July 29, 1987, p. 52.

SackRider

SackRider lived in the Nordegg area for close to 40 years. Although he had a cabin and corrals in the Haven Creek area, he spent a great deal of his time wandering throughout the countryside and also visiting with the Stoneys who lived further west. On one particular day in 1950 he was in Nordegg visiting a friend, "Dirty Mike," who had a cabin below Bachelor Street, when the Catholic priest, Father Anthony Dittrich, dropped in to visit Mike.

A young priest recently ordained, Father Tony had arrived in Nordegg the year before. Originally a farm boy from east central-Alberta, he soon discovered that he was very compatible with mountain life. Eventually Father Tony Dittrich became a registered guide and outfitter. He made many good friends among the Stoney people and he liked nothing better than to sleep under the stars on the Kootenay Plains.

Father Tony and SackRider got to talking, when suddenly SackRider presented a proposition to the young priest; he asked Father Dittrich to come with him to where he had found gold. SackRider showed Father Tony a letter he had received back from Ottawa, a response concerning gold samples which he had gotten by drilling into intrusive rock, and then forwarded to Ottawa for assessment. The letter from Ottawa stated that the samples appeared to indicate a good find, and it also suggested that SackRider drill a few feet deeper, as it was expected the gold quality would improve as he went further into the ground.

SackRider also told Father Tony that, as well as gold, he also had located crystal-quality sand, the type used to make fine glassware. SackRider wanted the priest to accompany him when he returned to the location where he had found the gold. Although he did not divulge the location of his find, Father Tony got the impression that it was in the mountains to the northwest, toward the Brazeau River. Apparently SackRider had had plenty of offers from various miners to accompany him, but he was being very cautious. He knew what the idea of gold could do to men. However, he figured that the Catholic priest was about as safe as he could get. Father Tony agreed to go with SackRider on his next trip into the mountains.

At this time the young priest was in the process of digging a basement for the house he would later construct west of the church. Working through some rainy weather had caused him to develop severe bronchitis and he was seriously ill through part of that spring and all of that summer. The two men realized it would be necessary to postpone their trip until the following summer. SackRider then decided that, while waiting for the priest to recover, he would take the opportunity of returning to Minnesota to visit with his brother.

SackRider never returned to Nordegg; he died while visiting his family in Minnesota.*

*Father A. (Tony) Dittrich, interview, Aug. 6, 1993; July 7, 1994.

geological formation, which is widespread throughout the mountain regions, as well as the geological Nordegg formation, which has scattered outcrops in the Nordegg area, supplied places where good chert could be located.[9] This was used to make arrow and spear heads for the nomadic hunters. The quarry area on the south slopes west of Shunda Gap was a prehistoric site located along one of the routes from the prairies to west of the Rocky Mountains. This quarry area supplied good chert from Mississippian age limestone. This chert varies in color from grey to brown, and is found embedded in the lighter colored limestone. The Shunda quarry site, which was on one of the routes used by Natives passing through Shunda Basin, held excellent archaeological possibilities because of the good composition of the chert in that particular spot, but construction and quarry activity destroyed the archaeological value of this location. This stone quarry was developed by the railway during the early years of the Brazeau Collieries and was located on the northeast lower slopes of Eastbush Mountain, where the railway route into Nordegg was established.

The Upper Saskatchewan River Corridor traditionally is First Nations territory. Extensive use of this area has been made by numerous First Nations tribes, as the number of identified grave sites, sacred places, and historic and prehistoric campsites bear witness. Although very little archaeological exploration has been done in the Upper Saskatchewan Corridor, available data indicates that it has a human history of close to 10 000 years.

Kootenay Plains, once known as "Kadonnha Tinda" (Ke-don-ne-ha Tin-da) or "Meadow of the Winds," was a major attraction to the Native people of the Upper Corridor.[10] With their nomadic lifestyles, it was used extensively by various First Nations people as a meeting place where they traded, danced, and feasted. David Thompson's manuscript frequently mentions Kootenay Plains when he is discussing Saskatchewan River Corridor country. At one point his notes refer to the region as "Kootones," which may have been Thompson's closest attempt to interpret the rapid and flowing Stoney pronunciation of Kadonnha Tinda, rather than the generally accepted belief that these Plains were named for the Ktunaxa, the original Kootenay First Nation name (pronounced kTu-na-ha).[11] Thompson had been attempting to reach the Kutenais for some time and he was aware that this route through the mountains was used by the Ktunaxa. Upon hearing the Stoney term, Kadonnha Tinda, Thompson may have thought that the very similar sounding term was the name used by traders when referring to the First Nation tribe, the Ktunaxa (Kootenay). But Native place names, for the most part, tended to be descriptive of the spot so that recognition was simplified. Kootenay Plains, the "Meadow of the Winds," is one of the trans-mountain corridors susceptible to fierce and unpredictable winds.

The Ktunaxa appear to have been located west of the Rockies by the time of European expansion into the Upper North Saskatchewan River Corridor, and were not part of the territory of the eastern slopes. The Kadonnha Tinda has been used extensively over the course of centuries by numerous other First Nations tribes, of whom the Kootenays were one. Kadonnha Tinda is a unique ecological feature with a warm, dry climate. It is noticeably warmer during the winter months than the surrounding area, and it receives less snowfall. It is a large, flat valley, rich in grass and winter feed, but it is also characterized by aspen, Douglas fir, and patches of lodge-pole. It has indefinite boundaries, and varies from large open stretches to heavily treed areas. The region now called Kootenay Plains Ecological Reserve/Natural Area is much smaller in size than the original Kadonnha Tinda territory.

Since 1972, the Plains also has included the upper regions of Lake Abraham. This lake now extends approximately 20 miles (32 km) behind Bighorn Dam. The Kootenay Plains, which are a large part of the transverse valley lying west of the Front Ranges of the Rocky Mountains, are surrounded and sheltered by the towering peaks of the snow-capped Rockies, making it one of the most picturesque spots in North America.

This was a favored wintering spot of the Native people, affording excellent hunting. The Upper Saskatchewan Corridor was a land of plenty for the various nomadic tribes frequenting this region over countless centuries.

Department of Mines, Geological Survey, 1934, Map 302A.

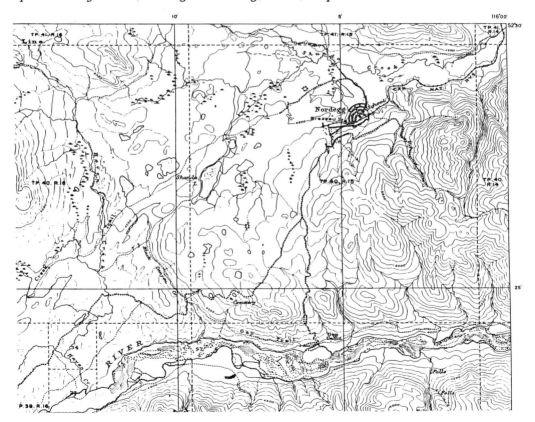

During later periods of prehistoric time, the Upper Saskatchewan River valley was part of a main east/west trans-mountain route followed by interior tribes coming eastward to hunt buffalo. First Nations people from what is now Alberta also used this route extensively while hunting throughout the valley, and they frequently crossed the Rocky Mountains to trade with tribes to the west.

One of the many north/south First Nations' trails that wove throughout the Upper Saskatchewan Corridor passed through Kootenay Plains and north into the Cline River valley. It then continued on to the Athabasca/Jasper area, following the Cline (Whitegoat) River and Cataract Creek, which flow into the Saskatchewan River from the northwest. This trail was a main route to the Athabasca region. West of this trail lay the beginning of another lateral valley through which Alberta's present Icefields Parkway eventually was constructed. As recently as 1870 the present route of the Icefields Parkway was still covered by glacial ice. In earlier years this area between Howse and Athabasca Passes was not well known or explored west of the Cline River trail; this was a formidable, ice-covered region containing 11 of the 24 highest peaks in the Canadian Rockies. The Cataract Creek trail runs east of, and roughly parallel to, the present Icefields highway. Further northwest this trail intersects with the Brazeau River not far from one of its mountain sources southwest of Brazeau Lake. The pattern of movement throughout the mountains of this region placed the Kootenay Plains in a central location for both east/west and north/south traffic.

As the North Saskatchewan River travels eastward, it is joined by numerous tributaries which flow into the river from the various ranges of the Rockies. South of the river, as it passes through the Front Ranges, there lies a distinctive mountain with a crooked talon pointing skyward. This mountain, the northern-most point of the Ram Range of mountains, was named Mount Michener in 1976. On the northwest side of the river is Windy Point. Between these two locations there once lay a wide, flat valley through which the North Saskatchewan River meandered, cutting numerous channels along the valley floor, but which now is filled by the man-made Lake Abraham. To the east, the Brazeau Range's northern outlier mountains can be clearly seen along the north-eastern horizon, as viewed from the David Thompson Highway viewpoint located just north-east of Windy Point, as well as from the bridge across the Cline River, further to the south-west, and at points between. It is in the shadow of these Brazeau outlier mountains that Nordegg was built.

These outliers are part of the chain of the most eastern edge of the Brazeau Range which, in turn, is the most eastern of all the mountain ranges that run through the Upper North Saskatchewan River Valley. Looking eastward from the tops of these mountains the land is relatively flat, although heavily wooded. From the tops of these mountains the lights of Rocky Mountain House are visible on a clear night.[12] When the forces of nature created the Rocky Mountains it caused the land to buckle in such a way that the mountains lying the furthest east were created from land that was forced up from the greatest depths of the earth. These mountains are composed of materials that were deposited hundreds of millions of years ago, when this land was covered by shallow seas. Early residents of Nordegg marvelled at the great number of fossils to be found along the rocky ridges at the upper level of Coliseum Mountain. The Brazeau outliers at Nordegg are the distinctive mountains which lie north of the David Thompson Highway. To the south, and running roughly parallel to the highway, the Brazeau Range is clearly visible from heights of land east of Nordegg, along the David Thompson Highway.

The Brazeau outlier mountains lie within the geographically distinct region of Shunda Basin. The Basin is characterized by a wetland environment with a considerable amount of muskeg; thus the areas which could be occupied by the prehistoric and historic Native people would have been limited to the higher areas and the dry edges of the Shunda Basin. The town of Nordegg was built on the southern up-slope of the wide, flat valley of Shunda Basin drainage area. A translation of one of the Native names for the Nordegg region was Lake Mucky Swamp, because of the great amounts of muskeg found throughout the flat expanse of the lower valley. Shunda Basin was well utilized for hunting, fishing, and trapping. It was an area rich in game, including the favored bison which roamed throughout this region; David Thompson's 1807 journals made mention of these animals wintering in the Shunda Basin area.

Shunda Basin is drained by Shunda Creek, which rises in the mountains north and west of Nordegg. The Natives called it Big Fish Creek or Fishing Creek.[13] The Shunda, actually more than a creek but less than a river, flows through the Shunda Gap and empties into the Saskatchewan River about 15 miles (24 km) east of this mountain gap. David Thompson referred to this creek in his journals as both North Brook, for the direction from which it flows into the Saskatchewan, and as Jaco's Creek. The latter name was in reference to his Metis horse-keeper, Jaco Cardinal, who was based out of Rocky Mountain House but who ranged the horses along the Saskatchewan River west of the Fort. In the later years of the 19th century this creek appeared on maps as Mire Creek and, in 1912, it was named Shunda Creek.[14] Shunda is the Stoney Indian word for mire or swamp.

The trail network of the First Nations included the north/south Big Fish Trail or Fishing Trail along the Shunda. This trail passed through the general area of the Wapiabi, a Stoney term meaning grave. It then cut through the Blackstone/Chungo regions before continuing toward Athabasca country. For the Natives, this was a well used route of travel from Shunda to the Athabasca River. As well as this north/south route, the network included east/west routes which travelled through the Shunda Gap and Nordegg regions, toward Bighorn and the Kootenay Plains, and through Howse Pass to the western slope of the Rockies.

The Saskatchewan River between the Shunda and Tershishner Creek was a difficult section for water travel. South of Nordegg, and up-stream from its confluence with the Shunda, the Saskatchewan swings to the southwest and is rough and swift-flowing, passing between high canyon walls. It was impossible for horses to follow along the main river during the years of the fur trade because of thick undergrowth and immense piles of wind-fallen wood which covered banks on either side of the river. The river banks themselves move nearer to the river's shores, closing in to become high walls of rock intersected by deep valleys. For this rugged region of the Saskatchewan River both the river route and the overland trail system were used, depending upon the time of year for travel. In winter the river ice could be followed with dog teams, but if the weather was warm and the river was not frozen, or if the river ice was not sufficiently smooth, the overland system was the easiest to follow.[15]

The overland route followed the Natives' Big Fish Trail from the mouth of Shunda Creek through Shunda Gap at the eastern edge of Shunda Basin, just east of where Nordegg later was constructed. Shunda Basin was a crossroads area; the overland route split into a number of different routes at this point. Because of the considerable amounts of muskeg within the Shunda Basin, the First Nations' trails tended to keep to higher ground at the base of the mountains along both the north and south edges of the Basin.

To the west-northwest lay the Big Fish Trail and Athabasca country, while to the west-southwest other routes angled the traveller back toward the Saskatchewan River, crossing out of Shunda Basin by passing through the location where Nordegg later was constructed, then angling southwest of the Brazeau Collieries mining complex. At The Forks, approximately two and one-half miles (4 km) south-southwest of the mine area, this overland trail split into two different routes.[16] One branch of this trail extended to a small plain along the Saskatchewan River, west of the present Forestry Trunk Road bridge. Alexander Henry the Younger commented upon this overland route when he wrote in his journal that "the trail rejoins the river, having made a long circuit in a gap in the mountains." Henry and his men were among those travellers and explorers who camped at this location. His journal entry for February 4th, 1811, concerning the location where this overland route rejoined the river, included the comment: "About where this track comes out appear several spots of meadow on the rising grounds. The grass is . . . excellent for horses. Buffalo are frequently seen here."[17] This general area later became known as Brewster's Flats, named for George Brewster, who built a homestead and small horse ranch in this region during the first part of the 20th century.

The other, longer branch of the overland route continued in a south-westerly direction toward the Saskatchewan River, passing through Black Canyon before continuing on toward the Bighorn River. The remnants of this trail still can be seen from the Forestry Trunk Road/Bighorn Highway. This Saskatchewan River overland route rejoined the North Saskatchewan near the mouth of the Bighorn River, extending westward from there through the Kootenay Plains. A more inland Native trail westward remained a distance north of the river; this was the route later improved for vehicular traffic westward to Windy Point. This trail returned to the Saskatchewan River at Tershishner Creek (near the east end of the present Bighorn Reservoir), then extended west through the Kootenay Plains. The Bighorn/Tershishner Creek area was another major intersection for a number of Native trails. Tershishner is Stoney for burnt timbers.

The routes of these trails made the Nordegg region an important location. This was a central point for a number of the trans-mountain routes, regardless of the direction being travelled, and several camping areas were established in the area. Although traditional Stoney campsites have been identified throughout the region, three prehistoric sites were identified north of Nordegg.

One of these campsites northwest of Nordegg was a major prehistoric and historic Native campsite. This site was situated close by the intersection of a number of trails from various directions. It was located on a terrace overlooking the Shunda, and was used consistently by the Natives as a summer campground. A second site was located further northwest along Big Fish Trail, where the Brazeau Collieries later constructed a timber camp, known locally as Grouch Camp. A third site on the route to Athabasca country was situated further northwest along the Chungo, a Stoney word for trail.[18]

The grave sites, sacred places, and historic and prehistoric campsites throughout the Upper North Saskatchewan River Corridor, along the Bighorn/Kootenay Plains Trail, the Big Fish Trail, and the Saskatchewan River itself, as well as the numerous well-defined trails and deeply embedded pathways throughout the vicinity, bear testimony to the many feet which trod this same ground during countless years prior to the intrusion of Europeans into the Upper Saskatchewan River Valley and the Shunda Basin. The knowledge of the country which the First Nations people had developed over countless centuries of ranging throughout this region was shared with the European explorers who used Native guides and followed established Native trails. These routes became the Fur Brigade Trail of early European exploration. Explorers, including David Thompson, followed these trails overland beside the Shunda, continuing along to Bighorn region and the Kootenay Plains.[19]

In later years these same trails became forestry patrol routes throughout the entire Upper Saskatchewan region. The majority of Nordegg's original roadways prior to highway construction followed routes developed by the First Nations over centuries of inter-mountain travel. The generalized route of our present-day David Thompson Highway was well established as an inland route to the Kootenay Plains long before the first Europeans had journeyed this far into the west. The historical value of the overland trail(s) "lies in the events which it commemorates. It is a tangible memorial to the first crossing and exploration of the Rocky Mountains, and . . . equivalent in value to the designated Lewis and Clark Trail in the Northern United States."[20]

As Long as the Sun Shines . . .

*T*he Natives of the Upper Saskatchewan Corridor were familiar with the mountain passes and the trails that wove throughout this territory, and they designated special places to be used for both religious and ceremonial purposes. They led a nomadic life – gathering, hunting, and fishing – living in harmony with nature. The First Nations people were, and are, as much a part of this country as the valleys and the mountains, the wildflowers and the early snows. Over the years, the Upper North Saskatchewan River Corridor has been familiar territory to many Native tribes, but in historic times, two tribes, the Kutenai and the Stoney, have lived in this region.

A. Belliveau collection.

Kutenai camps seen by Alexander Henry the Younger during the winter of 1811-12 were located about half-way between Whirlpool Point and the present location of the Bighorn Dam, on raised areas of land on both sides of the Saskatchewan River. The Kutenais were relatively gentle and friendly people, with a language that appears to be unique. Their speech was so different from that of other First Nations people that it was noticed and commented upon by the earliest traders.[1]

According to records of Peter Fidler (1792) and Alexander Henry the Younger (1811), the Kutenais were originally located along the foothills and eastern slopes of the Rocky Mountains, but were forced further westward into the mountains by the Peigans during the early 18th century. In the early 19th century, the Peigan Indians patrolled the eastern portion of the Saskatchewan Corridor in an attempt to discourage the fur traders, notably David Thompson, from trading with the Kutenais and other tribes located west of the mountains. The Kutenais had moved west prior to early white trading contact, but they returned a few times each year to hunt buffalo and to trade. One of their routes through the mountains was along the North Saskatchewan River.

The Shuswap, Blackfoot, Peigan, Blood, Sarcee, Stoney, Cree, and Kutenai all hunted and fished areas of the Upper Saskatchewan at one time or another, even though some of these tribes were Plains Indians who disliked, and even feared, the mountains, hills, and woods.[2] However, the historically-identified occupants of this area were the Stoney peoples, and their traditional territory extended from Shunda Gap, approximately 4 miles (7 km) east of where Nordegg later was located, west to the general area of Saskatchewan River Crossing at the Banff/Jasper Parkway.

Alberta's Stoneys are Assiniboine (Nakoda); they are members of the Siouan linguistic family.[3] Since available resource material is limited, it is difficult to trace the movements of these Native bands. According to Stoney tradition, small bands had begun to break away during a smallpox epidemic. Two such splinter groups, who later became Alberta's mountain Stoneys, separately migrated westward during an extended period of time.[4] Separating in the North Dakota/Manitoba regions, they were reunited once again after reaching the foothills and mountains of Alberta.

One group whose descendants have separated into two bands, the Bearspaw and Chiniki bands, eventually moved along the eastern slopes of the Rockies into regions extending from west of Lethbridge to west of Calgary. The other band, whose descendants later became the Wesley Stoneys, moved first to the north and then westward into the mountains along the Red Deer, Clearwater, North Saskatchewan, and Brazeau Rivers.[5] The Upper North Saskatchewan River Corridor became home to the Wesleys. Over the years the Wesley band had been known as Swampy Grounds Stoneys, Woods Stoneys, Jacob's band, Goodstoney band, and Wesley band.[6] In May, 1987, they reverted back to the name Goodstoney band, but in 1993 they again took the name Wesley Band. They were a small tribe surrounded by enemies, but they managed to survive without becoming fully allied to other tribes, thus retaining their language and customs, and many of their original traits. Although the Stoneys usually did not ally themselves with white society through marriage, they developed genuinely warm feelings toward white people.

The designation "Stoney" is a rough English translation of the name "Assiniboine," which, in turn, refers to their method of cooking with hot stones. While the buffalo supplied all the needs of the Plains people, the Stoneys, who lived in the mountain regions, were more dependent upon the moose. The Wesley Stoneys subsisted upon the game that was so plentiful in the Upper North Saskatchewan River Corridor. It was not necessary for them to follow the buffalo herds or to collect into large bands for the hunt – the Corridor was a land of plenty.

The woodlands of the Saskatchewan Corridor also offered a plentiful supply of fish, berries, and roots. A variety of berries grows throughout the area, as do various roots and green-leafed plants. At the lower and mid-level of the mountains encircling the Shunda Basin, as well as in other areas of the Saskatchewan Corridor, there grows the colorful tiger-lily, which provided the Stoneys with an edible bulb which could be baked, boiled, or dried.

During the warmer months, families and extended family groups migrated throughout the foothills in search of food, but the size of the band was not a direct influence upon survival, as it frequently could be for the people of the Plains. The patriarchal family unit was the most important in the Stoneys' social structure. During the winter, Stoney families came together in their chosen, protected camping areas.

Since using a horse was not very practical when hunting big game animals in forested and mountainous country, Stoney hunters became swift and agile, chasing their quarry on foot. They used a relatively short spear, with a head of either bone or stone. They also preferred a short bow for hunting. The Stoneys developed an excellent reputation for skill and courage, and they were able to use a bow and arrow with tremendous strength and accuracy.[7]

One personal item which survived the test of time and changes brought by Europeans was the elaborate, long, feathered headdress which became universally known and recognized. This type of headdress is Dakodan (Siouan) in nature; the Stoneys used eagle feathers in varying numbers to indicate different successes or honors of the wearer.

The Dakodan long, feathered head-dress was worn by Stoneys on special occasions. Maggie Morris Collection.

The Stoneys were respected by other tribes. Prior to missionary influence, the Stoneys were "held in dread by the Blackfeet [sic], who rarely venture[d] into their country."[8] The Blackfoot did not pick a quarrel with the Stoneys or steal their horses because it was known that Stoney warriors would fight to the bitter end. The Blackfoot referred to the Stoneys as "cut-throats" because they would cut off the heads of their enemies.[9]

Although it is possible that French traders reached Rocky Mountain House around 1750, it was the early years of the 19th century fur trade which brought a number of European traders, as well as great changes, into traditional Native territory. Missionaries had made their way into the west shortly after the first explorers and fur-traders. In 1840, the Wesleyan missionary, Reverend Robert Rundle, became the first missionary to visit the Stoneys at Rocky Mountain House, beginning the process of a major change in Stoney lifestyle. Rundle had had limited success with the Plains tribes, but the Stoneys readily accepted him.[10] Other missionaries, including the respected Father Lacombe, made contact with the Stoneys at the Rocky Mountain House fort during following years.

The story is told that the Stoney Chief, Mah-Min, and his brother were praying to the gods when the voice of their traditional god told them a white man would come and bring them a new god in which they should believe. When Mah-Min met Reverend Rundle at Rocky Mountain House, the Indian Chief saw in the missionary the fulfilment of this prophecy and he became an instant convert. It was through missionary influence that Native names ceased to be used and western-European and biblical names took their place. Mah-Min, who was immortalized in a magnificent painting by artist Paul Kane, has descendants with family names of Twin and Wildman.[11]

The legendary Stoney chief, medicine man, war leader, and prophet, Tchatka, who "through superior cunning and dream power"[12] kept his people victorious in fierce conflict with the Blackfoot, was also one of the early converts to Christianity at Rocky Mountain House. Of all the Assiniboine chieftains, Tchatka attained the greatest reputation and respect. For the span of a generation, he guided his people into prominence, making them a force to be reckoned with by other tribes. In later years, Tchatka became such a strong believer in Christianity he would begin fasting when he heard about war and killing.[13] A son of Tchatka, Calf Child, who was a mystic and a gifted healer in the early 20th century, was assigned the name Hector Crawler. The name Crawler, among a nation skilled in stalking both man and beast, denotes outstanding ability or skill as a hunter.[14]

Another surname taken by the Stoneys was that of House (or Howse). This name was said to have been taken by Native men who worked with the fur trade companies along the upper North Saskatchewan River and through the Howse Pass area. The surname Hunter was taken by the Stoney who was the official hunter for Rocky Mountain House. However, the Stoneys continued to take a name in their own language as well as having a second, official name for government records.[15]

A great many of the Stoneys had accepted the ideas and doctrines of Christianity by the late 1850s. Native lifestyle, which interwove religion into everything they did, left them ripe for missionary teachings. Bands located in areas where there was constant conflict were less likely to look upon teachings of brotherly love as being realistic, but the Stoneys, who lived their lives in relative isolation along the North Saskatchewan, were more open minded about such teachings. In the years prior to signing treaty, these Natives had become known as good, quiet, peaceable people.

During the mid-19th century, Paul Kane travelled throughout the west, interpreting the land and people through his paintings. He visited Rocky Mountain House in 1848, a few years after the Stoneys had first been exposed to Christianity. Kane made the statement that the Stoneys were the most kind and honorable tribe he had met.[16] Almost every journal report of early explorers and missionaries makes reference to the high principles and fine character of the Stoneys.

The Stoneys combined many elements of Christianity with ancient customs and beliefs, creating their own form of mysticism; they held onto their strong belief in dreams, omens and a world of spirits. The Stoneys continued to maintain their legends concerning the little people who live in caves in the higher hills. Tribal members would not go near such caves without first performing a ritual meant to reassure these little cave dwellers that no harm was intended.

The Stoneys believed in Christian teachings, but often followed their own tribal marriage customs; a church ceremony formalized the marriage while the bride price finalized it. It was not Christianity, but governing officials after Treaty signing who did away with the custom of a man having as many wives as he could support. However, during a large part of the 19th century, the Stoneys of the Upper North Saskatchewan River Corridor were not greatly influenced by the coming of the whites, except for their immediate and whole-hearted acceptance of Christianity. They continued to roam the mountains, along the foothills and onto the plains, coming together for the winter at special locations, one of which was the Kootenay Plains, known to them as Kadonnha Tinda.

When, in 1873, Methodist missionaries George and John McDougall moved into Stoney country to establish a permanent mission, they selected a traditional Stoney winter camp-ground, now Morley. Soon, a school was opened. The Morley area came to be looked upon by the dominant society as the central point of Stoney life while, in reality, it only was one of the Stoneys' wintering locations.[17]

Canada became a nation in 1867 and, three years later, acquired the Hudson's Bay Company's claim to Rupert's Land. To hold together this vast territory, the government decided to attract settlers to the prairies by offering free land. The First Nations peoples' territory, through which the fur trade had advanced and flourished, now was to be turned into an agricultural hinterland.

Since good eastern farm land was becoming scarce by this time, the idea of creating a new world in the new west appealed to many settlers from central Canada and Britain. This vast land would be linked together by the railway stretching across the prairies and through the mountains. In 1872, the North Saskatchewan River Valley was one of the routes being considered for the transcontinental Canadian Pacific Railway.

However, before the western interior could be settled, the government thought it necessary to establish some control over both the land use and the Natives of the prairies. Considerable unrest was evident in the northwest at this time, and confrontations between European, Mixed Blood, and Native were becoming serious. Whiskey traders had moved into the region and lawlessness was more common. A military-style organization, loosely disguised as a police force, was formed under the name of The North West Mounted Police. By 1874, this Force reached territory that now is Alberta, helping to defuse the tensions.

Between 1871 and 1877 there were seven treaties made with First Nations tribes of what was then known as the Territories. These treaties required the Natives to sign away

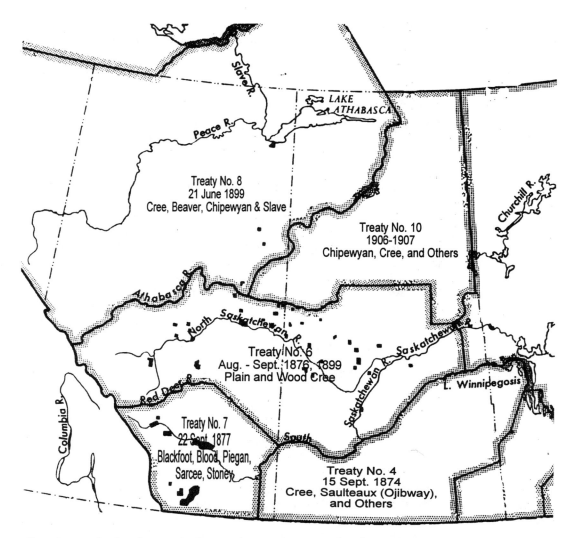

all rights to the land specified in each treaty, except for the regions specifically set aside for Native settlement and use. The missionaries, who had established a Stoney mission at Morley, planned to introduce these nomadic hunters to an agricultural lifestyle.

However, not all Stoneys wanted to live in the Morley area. In 1909, John Abraham stated to the Secretary of the Department of Indian Affairs that, prior to designation of Morley as the Stoney Indian Reserve, John's father had "told the commissioner and Reverend McDougall that he was taking treaty for that land at the head of the Saskatchewan in the Mountains."[18]

The Stoneys were asked to sign Treaty 7 in 1877. This treaty dealt with land in the Morley area, but did not include the Kootenay Plains-Bighorn region – traditional Stoney land. The northern boundary of land being signed away by the First Nations in

Treaty 7 was the Red Deer River, which is considerably south of the North Saskatchewan River area, while the land of Treaty 6 had covered a vast area of what is now Saskatchewan and central Alberta. This included Shunda Basin and Bighorn land, but not the Kootenay Plains. It wasn't until Treaty 8, in 1899, that the Plains was included under any land treaty. This is an important distinction, because much of the Upper Saskatchewan Corridor was included in Treaty 6. When the Stoney representatives signed Treaty 7, it inadvertently began a dispute which has never been fully resolved. There is some question as to whether the entire Stoney tribe was represented at the treaty signing, and indications are that they were not. A significant number of the Stoneys were permanent residents of the Kootenay Plains and it is unclear from the official records whether Chief Jacob Goodstoney was appointed to speak on behalf of those who were absent.[19]

The omission of the Kootenay Plains area from both Treaties 6 and 7 may have been due to ignorance on the part of policy makers in distant Ottawa — boundaries were defined in general terms. It also may have been because the "fertile belt" of the North Saskatchewan River, as reported by the Palliser Expedition, was expected to be one of the first areas to be developed. During 1876 and 1877, when Indian treaties 6 and 7 were being signed, the railway route through the mountains still was uncertain. At least six passes through the Rockies were assessed, but none had yet been designated, although Howse Pass was considered one of the easier slopes through the Rocky Mountains. The region of the Upper North Saskatchewan River Corridor had been the focal point for Canadian exploration from the 17th century onward and, during the 19th century, on a number of separate occasions, it had been considered as a logical route to carry the traffic of the nation.

Published reports indicating the coal potential of this valley, and the gold-rush fever of the mid-to-late 19th century, created interest in such possibilities existing in the Upper Saskatchewan region. Sir William Francis Butler, who spent some time in Rocky Mountain House late in 1870, commented in his report to the Lieutenant Governor of Manitoba that, based upon conversations he had had with both prospectors and explorers, he believed that in the near future there was "a very strong probability of the discovery of gold-fields in the Upper Saskatchewan," and he pointed out that this would have "the utmost consequence" upon the whole Western territory.[20] This region of the Northwest Territories was expected to be in the forefront of development.

Was it by accident or design that no Native reserve land was created in the Upper North Saskatchewan River Corridor?

The land at Morley was not suitable for cultivation, so the Stoneys continued in their old ways of hunting, fishing, and trapping. This saved the government ration money, so the practice was condoned, even though Indian Affairs policy was to keep Natives on the reserves through threat of being jailed if they left without a pass. In 1894, Peter Wesley, discouraged and disgusted with the deterioration of life on the reserve, led approximately 100 band members back to the Kootenay Plains to live, in defiance of government regulations.

Peter Wesley, or Man-Who-Walks-Against-The-Wind, was born in 1840 in the Bighorn area, approximately 15 miles (26 km) west from where Nordegg later was built. Wesley was a strong, forceful character and an ardent Christian who worked continu-

34 *Small Moments in Time*

Peter Wesley in 1904. Tom Wilson III Collection.

ously for the advancement of his people.[21] The Indian name he was given as an adult was Ta-otha, or "the one who provides."

Accompanying Peter Wesley to the Plains were the families of Abraham, Beaver, House, Hunter, Wildman, and Wesley.[22] Later, Peter Wesley was elected chief, and the band became known as the Wesley Band. The government did not take action to force their return to Morley, and so these people once again took up their lives in the land they had always considered theirs. They were relatively isolated in this area, as it was a three day trip from Morley.[23]

Despite the controversy and misunderstandings resulting from the Stoney Indian signing of Treaty 7 in 1877, members of the Wesley band were able to maintain their independence, and continue in their traditional lifestyle in the Upper North Saskatchewan River Corridor. For almost a century after having been requested to make treaty with the immigrant nation, the Stoneys carried on their lives with relatively little contact or interference from the dominant society.

Native and Immigrant

*I*n 1883 the final decision for the Canadian Pacific Railway's route through the mountains was made in favor of Kicking Horse Pass. For 11 years, until 1894, when Peter Wesley led a small band of Stoneys back to the Kootenay Plains, the land of the Shunda and the eastern regions of the Upper Saskatchewan Corridor saw less human occupation than any other time in its extensive history.

Once the railway was constructed along the Bow Corridor, opening up the Rockies well south of Howse Pass, travel in the mountains was concentrated largely in the southern regions. Expeditions into, and through, the mountains followed a more north/south pattern through the passes and lateral valleys.

The western regions of the Upper North Saskatchewan River Corridor, in particular the Kootenay Plains and Howse Pass, frequently were visited by explorers and adventurers, usually accompanied by guides and outfitters who based themselves out of areas along the railway. Sportsmen and tourists began venturing into the Canadian Rockies. The only transportation into the mountains was by railway or by horse. However, east of Kootenay Plains, the trans-mountain valley of the North Saskatchewan was left silently sleeping. By the turn of the century, the Stoneys, who once again roamed their territory along the Saskatchewan despite their inclusion in Treaty 7, were the sole permanent inhabitants of the Corridor; it remained a land relatively untouched.

In 1903, guide and outfitter Tom Wilson moved onto the Kootenay Plains, setting up wintering quarters that were a combination horse-ranch and trading-post in the heart of Stoney territory. In 1885, Wilson married Minnie McDougall, cousin of missionary John McDougall.[1] Many of the Native people knew Wilson and, during one Banff Indian Days, Tom Wilson held a meeting with the Stoneys to see if they were interested in his setting up a Trading Post on the Kootenay Plains. He said he would organize this if the Natives would sell him all the furs they trapped.[2]

The trading post, located where White Rabbit Creek flowed into the North Saskatchewan, consisted of three sod-roofed log buildings and a corral built by Silas Abraham, and improved by Tom Wilson.[3] Wilson had the close cooperation of the Natives for a number of years and he spent each winter with them on the Plains.[4] In 1906, E. C. Barnes brought a herd of pure-bred Clydesdale horses up the river valley from Innisfail and set up the Kadonna ranch on the opposite side of the river. The name of this ranch appears to be another variant of the Stoney pronunciation of Kadonnha Tinda. In 1908, Barnes gave up the venture, sold some of his herd to Tom and moved south of Morley.

By 1909, Wilson had built up his ranch to a considerable size. He asked the Stoneys who were living near White Rabbit Creek to move from the area, and a number of them relocated to the Windy Point/Bighorn region. Wilson wanted to fence and control large areas of the Plains, but he was unable to register a homestead claim. In 1911, he attempted to get an exclusive grazing lease on the Kootenay Plains.[5] Meanwhile, massive amounts of correspondence were exchanged concerning creation of a reserve for the Stoneys along the Saskatchewan, and it nearly became a reality during these two years.[6]

Then, after years of Stoney petitions to government for a reserve along the Saskatchewan, the government, in 1910, suggested that new land which was to be granted the Stoneys might be on the Kootenay Plains.[7] John McDougall supported this, but the Indian Agent contended that it would be difficult to distribute rations there, despite Stoney protestations that they did not require government ration supplies. Agent Fleetham concluded that the land on the Plains would fulfil conditions of the treaty and he suggested that the Geological Survey Branch might help in establishing boundaries.[8]

John House, Silas Abraham, and Job Beaver, 1904. Kootenay Plains Natives did not require government ration supplies. Tom Wilson III collection.

D. B. Dowling, the Chief Surveyor of the Geological Survey Branch in Ottawa, was called upon for information and he lent his support to the idea. He supplied a detailed plan of the Kootenay Plains showing the location of all cabins, including the horse ranch of Tom Wilson on the southeast side of the Saskatchewan and the Kadonna Ranch on the northwest side. Dowling had surveyed the Kootenay Plains and area in 1906, and again in 1907 when he came west with German entrepreneur Martin Cohn (Nordegg) who, at that time, staked claims to coal fields in the Bighorn region and in the Brazeau River area to the north. By 1911, the information was ready, but that summer the Department of the Interior was reorganized, new branches were created and new policy was devised: the Forestry Branch considered it inadvisable to grant a reserve on the Kootenay Plains. The almost-decision to grant the Plains to the Stoneys was dropped in 1911 when the Forestry Branch, also of the Department of the Interior, requested the Kootenay Plains for grazing land and as a Ranger centre because of its central location within the Rocky Mountain Forest Reserve. The forestry department took over both the Barnes and Wilson ranch areas during 1912. Eventually the ruins of the Barnes ranch were burned.[9]

While two-thirds to three-quarters of the Stoney band lived at Morley, a small group continued to maintain their traditional lifestyle in the Upper North Saskatchewan River valley. The Stoneys had built houses and planted gardens, they had horses and cattle there, and family members had been buried there. This was their home. In 1912, John McDougall petitioned Ottawa on behalf of the band, supported by a letter from the band chief and councillors, and a list of names agreeing to surrender a portion of the Morley reserve in exchange for a reserve on the Saskatchewan.[10] Nothing was done.

By 1913/1914, it was estimated that 200 people with 40 homes were living in the Kootenay Plains/Bighorn regions. The Stoneys regularly petitioned Ottawa for this land, while the Forestry, in turn, submitted suggestions and plans to get the Natives off the Plains. The Morley Reserve was too small and too poor to support all the Stoneys, even if they had agreed to move back, but no mutually acceptable alternative location could be established.[11] During the following years further petitions were made to the government for the land at the Kootenay Plains, but there are only a few documents recorded from 1920 to 1945. This was a period of relative stability for the Wesley Stoneys, during which they made Nordegg their base of operations, outside of the Kootenay Plains/Windy Point/Bighorn regions.

The first, and only, sizable European settlement to be constructed in the Stoney territory of the Upper North Saskatchewan Corridor began to take shape in the early 20th century. In the fall of 1910, Martin (Cohn) Nordegg, while following the Native hunting trail east to Shunda Gap, had located coal. A mining complex and town took form just west of Shunda Gap.

When Martin Nordegg first came west in 1907, he had met and liked Stuart Kidd, factor of the Morley store. The Stoneys liked Kidd too, and they appreciated that he had learned to speak their language. In 1911, Kidd was hired by Martin Nordegg as purchasing agent for the new coal company, the Brazeau Collieries. In 1913, Kidd became head of the provisions and supply department and, when the town of Nordegg was constructed in 1914, Stuart Kidd became general manager of Nordegg's company-owned, all-purpose general store, the Bighorn Trading Company.[12] The Stoneys, knowing Kidd, soon began riding into Nordegg to visit.

Kidd set up the store so that furs could be brought into Nordegg and traded for either money or goods.[13] Stoney families began travelling into town by buckboard wagons pulled by two horses, while individuals rode into town on horseback. Behind the Bighorn Store was a grove of evergreen trees used for hitching the horses. There was relatively easy access to Nordegg for trading, supplies, and medical care, and they used one of the old overland trails as a wagon road to connect with this settlement. The Stoneys rarely spent a great amount of time in the town of Nordegg, but during summer months they often camped for weeks in nearby locations. A favorite spot was the prehistoric site of Shunda Flats, north-northwest of town. Nordegg people occasionally used the Flats for picnicking and camping also, but there was an unspoken understanding that this was a Native camp area and the Natives had prior rights for its use.

Nordegg town now supplied the Stoneys with whatever they needed. During the 1918 flu epidemic, Stuart Kidd made sure the Stoneys had proper medical attention through Nordegg hospital facilities, beginning a custom which continued throughout the life of the town.[14] Kidd also became the unofficial Indian Agent, distributing treaty money, trading supplies for furs, and giving advice when it was asked for.[15] In 1927, he was made the first honorary chief of the Stoneys, a tribute to his service to these people.[16]

Ottawa gradually began to refer to the region where the band continued to live as the location of the Nordegg Stoneys.

Probably the most widely known member of the Wesley band was Morley Beaver, also known as Chief Walking Eagle, a Stoney medicine man. He was born in approximately 1882, and was one of the band who came to Kootenay Plains with Peter Wesley in 1894. Morley was tall and slim, and wore his hair in long black braids hanging over each shoulder. He and many of the Stoneys knew a great number of Nordegg people by sight, even if not always by name, and Morley's little smile and quick nod of greeting was a familiar sight in the town. He became one of Canada's most famous First Nations people through his accurate weather forecasting. His prowess in this area was well publicized by the editor of the *Rocky Mountaineer*, Grace Shierholtz; eventually this was noted in *Time* magazine.[17]

Tom Wilson and Morley Beaver (Chief Walking Eagle) on Kootenay Plains, 1904. Tom Wilson III collection.

Some Stoneys hired on for short periods of time at the Brazeau bush camps, cutting timber for the mine, but for the most part they were self sufficient. As well as coming into Nordegg for supplies and medical care, the Natives occasionally attended a movie or church. They also played a large part in the festivities of Sports Days, held three times a year on the Flats at the northern edge of the town. They dressed in traditional costumes and took part in the day's events. However, for the most part, the Stoneys lived their own separate lives, a distinct society living in harmony with the immigrant society now in their midst. The Nordegg Stoneys were a good and a gentle people who lived by a code that kept them in harmony with the natural environment. The townspeople learned from the Stoneys and, in a number of instances, the lifestyles of both took on strong similarities. Roads were nearly non-existent, so horses were the mode of travel. This afforded a great deal of freedom and mobility and, before long, both Stoneys and

Nordegg inhabitants could be found wandering on horseback throughout the area. Soon the immigrants, as well as the Indians, were reading the weather and identifying directions by physical signs. Both gathered from the land, fished the streams, hunted game for food, and bought or traded for what they required at the same Bighorn Trading Company.[18] Both used the local hospital and doctor for severe illnesses, but looked after the mild ones themselves.

Two areas of the Native philosophical approach to life also became an integral part of the collective personality of the white immigrant society. The unity and cohesion of the Native band, with their extended family system guided by a band council, was in many ways similar to the system which evolved in the white society of Nordegg. An individual who belonged to Nordegg became part of an extended family which cared about, and looked after, its own. This was influenced by the isolation and inter-dependency which was an accepted part of life in Nordegg, in the same way that it had characterized Native life.

Another area of similarity in philosophy was the Natives' approach to "territory" as an extension of "dwelling." This concept also was adopted by many members of Nordegg. This was especially true of later generations who grew up in the area, and who developed a strong territorial feeling about the entire region. The town was not viewed as an enclosure within the mountains; the entire region was an extension of "home." The term "Nordegg" did not signify any definite boundary. The Stoneys and the people of Nordegg shared this beautiful wilderness, living separate but similar lives in close proximity.

A. Belliveau collection.

The Stoneys continued to petition the government, hoping that, somehow, someone with authority would correct the injustice. In 1947 a tiny reserve was created for the Wesley band at the confluence of the Bighorn and the North Saskatchewan Rivers. The

5000 acre Bighorn Reserve is less than one-half the size which should have been granted, based upon original treaty terms. This stated there would be 640 acres for every 5 people; there should have been 12 800 acres for the approximately 100 people who were to live on the Bighorn Reserve.[19]

Other small Native bands gravitated toward the Saskatchewan Corridor during the 20th century. Two groups of the Ojibwa tribe eventually had reserves created for them northwest of Rocky Mountain House – the Sunchild Band (1944) and the O'Chiese band (1950). In 1968, Chief Smallboy's break-away band of Crees from Hobbema Reserve also took up their traditional Native lifestyle in Big West Country.

Despite the controversy and misunderstandings resulting from the Stoney signing of Treaty 7 in 1877, members of the Wesley band were able to maintain their traditional lifestyle in the Upper North Saskatchewan Corridor until the mid-20th century, while unceasingly petitioning the government for land which they understood was to be theirs with the signing of the treaty. However, since the mid-20th century, the accelerated pace of expansion and development has caused the Wesley band great difficulty.

The National Resources Transfer Act of 1930 had transferred Crown lands to the provinces, thus giving them power in matters concerning land utilization or settlement by Native bands. Legislation was passed setting up registered trap line areas. The long arm of the dominant society's rigid structuring had reached deep into the western wilderness and found the Stoneys. By 1965 no Stoney had indicated that he was hunting or trapping in the Shunda Basin, or anywhere east of the Bighorn Range of the Rockies.[20] The 1947 Transfer Agreement, which created the Bighorn Reserve, included a condition which limited to a minimum the number of horses for which Native ownership could be claimed. Herds of wild horses had ranged throughout the mountain regions since at least the days of David Thompson, who commented upon them in his journals. The herds had been increased by horses strayed from the Wilson and Barnes ranches on the Kootenay Plains. Adding to this herd were horses from George Brewster's homestead and small ranch south of Nordegg, near the end of the short branch of the old Fur Brigade Trail. Some local horses, including those of the Stoneys, often ranged with this band. Some of these horses were lost when the Forestry began a program of cutting back on the wild and semi-wild horse population by rounding up and killing many of these horses that ranged throughout the Saskatchewan and tributary valleys, and along the meadows and flats of the Corridor. However, despite the control measures taken over the years, wild horses continue to roam the region, as they have done for centuries.

In early summer of 1955, the coal mining town of Nordegg was closed, removing from the Upper Saskatchewan Corridor the support system and familiar faces with whom two to three generations of Stoneys had dealt. Major supplies and medical care now were centred in Morley, a three day trip by horse, or at Rocky Mountain House, between 75 and 100 miles (between 121 and 161 km) east by car on a not-always-passable road.

Despite the ongoing intrusion into the Upper North Saskatchewan River Corridor of seismic crews, a few oil exploration rigs, big game hunters, a minimum security prison, and some hardy tourists and back-packers, the years to the early 1960s continued much as had the previous ones – but the clouds were gathering. The late 1960s and 1970s were most disruptive and destructive to the Wesley Stoneys as, with complete disregard for the traditional Stoney inhabitants, the institutions and structures of the dominant society took over their lives.

Wilderness areas were created by the government to preserve and protect the wilderness for future generations; these areas are exempt from all hunting and fishing. Two of Alberta's four Wilderness areas are located in the Stoneys' original hunting territory. First Nations people living on reserves were required to obey laws, including the hunting and fishing laws of general application, as passed by the provincial Legislature. This effectively curbed the Stoneys' ability to maintain their traditional lifestyle.

In 1975, the David Thompson Highway officially opened, creating a hard-surface, all-weather connector from Red Deer to the Icefields Parkway. The David Thompson Highway was connected with the Edmonton/Jasper Highway to the north and the Calgary/Banff Highway to the south by the Forestry Trunk Roads. These roads, carved out of the bush, angled across both the Big Fish trail and the First Nations/Fur Brigade trails to the Saskatchewan River. Civilization was intruding.

The prehistoric/historic campsites located in the Shunda Basin and along Shunda Creek had been locations used by the Wesley Stoneys; in the early 1960s a Youth Hostel was set up at the north site, and the Upper Shunda Recreation Area was established at the Shunda Flats location. In 1970, this latter area became a public campground. The European world had intruded once again, claiming sites which had always been Native campgrounds. Along the Chungo, tourists and campers, looking for a place to run dirt bikes, moved in on a third prehistoric campsite location.

Just over 20 years after getting their small reserve, the Stoneys learned that a Calgary Power (TransAlta Utilities) Dam was to be constructed in this same area. A 20 mile (32 km) man-made lake was to be created, flooding a portion of the historically significant Kootenay Plains, and removing much of the Stoneys' traditional hunting grounds. During construction of the Bighorn Dam, Native graves were stripped open by bulldoz-

Kootenay Plains Indian burial ground, flats where Tom Wilson's Trading Post buildings were relocated when the dam began to fill, and the original location of Barnes' Ranch, 1906. A. Belliveau collection.

Sasquatch – "wildmen of the woods"

Mammoth creatures have been part of Native folklore for centuries. Since the late 19th century there have been over 300 eye-witness reports of the Sasquatch, all indicating similar characteristics. The Sasquatch seldom indicates aggressive behaviour, usually standing quietly and staring without expression, or else fleeing from the encounter.[i] A central location for the Sasquatch would appear to have been the Bighorn/Windy Point area west of Nordegg in the Upper North Saskatchewan River Corridor. Chief Smallboy's breakaway band of Crees was living in the Upper Saskatchewan area in 1968 when Lazarus Roan reported that a large animal had been disturbing the camp and exciting the dogs. Footprints were noticeable the morning after the disturbance and they were located an inch deep in soil which was firm enough to resist any impression of human feet. The prints were between four and five feet apart.

The *Edmonton Journal* reported that Morley Beaver, also known as Chief Walking Eagle of the Bighorn Stoneys, had told people of sightings in earlier years. According to the *Calgary Herald*, in April of 1969, Native people had said there were enormous creatures sighted in the mountains around Nordegg. Some of Chief Smallboy's band told of seeing strange figures in the Windy Point region in June of 1969, and a hairy, man-like creature was also reported at White Rabbit Creek on Kootenay Plains.[ii] Legend has it that the whole area was once populated by the creatures.[iii]

Calgary Power Company, now known as TransAlta Utilities, began work on construction of the Bighorn Dam in 1969, and a number of sightings took place during that summer. One theory is that the creatures, fascinated by the construction noise generated in this normally quiet region, ventured closer to investigate.

In late August 1969, five workmen were clearing timber, building access roads and setting up the construction site prior to creation of the Bighorn Dam on the Saskatchewan River. On this particular morning they were working on the pump-base of a well at the river when Guy L'Heureux, of Rocky Mountain House, and Harley Peterson, of Condor, noticed someone on the high ridge to the south of the river. Harley's father, Stan, who was also the foreman, joined the others at their work and he was asked if he had noticed the fellow sitting up there on the ridge watching them work. Stan acknowledged having seen him, and the boys commented on his seemingly large size.

After a considerable period of watching the activity along the river bed, the creature stood up and then moved off into the trees. When it stood up, the size difference was immediately apparent; it was bigger than any man. Later in the day, two of the men went up on the ridge so those below could get a comparison sizing. It was then that the men at river level were able to see the enormous difference in size between the men who had climbed the ridge and the creature which had sat there, watching them work.[iv]

[i] Henderson, p.253
[ii] *Edmonton Journal*, Aug. 30, 1969
[iii] *Calgary Herald*, Aug. 30, 1969
[iv] Stan Peterson, oral interview.

ers doing clearing operation; grave markings were destroyed, and some locations were lost. Because of lost grave markings, a number of these graves, which were relocated to upper Kootenay Plains near Two O'Clock Creek, where Barnes' Kadonna Ranch had been built in 1906, then had to be marked as "Wesley Stoney" or "Wesley Stoney Child."

A rushed archaeological survey was done on the area from Bighorn to the west edge of the Kootenay Plains prior to Power Dam operation and flooding of the Plains. It was this survey which established and recorded the 61 Kutenai campsite locations, now submerged under Lake Abraham, in the Bighorn Reservoir area. These had been small winter hunting camps based out of camps further upriver on the Plains. Traditional trapping, hunting, recreational, grazing, and religious areas were flooded as the dam began to fill in August, 1972. The activity and noise created through dam construction contributed to the disappearance of wild animals from the area, and the Bighorn Stoneys, always the most independent of the Stoneys, finally were forced to take welfare in order to survive.[21]

An information package issued concerning the Bighorn Dam had a heading, "Effects on Communities"; the first settlement mentioned was Rocky Mountain House. Mention also was made of the few farms west of Rocky Mountain House, along the river.[22] However, no mention was made of the Natives nor of the Bighorn Reservation, which is located at the confluence of the Bighorn and the Saskatchewan Rivers, five miles (8 km) downstream from the Bighorn Dam. The close proximity of this massive storage structure, and its potential for destruction, was frightening to the Stoneys. They listed this among other concerns, which they itemized and forwarded to the Premier of Alberta, to the Chairman of Human Resources Development Authority, and to others. Itemized concerns included disruption of the Native way of life, flooded homes and land, loss of grazing land, loss of trap-line areas, loss of traditional areas for the Sundance, loss of recreation areas, disruption and loss of historical and cultural aspects, and flooding of sacred areas and graves. They received sympathetic lip-service, but no action. Again.

Even to the territorially-minded ex-Nordeggers, construction of the Bighorn dam was a severe psychological blow, despite the intervening 17 years since the town had closed. To the Stoneys, who watched their traditional home being taken out from under them, this was catastrophic.

This region is among the richest, historically, in North America, as well as being the traditional home of the Stoneys, but the Bighorn Dam construction was looked upon by the people of Alberta as just one more project along the road of progress. The reply of the Chairman of the Human Resources Development Authority to Chief John Snow's concerns included the comments:

> *It is always regrettable when the progress of civilization changes historical and cultural patterns. Nevertheless, it is inevitable . . . the advancement of civilization cannot be stopped.*[23]

The advancement of civilization, in the creation of this dam, resulted in desecration of this historically rich area of land and total demoralization of the Stoneys.

West Country Legend

From the time Europeans began exploring and trading westward into the continent, the focus of activity north of the 49th parallel was toward the headwaters of the Saskatchewan River. Indian middle-men told of a swiftly flowing river issuing from the mountains, and European exploration gradually moved westward, looking for the source of this river and for the route to the Western Sea.

View of the Saskatchewan River, west from Windy Point. A. Belliveau collection.

A memoir of a French post commandant that has created considerable interest and controversy among historians is that of Jacques Repentigny Legardeur de Saint Pierre who, in August, 1752, forwarded an account of the founding of a French fort to the Governor-General in Quebec:

> *The order which I gave to the Chevalier de Niverville, to establish a post three hundred leagues above that of Paskoya, was executed on the 29th May, 1751. He sent*

off ten men in two canoes, who ascended the river Paskoya (Saskatchewan) as far as the Rocky Mountains, where they made a good fort, which I named Fort LaJonquiere . . .[1]

Is it possible that Anthony Henday, of the Hudson's Bay Company, was not the first European explorer to see the Alberta Rocky Mountains?

And where was Fort LaJonquiere constructed?

There are no definitive answers to these questions and, quite possibly, there never will be. However, we can consider the portion of the puzzle which is complete, and speculate about the missing parts.

The Hudson's Bay Company policy of encouraging the Natives to bring furs for trade to the Hudson's Bay Company Headquarters was countered by the policy of the French, who went inland to the Natives for trade. The French lay claim to all the land they travelled through, although these sovereignty claims were aimed at the English. As far as the Native people were concerned, French rule was limited to within the walls of the posts they constructed.

Prior to 1761, those *voyageurs* who manned the French thrust westward were nearly all Canadians by birth, from *habitant* families who "were in constant association with the Indians," and from Metis. These men became experienced woodsmen, knowledgeable about the country, its people and the languages spoken.[2] Many of them had a common bond with the First Nations people through whose territory they passed. The Canadians, backed by the French, became extremely successful, winning both the good-will of the First Nations and a large share of the best furs. The posts were called French but, in reality, the majority of the manpower was French Canadian and Metis.

The French centre of operations was Montreal, and the supply route was long and arduous. The commissions of western post commandants included the stipulation that the men were to go west "to the legendary sea," but little thought was given to the difficulty of this. The French government ordered the westward search, but did not supply funds to achieve this, insisting instead that the cost be covered by profits from the fur trade.

The environment was hostile and posts were isolated, winter was spent in drafty huts and morale was always a problem. Food supplies were scarce because of transportation, and the men were expected to live off the land as much as possible. Illness was a constant worry, while European medical practices of the time, such as blood-letting, made it extremely dangerous to become sick.[3]

Inter-tribal wars posed another problem: if the Europeans showed support for one tribe, it incurred the enmity of the opposing tribe. The famous French explorer, Lieutenant Pierre Gaultier de Varennes et de LaVerendrye, paid a high price for his support of northern tribes when, in 1736, a retaliatory massacre on the part of the Dakoda (Sioux) resulted in the death of his eldest son, Jean-Baptiste.

By 1749, the French government had decided it was important that the Canadians of New France extend their claims as far as possible in the search for the Western Sea, and France agreed to finance the voyages of discovery reaching beyond their advance posts so that the men would be concerned with exploration, not trade. Sixty-two-year-old LaVerendrye was selected to push the thrust westward but, while preparing for this concentrated effort, he died. His sons were denied their request to carry out the journey and LeGardeur de Saint Pierre was appointed to carry out the task. Saint Pierre had a distinguished military career, good control over his men and he was adept in his dealings with the First Nations.[4]

Of Saint Pierre's thrust to the western Sea we only have a summary of the information, as forwarded to his superiors; his actual journals never have been located. This summary states that a fort, which he named LaJonquiere, was established on a small island at the Rocky Mountains. Saint Pierre's memoir has generated controversy among historians who have both accepted and rejected the statement of expansion as far as the Rockies. Consideration first was given to the South Saskatchewan as the route taken, and Calgary as a possible location for the fort. The north branch, however, followed the woods where furs were plentiful, and flowed through land inhabited by Natives who spoke Cree, which was the working language of the fur-trade. Saint Pierre's account indicates that contact was made with Natives who were going by a river that issued from the Rocky Mountains to trade with the French.

The original instructions to Saint Pierre's lieutenant, Joseph-Claude Boucher Chevalier de Niverville, to proceed westward upriver for 300 leagues, does not include mention of the Rockies. The mountains become part of the statement only with Saint Pierre's additional information that the men followed the Saskatchewan River as far as the Rocky Mountains.

Noted historian W. J. Eccles of the University of Toronto has stated that "it would have been utter stupidity . . . to fabricate this tale of a post at the Rocky Mountains" in a journal to be submitted "to the governor-general" when de Niverville, or any of the men, could have exposed it. Eccles further states "one of the acknowledged rules of evidence" is that historians cannot dismiss the statement of Saint Pierre that a fort was established at the Rockies in 1751 and "unless convincing evidence can be produced that Saint Pierre's men did not reach the Rocky Mountains, his statement has to be accepted."[5]

When de Niverville was unable to make the journey, having fallen ill himself, he remained at Fort Paskoya (The Pas, Manitoba) and sent his men ahead to establish the fort, expecting to join them within a short time. Some scholars have questioned the ability of 10 men, without either of their superior officers, making this journey. However, the hardy *voyageurs* who "gloried in feats of endurance that made Europeans blanche,"[6] were used to paddling from dawn to sunset, portaging as much as 9 miles at a stretch, carrying at least two 90-pound loads at once, living off the land and living with the unexpected as commonplace. They would have had little trouble making such a journey. These *voyageurs* no longer would be slowed by either pace or requirements of superiors, and a natural leader, if not already appointed by de Niverville, soon would emerge from within the group to direct the proceedings. Besides, the *voyageurs* had a vested interest in completing given instructions. When they were hired to extend French interests into the west, they were under contract for which they did not get paid until they returned to Montreal after completion.[7]

The distance of 300 French leagues translates to mean approximately 750 miles or 1250 kilometres from Paskoya, placing a final destination some distance upriver from Edmonton, if the North Saskatchewan River was the route of choice. Tracing the North Saskatchewan River's route eastward from the Rocky Mountains, the River continues to flow eastward until it passes to the southwest of Rocky Mountain House, where the river then makes an abrupt turn to the north. It follows this direction for close to 75 miles (125 km) before again turning east on its eventual way to Hudson Bay. For anyone coming upriver, toward the mountains and away from the prairie regions, the Rocky Mountains would not become visible until near present-day Rocky Mountain House, due to the direction of river flow and to the northwest/southeast angle along which the mountains lie.

Imagine the frustration of these early *voyageurs* as they paddled up the river which had led them so many miles into the west, only to have it turn as though the river was coming from the south. Eventually, by climbing a tall tree or from a height of land, they would be able to see the mountains in the distance, but their river would appear to be flowing parallel to these mountains.

Would they have explored up the Brazeau River which flows into the Saskatchewan from the west, near the bend in the river which would turn them south? But the mountains are still distant at this point.

Or would they have forsaken their upstream pull when they arrived at the confluence of the Baptiste and the Saskatchewan Rivers? A possible indication that these *voyageurs* reached, or passed, this point on the river is that, many years afterward, the early traders at Rocky Mountain House were told by the Natives that this particular river was called Baptiste. That also is the name given it, but without explanation, in the journals of David Thompson and Alexander Henry.[8]

Concerning the giving of place-names throughout the west, the Geographic Board of Canada, 1928, comments that "it is remarkable that the traders themselves applied names only when it was absolutely necessary to do so, as when they established trading posts."[9] Is there any special significance to naming this one river?

However, Baptiste is a relatively common French name. But might it be possible that a *voyageur* of the mid-18th century gave the river its present name? And is that name in any way connected to Jean-Baptiste, the eldest son of LaVerendrye, killed in 1736?

Were some of these *voyageurs* the same men who had worked with LaVerendrye and his sons during their search for the Western Sea? Could this be the *voyageurs*' way of leaving the LaVerendrye mark upon the land for which they searched but never saw? Would the early *voyageurs* have known from Native or other sources that the large river upon which they were travelling was the one they sought?

Saint Pierre's account states "ten men in two canoes . . . who ascended the river . . . as far as the Rocky Mountains."[10] Does this mean "near" or "into" these mountains? The Baptiste River would not take the *voyageurs* into the mountains but it would take them reasonably close. If they did continue upstream on the Saskatchewan, did they build their fort at Rocky Mountain House where both the Northwest Company and the Hudson's Bay Company constructed their posts half a century later?

Saint Pierre also stated that Natives were "going by a river which flows from the Rocky Mountains, to trade with the French, who had their first establishment on an island at a small distance from the land." The topography of the land where the Upper North Saskatchewan River Corridor ends in an abrupt turn of the river from east to north, the area where the Rocky Mountain House forts later were constructed, indicates the possibility that part of this area once could have been an island. The North Saskatchewan River is a river of many channels; this creates small islands throughout the valleys where it flows, as still evidenced in the upper reaches of the Corridor, where the river flow is unaffected by the flow control of the Bighorn Dam. Any river in flood, or under heavy ice pack, changes its channel routes on a semi-regular basis, especially in areas where there is even a slight directional change of the water flow.

> *Since fur traders had a tendency to build their posts on the site of earlier existing ones, Fort LaJonquiere may well have been built where Rocky Mountain House later stood. All that is needed to prove the hypothesis is sound evidence.*[11]

The 1963 archaeological excavations of the first Rocky Mountain House site unearthed some items which seem to pre-date the 1799 construction date of this fort. Within the excavated area 19 loose nails were found in building II, of which six were dated pre-1800. All six were found in the western part of the building, in the area of the double hearth fireplace.

> *The distribution of the early nails restricted to the western end of building II as opposed to the wider over-all distribution of the later nails is of note. This is highly suggestive of the presence of an earlier structure in what later became the western end of the Hudson's Bay Company building.*[12]

Five brass buttons also were found, of which four were considered the type to date between 1720 and 1785. These four buttons were found both in, and near, building II, with the largest being found near the double hearthed fireplace.

Also located during excavation was a well preserved two-tined steel table fork, fitted with a straight-shanked two-piece antler handle. This fork, found near a drainage outlet west of building II, was a type of fork of the period 1720-1780, and was known from archaeological excavations at Fort Michilimackinac.[13] Michilimackinac, situated between Lakes Michigan and Huron, was the main French trading depot between Montreal and the western outposts during the days of LaVerendrye and Saint Pierre.

Pits of varying sizes and functions were excavated and they yielded a great variety of artifacts. Pit #4 was a 22 inch (56 cm) deep pit located below the floor of the northwest corner of building II. At a depth of 21 inches (53 cm) "a tan spall gunflint of French style was uncovered."[14]

Could it be that Fort LaJonquiere lies underneath the northwestern section of the first Rocky Mountain House fort?

Or did these *voyageurs* portage past the Brierley Rapids west of Rocky and continue upriver until they were actually within the mountains before building their post? This would have required another 50 or more river miles (85 or more km) of travel up the river to the Saunders/Alexo region. This is near the Gap, and is the east end of the difficult section of the Saskatchewan River as it passes through the Brazeau Range. It even is possible that the *voyageurs* passed through Saskatchewan Gap into the wide, flat valley of the Brewster's Flats area. The French post was reported as constructed by May 29, 1751, early enough in the season to pass through the Gap prior to heavy spring run-off in this part of the west country.

*T*he eastern portion of the Upper North Saskatchewan River Corridor, including both the area at the mouth of the Shunda and the territory around the Rocky Mountain House forts, was a region frequented by both the Blackfoot (Yhatchelini) and the Stoney (Assiniboine), and the report of Saint Pierre mentions both of these tribes. Saint Pierre writes about leaving Fort La Reine (present-day Portage la Prairie, Manitoba) to visit the new fort, when he learned that the Assiniboines, who had travelled to the Rocky Mountains to visit the newly-established French fort, found the Yhatchelini already camped there. Saint Pierre was forced to abandon the idea of maintaining this newly-created outpost when there was a renewal of inter-tribal warfare after the Assiniboines attacked the Yhatchelini. This communication of Saint Pierre suggests that a band of Blackfoot Natives had located themselves around the newly established fort in the Rocky Mountains.

John Ewers, an authority on the Blackfoot, has stated that "Frenchmen must have been the first whites these Indians met."[15] Ewers states this is "strongly suggested in name for Frenchmen which has survived in the language of the Blackfeet(sic)."[16] The term for Frenchman is *Nitsapikoan*, meaning "real white man," or "real or original Old Man People." The term for northern whiteman is *Napikoan*, meaning "Old Man People." Both terms are a reference to a superhuman figure, Napi, or "The Old Man" (in Blackfoot). However, the French term indicates earliest contact. Native oral tradition also tells a tale which would seem to support Saint Pierre's report concerning construction of a fort far up the Paskoya River. George Bird Grinnell collected a number of traditional Indian stories and, in 1911, he published a book of these tales. One such tale is "The Coming of the White Man." It was told by a man nearly 70 years old when the tale was collected, sometime before 1911. He had heard the story when he was a boy, from a tribesman who was then an old man, and the old man, in turn, had heard it from his grandfather, who was one of the party who met the white people.

The Blackfoot story tells of a war party which came to the Big River (Saskatchewan) and discovered what looked like strange beaver work. Upon investigating, they came to an open spot on the river bank and saw what looked like bears lifting logs and piling them up. Upon closer inspection it was decided that these creatures looked like people except that they had wool on their faces, and they were not wearing robes. The story mentions that these creatures were wearing what appears to have been brightly colored sashes which the Natives admired.[17] It was then decided that these creatures were "water people" whom the Natives feared.

Eventually the two groups made contact with each other. The Blackfoot party "stayed with the white men some days, camping nearby" before returning to their camp. "Afterward, many others visited the whites."[18]

This Blackfoot story of the first meeting with the white man does not relate a story about a solitary white adventurer who visited the Natives in their camps, as Anthony Henday did, but rather it suggests the presence of a group of white men constructing a fort on the banks of a river in approximately mid-18th century.

*I*n the story of the "missing" Fort LaJonquiere, not all pieces of the puzzle are available to us. It is history, but must remain partly legend. Unless the fort eventually is located, or new information is unearthed, that is how it will remain.

Could it still be possible to find the ruins of a small fort constructed well over two centuries ago?

Through the Shining Mountains

*B*y 1760, French fur trade activity in the west had ceased. The St. Lawrence fur trade was reorganized under Anglo-American, British, and French merchants, and fur trade competition continued once again. During the later part of the 18th century, the NorthWest Company and the Hudson's Bay Company continued to extend their trading posts further into the west along the established First Nations routes, competing with each other for the Native trade and the best furs. Both companies had men who journeyed ahead of the main thrust, exploring the still-unknown land. The North Saskatchewan River route into the mountains continued to be one major area of focus.

As one fur trading company moved upriver, the other followed closely behind, playing a gigantic game of high stakes leapfrog across the west. By 1795, both the Nor'westers and the Hudson's Bay Company were established along the North Saskatchewan River as far west as the Edmonton region, where the Hudson's Bay Company built Fort Edmonton and the NorthWest Company constructed Fort Augustus.

In the summer of 1798, John McDonald of Garth took six men in a canoe to explore the land upriver from the Edmonton area. They passed the confluence of the Clearwater and the Saskatchewan Rivers, and a short distance above this point they came in sight of the Brazeau Range of the Rocky Mountains. The men continued their journey for two more days but found the river was becoming unnavigable. This was the first officially recorded journey of Europeans into the eastern portion of the Upper North Saskatchewan River Corridor.

Both the NorthWest Company's Rocky Mountain House and the Hudson's Bay post of Acton House were established in 1799, just above the confluence of the Saskatchewan with the Clearwater River. There is "a grand view of the Rocky mountains, lying nearly S.W."[1] from the site of these first Rocky Mountain House forts. This became the jumping-off point for Nor'wester voyages westward through the mountains, although the hoped-for wealth of furs never fully materialized.[2] These posts saw little of the Kutenais but became an important post for the Peigans and, to a much smaller extent, for the Stoneys.[3]

John McDonald of Garth, who is credited with establishing the first of the Rocky Mountain House forts, spent the winters of 1806-07 and 1810 at this fort. David Thompson, a brilliant surveyor with the Hudson's Bay Company, had switched his allegiance to the Northwest Company in 1797. In 1800 Thompson and his young Metis wife, Charlotte Small, took up residence at Rocky Mountain House, and their first child, a daughter, was born there in June of 1801.

During the fall of 1800, a small band of Kutenai arrived at Rocky Mountain House where they traded their furs.[4] These Natives planned on returning to their western territory by travelling along the north bank of the Saskatchewan River Valley, so when it was time for these Kutenais to leave, Thompson sent two of his men, Lagasse and LeBlanc, with the Natives. Although it is not documented as such, it is possible that these two men were the first Europeans to reach as far west as the Nordegg region within the Saskatchewan Corridor, and to reach the western slopes of the Rocky Mountains by way of this route.

In 1800, the Rocky Mountain House Fort had come under the command of Nor'wester wintering partner, Duncan McGillivray, who had taken over the post from John McDonald of Garth. McGillivray strongly believed in the necessity of finding an economical route to the Western Sea and he had every intention of being the person responsible for locating a passage through the mountains. Therefore, in December of 1800, McGillivray set out once again, this time covering regions to the north. He followed the Saskatchewan for eight miles (13 km) and then went cross-country, probably following the Native trail that traced a route to the Brazeau River. He then followed the river to Brazeau Lake and beyond. However, this was not the type of route for which he was searching; he declared it impassible for horses. McGillivray had forced himself too hard in the process of exploring for access to the western sea and his resulting illness obliged him to return to Montreal in the spring of 1801. Prior to leaving the post, he left instructions that the men were to try again to find a practical route through the mountains.

James Hughes, a NorthWest Company partner, was left in charge of the Rocky Mountain House fort when McGillivray returned east. In June 1801, Hughes and David Thompson attempted to journey westward through the mountains. The party, guided by a Cree who, apparently, was not too familiar with this part of the country, travelled by horse along the bank of the Saskatchewan River, turning southwest up the valley of the North Ram River, a tributary of the Saskatchewan. Struggling through fallen timber and wide expanses of muskeg, they followed the north fork of the Ram River to the river's lake source, in a mountainous and wooded area southwest of Onion Lake, before admitting that the route they had chosen was impossible.

David Thompson was not yet familiar with this part of the country, but he calculated (correctly) that the route of the Saskatchewan for which he was searching was close by, and running parallel to the route they had followed. The north branch of the North Ram River is only about 15 miles (24 km) from the Saskatchewan River, along which stretched the Native trail toward Howse Pass and through the mountains. After reaching the headwaters of the North Ram River, Thompson and two men continued to explore on foot around the lake and into the upper valley on the east side of the mountains which border White Rabbit Creek, before turning back.[5] Again, they were close to the First Nations' Saskatchewan route, but separated from it by extremely rugged country.

Thompson and Hughes decided to give up this attempt to penetrate the mountains by way of Ram River and they retraced their route to the confluence of the Ram and the Saskatchewan Rivers. They camped at the mouth of the Ram for a few days while constructing a canoe for a further attempt at exploration, this time along the Saskatchewan itself.

By June 23rd, they were ready to launch themselves westward. Hughes, who was worried about being absent from the fort for too long a period, elected to return to Rocky Mountain House, which lay at a distance only 28 miles (47 km) east, as the crow flies. Hughes was accompanied to the fort by a small portion of the party, including the Cree guide. Thompson and the remainder of the party continued the attempt to penetrate the mountains, this time by paddling upstream along the Saskatchewan. However, snow often lies late in the valleys and on the mountains of the Upper North Saskatchewan River Corridor and the normal melting from the warm weather of late June, which that year was combined with unusually heavy rains, had caused the river to become a swollen torrent. It had risen until it stretched from bank to bank in places and was filled with great quantities of floating debris.

Within a few days, Thompson and his party, realizing the attempt was hopeless, gave up the battle against the raging river. He and two of the men walked a distance westward until they were well within the area of the river's passage through the first great chain of mountains. They came to a spot where they could go no further; the river closed in between high banks of rock which rose from the river to a height of 300 to 500 feet (92 to 152 meters). Yet, to their frustration, just beyond these perpendicular rock walls they were able to see green hills and an open valley where the river widened.[6]

At this point they would have been in the vicinity of the Saskatchewan Gap, south and east of Nordegg, where the North Saskatchewan flows through the Brazeau Range of mountains. The open valley that was ahead of Thompson and his men was near the Natives' overland trail, which rejoins the Saskatchewan River. No further attempt to follow the Saskatchewan appears to have been made until a few years later.

The Rocky Mountain House forts were closed in 1802 because the Kutenai trade had not come to these posts, but both posts were reopened again three years later. For over three-quarters of a century, Rocky Mountain House was opened and closed on a regular basis. David Thompson had been promoted to wintering partner in 1804, and in 1806 he was reassigned to Rocky Mountain House by John McDonald. McDonald, by this time, was in charge of the Saskatchewan district posts. He also had become Thompson's brother-in-law through marriage to Nancy Small, the sister of Thompson's wife Charlotte.

The Nor'westers were determined to cross the mountain barrier and they were convinced the venture would be profitable. The Hudson's Bay Company, on the other hand, did not believe that they would profit by taking their trade further west, so they did not attempt to do so.

During this first decade of the 19th century, the Peigans kept careful watch on the activity of the traders in order to prevent European trade with the Kutenai. Members of the Blackfoot Confederacy had been able to sell European trade goods to the Kutenais and other tribes beyond the mountains, making good profits for themselves, and they did not want this lucrative market to be taken from them.[7] However, when word reached the Peigans that Captain Lewis, of the Lewis and Clark expedition in the United States, had killed two of their tribesmen, the Peigans left for the Missouri River area to avenge these deaths. This gave Thompson the opportunity to follow the Saskatchewan River route across the mountains and to the Columbia River in the spring of 1807.

Finan McDonald took five men and supplies up the Saskatchewan to the Kootenay Plains; the remainder of the party travelled by horseback along the overland route, meeting the others at the Plains.[8] This group included Thompson, his wife Charlotte, and their three small children, ages 14 months, three years, and five years, as well as the family of one of the *voyageurs* who had gone ahead by canoe, one other woman, and three *voyageurs*. The few Europeans who, by this time, had crossed the mountains via the Saskatchewan River valley, may or may not have travelled through the Shunda Basin; David Thompson and his young family were the first European explorers on record as having taken the land route which follows close to the river, thus passing through the Shunda Basin in which Nordegg later was established.

Following the land route around Saskatchewan Gap afforded three choices of travel routes through the Shunda Basin area. After passing through Shunda Gap they may have chosen to keep to higher ground, following along the southern edge of Shunda Basin, passing south and above the area which later became Nordegg, and along the ridge under which lay the coal that would be mined by the Brazeau Collieries over a century later. Or they may have chosen to follow the trail north of Nordegg's later location, camping for the night at Shunda Flats, the traditional First Nations camp-

Thompson's latitude reading for their two day camp indicates Two O'Clock Creek Flats. A. Belliveau collection.

ground. The following day they would have journeyed south from Shunda Flats, possibly following the trail which later became Nordegg's Stuart Road, angling up the south slope of Shunda Basin and passing just east of where the hospital later was built. Slightly southeast of the eventual mine site, this trail merged with the route following the southern edge of Shunda Basin. Since they were taking the overland route, when the trail separated into two branches just southwest of Nordegg, they would have followed the route through Black Canyon, along the northwest side of the Saskatchewan. It also is possible, but much less likely, that they may have travelled west from Shunda Flats, along the inland route to the Kootenay Plains, an approximation of the present day David Thompson Highway route. However, this route is not close to the Saskatchewan River for approximately 35 miles (60 km).

On June 3, the land party rejoined the other members of their party who now were camped on the Kootenay Plains. Thompson's latitude reading for this location was 52° 2' N, which indicates that they were in the vicinity of Two O'Clock Creek, since all of the overland routes would have brought them to the Kootenay Plains along the northern bank of the Saskatchewan. In all probability, the area where they camped would be that later used by E. C. Barnes for his Kadonna Ranch, where the Native burial ground now is located. Three weeks later the entire party were on their way over Howse Pass, following the Blaeberry River to where it joins the Columbia River en route to the Pacific Ocean.[9] However, the Columbia at this point still flows northward, and does so for a considerable distance before taking a sweeping bend which begins its southwestern journey to the ocean. As a result of this characteristic of the river, Thompson did not suspect that this was the one he had been seeking.

*T*he Saskatchewan Corridor passage was the route followed by the fur brigade each year from 1807 to 1811, as they transported furs from, and supplies to, Thompson's base camp, now located west of the Rocky Mountains. Once David Thompson had been established at Kootenae House in 1807, Rocky Mountain House again was abandoned and furs from west of the mountains were brought to the forts built in what is now the Edmonton area.

In 1809, the Hudson's Bay Company also decided to expand into the Upper Saskatchewan River Valley and beyond, so Joseph Howse was sent to follow Thompson's route. Howse travelled through this area in 1809 and 1810 before heeding a stern warning from the Peigans to cease trading west of the mountains. Howse Pass and Howse River were both named after this man.

On June 19th, 1810, David Thompson was on his return voyage from the Columbia River when he and his small party camped on the Kootenay Plains before descending the Saskatchewan on their journey east.[10] Could this have been the day when he carved his name and 1810 into a tree on the southwest edge of the Kootenay Plains? Arturo Lucarelli, a contract miner from Nordegg and also a registered guide and outfitter, commented that, while hunting during the late 1940s, he had come upon a tree on the southwest end of the Plains that had David Thompson's name and the date, 1810, carved into it. Although Thompson did not know it at the time, this was to be his last trans-mountain trip via the Kootenay Plains due to the intense pressure being exerted by the Peigans, who were becoming hostile because this European trade had placed

Aerial photo of Nordegg, courtesy of the University of Calgary maps division. Stuart Road, which begins at the lower left hand corner of the photo and heads up and towards the right into town, was built over the original Indian/Fur Brigade trail back to the Saskatchewan River. Once past the railway station (top centre of the semi-circle) the trail continues on the same angle to Marcelle Avenue. Just north of and parallel to Marcelle Avenue, the Indian trail follows the southern edge of Shunda Basin from Shunda Gap.

arms, ammunition, and other trade goods in the hands of tribes across the mountains. This allowed these western Natives, who previously were at the mercy of the Blackfoot, to offer resistance to invaders or unwelcome visitors.

During the early years of the 19th century, while the Upper Saskatchewan River was still the only known route in this general region of the Rocky Mountains, the decision was made to re-open the Rocky Mountain House post. On October 5th, 1810, Alexander Henry the Younger arrived at Rocky Mountain House to re-open this fort. He immediately became involved in one of the more puzzling aspects of the race to the western sea. In recent years a few historians have begun to question the events of 1810-11 which resulted in the Pacific Fur Company, formed in 1810 by John Jacob Astor, reaching the mouth of the Columbia River ahead of David Thompson.

It has been suggested by some historians that Astor submitted a proposal to the NorthWest Company that the two companies make a joint settlement on the Pacific Coast at the mouth of the Columbia.[11] No record of this proposal was contained in the minutes of the Annual General Meeting of the NorthWest Company. However, scholars who have studied records dealing with the fur trade in the United States consider this proposal to have been a distinct possibility, and David Thompson's actions upon reaching the mouth of the Columbia River seem to support this. Following this Annual General Meeting of the NorthWest Company, Thompson had been dispatched westward once again to establish a post at the mouth of the Columbia. At that time, after dropping off his wife and family with her relatives living at the Lake Winnipeg post, David Thompson was at Rainy Lake, enroute to Montreal, when he received instructions to return to the west. He had been due to go on rotation to the east in 1808, but had continued his work in the west for another two years before leaving for his hard-earned vacation. Now, he was expected to waive his plans for a vacation, and return once again to Saskatchewan River country and the land west of the mountains.[12]

The Pacific Fur Company's venture into the west was to consist of 2 groups; one group was to proceed overland, while the second group would proceed via ocean travel. In early September, 1810, as David Thompson and his *voyageurs* returned to Rocky Mountain House, John Jacob Astor's ship, the Tonquin, was leaving New York harbor on its way to the mouth of the Columbia River, via Cape Horn and the Sandwich (Hawaiian) Islands. The majority of the expedition's members, and all of the leaders, were from the British territory which now is Canada; some members were former employees of the NorthWest Company. By April, 1811, the Tonquin had reached the mouth of the Columbia, and by the end of May there was the beginnings of a settlement which the expedition members named Fort Astor (now Astoria, Oregon).

The outcome of what may, or may not, have been a race to the Pacific is history, but the scanty available information about the race itself leaves some puzzling questions. Numerous and lengthy delays caused Thompson to "run his race as to lose it."[13] Thompson's characteristics of determination and persistence, which can be seen in his previous exploits, appear to be somewhat lacking during a short, but crucial, period of time during the fall of 1810.

David Thompson kept detailed notes during his years in the northwest, but Book 24 of his journals no longer exists. His diary ends on July 22, 1810, at Rainy Lake House, and his own records for that year begin again on October 29. The intervening three months are touched upon in a short three pages, written years later, when he compiled his *Narrative*. However, some information concerning events of this race westward is found in the journals of Alexander Henry the Younger, who played a major role in sorting out the confused events surrounding Thompson in October, 1810.

It was known by the traders that David Thompson would be leading a party across the mountains, en route to the mouth of the Columbia, but when Henry arrived at the fort on October 5th, the whereabouts of Thompson were unknown, including by Thompson's men, who expected to accompany him across the mountains. Attempts were made to send the canoes upriver, but the eastern regions of the Corridor seemed to be exceptionally well populated and patrolled by Natives looking to prevent this from happening.

When a group of Peigans arrived at the fort from the west, they had with them one horse which was known to belong to David Thompson, which the Natives said they had found three days previously. They also had a pair of leggings which Alexander Henry the Younger recognized as belonging to his cousin, William Henry, who had been travelling with Thompson. This convinced Henry that Thompson was somewhere upriver, probably at Kootenay Plains, waiting for his canoes to reach him.

After much difficulty and many interruptions by the visiting and watchful Natives, Henry managed to get the men and canoes launched for the trip upriver by 2:00 a.m., October 12th. By the following evening, William Henry arrived at the fort from down river with the news that Thompson was waiting for his people at the North Branch (Brazeau River), many miles to the north of Rocky Mountain House. The explanation was that in attempting to cross overland to the fort by horse, they had somehow miscalculated, ending up at the mouth of the Shunda where the Peigans were watching for up-river traffic.

Henry immediately sent a messenger up the river to stop the canoes launched previously. Henry was soon en route in the opposite direction, going down river to locate David Thompson, who had hidden himself on top of a hill, and in trees so thick that his camp could not be seen from more than 10 yards away. Henry, who by this time had completed his eventful first week at Rocky Mountain House, found Thompson starving but still waiting for his men, both those who were bringing the horses and those with the canoes.[14]

It is difficult to imagine David Thompson, who surveyed and mapped a large portion of the northwest with unerring accuracy, becoming lost or disoriented in the country of the Upper Saskatchewan which, by this time, he knew so well. It also is difficult to reconcile the image of Thompson, who previously had pressed on through numerous hardships, frustrations, dangers, and disappointments, now cowering in a secluded clump of trees, so afraid to move from concealment that he was starving. Might it be that the long years of toil and hardship had taken a severe toll upon Thompson's mental health, and the denial of his long-awaited vacation had caused him to suffer a stress- and fatigue-related breakdown?

Thompson would not attempt the Upper North Saskatchewan route, despite the fact that the river now was left clear and unguarded. Instead, Thompson insisted his men go northward to the Athabasca River and Athabasca Pass. If Thompson had taken his usual route through the mountains, he probably could have been established at the mouth of the Columbia River long before Astor's group reached this location. However, if he was not aware that his journey had turned into a race, he would not have seen the necessity for undue speed.

Some scholars have questioned the possibility of a secret deal between the Pacific Fur Company and the NorthWest Company, or even between David Thompson and the Pacific Fur Company. But would the strong, almost rigid, moral character of Thompson have allowed him to participate in such a subterfuge? The scanty documentation of these 1810 events make it difficult to understand. The possibility exists that Thompson believed the NorthWest Company and the Pacific Fur Company were working together toward the same end, in which case it would not matter which of the two Companies first reached the mouth of the Columbia.

Although changing to a new route through the mountains was very costly to David Thompson in relation to time, he succeeded in the very difficult task of crossing the mountains through Athabasca Pass during the depths of the 1810-11 winter. Even though Thompson had pioneered a new pass through the mountains, the North Saskatchewan was not abandoned immediately. In February, 1811, Alexander Henry the Younger and two men followed the frozen Saskatchewan River through the mountains as far as Blaeberry River, and then returned. When they were journeying westward, they stopped for breakfast at the mouth of Shunda Creek and then continued on through Saskatchewan Gap, where the mountains rise steeply on either side. Henry commented in his journal that after following the river through this enclosed region, the river valley suddenly opened to a width of nearly a mile from bank to bank, while the river separated itself into numerous channels.[15]

They camped where the short overland route rejoins the river. As Henry did not feel well they travelled only a short distance, and his men spent the remainder of the day hunting. However, they did not go far from the river since, as Henry wrote in his journal, the country was too rough, and the woods too thick to go any distance into the interior.[16]

Henry and his men camped on the (Brewster's) Flats near where the short overland route rejoins the North Saskatchewan. A. Belliveau Collection.

Henry commented upon the different land forms in the area – the low hills with open meadows and the rugged mountains behind them.

> *In summer, when these hills are covered with verdure, they must form a pleasing contrast to the adjacent mountains, which are very high and craggy, consisting of solid rocks, destitute of verdure or soil.*[17]

It was mid-July 1811 when David Thompson and his party reached the mouth of the Columbia, and the new settlement of Fort Astor. Thompson told the Astorians that he believed the two Companies were working together, and he showed them a letter, a copy of the resolution which the Nor'westers had passed the previous summer, consenting to a deal with Astor.[18] This would seem to indicate that Thompson was unaware that the agreement had either been dissolved or had never been ratified. The Pacific Fur Company was firmly established at the mouth of the Columbia; the race to the Pacific was over.[19]

Thompson retired from western exploration work in 1812. In later years he worked with the International Boundary Commission, helping to establish the divisional line between the United States and the British territory to the north. He believed that his explorations and surveys accomplished west of the Continental Divide created a legitimate claim for Britain to this land. He suggested a boundary along the 47th parallel from west of the Rocky Mountains up to the Columbia River. His suggested boundary then would extend down the centre of the river until it reached the ocean. This would have meant that Canada now would include northwestern Montana, the Idaho panhandle, and nearly all of Washington State, areas explored and mapped by Thompson during his years in the west. Thompson was furious when, in 1846, Britain ceded its claim to all the land south of the 49th parallel.[20]

Although David Thompson did not use the Upper North Saskatchewan River Valley as a route through the Rocky Mountains after his disastrous attempt in the fall of 1810, the partners of the NorthWest Company preferred to maintain this route. Recorded minutes of the General Meeting indicate that, after a full discussion, it was decided the new Athabasca Pass trail would be more difficult and expensive than the original, and trade was to be carried on by the usual passage of the North Saskatchewan River. Despite this statement of intent, the vigilance and constant harassment of the Peigans won out, and Athabasca Pass then became the fur brigade's portal through the mountains, regardless of the additional expense involved.

Members of the fur brigade had followed the North Saskatchewan route westward until the fall of 1811 when this trail was abandoned, leaving the Upper North Saskatchewan River Corridor off the main transportation and communication routes. This first and possibly easiest route through the Rocky Mountains was discontinued in favor of the more northerly route through Athabasca Pass, well beyond the territory of the angry Peigans. However, the North Saskatchewan River system, including the overland detour along the Shunda in order to pass Saskatchewan Gap, was the first practical route through the mountains for European explorers and traders, and the one which opened up the land beyond the shining mountains.

Explorers, Prospectors, and Other Visitors

By 1813, the Athabasca trade route was well established. In 1821, the rival North-West Company and Hudson's Bay Company amalgamated under the name of the latter, but the Nor'wester name of Rocky Mountain House was retained. The role of Rocky Mountain House was brief but important; "As a link in the network of posts that established British domination over the western territory, it served as a block against American penetration."[1] The Rocky Mountain House fort, closed in 1875, played a necessary and colorful part in the fur trade along the North Saskatchewan, thus taking its place as an important element in the larger context of Canadian fur trade history.

One of the more colorful characters of Rocky Mountain House was Joseph Edward Brazeau. It is this man's name which has been sprinkled liberally over the west-central Alberta area, giving identity to a river, a lake, a single mountain, a mountain range, a railway station, mining collieries, and two coal fields (the Main Brazeau and the South Brazeau coal fields). Of French and Spanish ancestry, Joseph Brazeau entered the fur trade in 1830, and worked along the Yellowstone and Missouri Rivers before hiring on with the Hudson's Bay Company. His attire was somewhat unusual and, according to a family description, he sported a cloak rather than a coat and wore a flat, black Spanish sombrero on his auburn hair. He could speak nine languages. Brazeau was also of considerable help to the Palliser expedition.

The Palliser Expedition, which took place between June 1857 and March 1860, had been organized to gather solid information on the territory of British North America west of the Great Lakes. This country seemed to promise a wealth of opportunities, but the expanse of land was almost beyond anyone's imaginings and little was known about it. There were numerous questions needing answers before further planning could take place and it was hoped this expedition would provide answers to these questions. Travelling, for the most part, over trails that long had been established, members of the Palliser Expedition covered an amazing amount of territory in their search for information about this vast land. This expedition created a comprehensive document concerning the territory they travelled. For many years this report was the authoritative guide for subsequent ventures into the Canadian Northwest.

Since the Rocky Mountain House fort was abandoned every spring and reopened in the fall, not much verbal information could be gathered about this part of the country by visiting it during the summer months. Therefore, in January 1858, some Expedition members, including James Hector M.D., the naturalist, geologist, and medical doctor of the party, spent some time at Rocky Mountain House, gazing at the mountains now so near, and exploring upriver as far as the ice would allow. Hector learned that Hudson's Bay Company men frequently planted vegetables at the fort before leaving in the spring, and the results indicated that "the soil and climate are very favourable to agriculture." Hector felt that this area might be preferable to Edmonton for a number of reasons. He commented upon the "soft winds from the west, which cause a rise in the thermometer." The Indians told Hector that the area also had a great display of wildflowers, and an abundant supply of butterflies and other brightly colored insects.[2]

One of the questions the Palliser Expedition was attempting to answer was if it was feasible to construct a road through the mountains to the Pacific while remaining in British territory. During August and September 1858, Hector crossed the Rockies and returned, exploring and assessing as he travelled. By September 15, Hector and his party had reached the Kootenay Plains. Hector's report on the area pointed out that the North Saskatchewan valley was much wider and more open, and the route from its mountain source was much more direct than that of the Bow River valley. He remarked upon the strong similarities in the longitudinal valleys and the mountains surrounding both of these river drainage systems.

During the summer of 1858, James Hector had covered considerable ground in, and through, the Rocky Mountains. Returning from these explorations, he followed the old fur brigade trail eastward through the Upper Saskatchewan Corridor from the Kootenay Plains. On September 18th, they passed Windy Point, where the river flows through the Rocky Mountains' Front Ranges on its way east. Hector noted that the country quite suddenly widened out and became fairly level in this valley between First Range and Bighorn Range, while the Brazeau range "formed a line of lower mountains" even further to the east. Hector commented upon the beauty of the country in this great valley.[3]

The group spent a week resting in the Bighorn area before setting off once again. On September 27th they passed through the Bighorn Range and into the Shunda Basin region, where they soon got into thick spruce forests and soft muskeg. They passed a number of streams and large lakes before reaching the Nordegg region, in the valley at the foot of Brazeau Range. They camped near Shunda Creek where: "North and south of us, were lofty bluffs of limestone rocks, the beds of which dip to the west at a high angle."[4]

This would seem to indicate they were relatively close to Shunda Gap, where the mountains close in, encircling the eastern edge of the Shunda Basin region both north and south. Possibly they camped in the area near, or slightly east, of Beaver Dam Flats, just east of where Nordegg later was located. Hector stated that they camped near the source of a stream flowing east. However, the Shunda, which is the only true eastward flowing body of water on the route they were following, actually rises quite a distance northwest, well off the route to Shunda Gap in the Brazeau Range. The Shunda, however, has an extensive drainage system, with many streams joining the eastward flow. The marsh, muskeg, and drainage in the area west of the gap, where the mountains close in on Shunda Basin, substantially increase the size and flow of this body of water.

Hector and his party followed the Shunda to the Saskatchewan, retracing the old fur brigade route to Rocky Mountain House and Edmonton.

The following year Hector returned to the western portion of the Corridor at the Kootenay Plains by way of Pipestone Creek and Siffleur River. He then followed the North Saskatchewan River westward, attempting to locate the pass through the mountains which had been used by the early fur brigade. James Hector declared Howse Pass to be lower in ascent than any others he had examined, with no difficult ridge elevation to be crossed. Although Howse Pass was heavily timbered, especially on the western slopes, it had relatively few obstacles to surmount. Its grade rises approximately 325 feet (100 meters) over a span of 15 miles (25 km), giving such a gentle climb that Hector and his party were unaware they had crossed the height of land until they noticed streams flowing to the west.

In February 1859, a request was made for copies of Palliser's Report to assist the Canadian North-West Transit Company to estimate construction costs for a projected road to extend from the Saskatchewan headwaters to the Pacific. The Saskatchewan route through the mountains, first choice of fur traders until turned northward by hostile Natives, was being looked upon once again as a logical choice for a trans-mountain route to the Pacific.

The Palliser Report had labelled a portion of the northern prairies as arid, unsuitable for agriculture, but it also had described a fertile belt, a rich zone which included the area drained by the North Saskatchewan River, and the eastern foothills of the Rockies. The Report also pointed out that the area which now is Alberta contained an abundance of coal, and the banks of both the Red Deer and the North Saskatchewan rivers were mentioned as containing a considerable supply. These items sparked interest in those looking to western expansion.

Palliser was convinced that the Hudson's Bay Company would not be able to maintain their monopoly upon this huge territory, and he was concerned about the First Nations people who soon would be exposed to the destructive effects of European extension into the Canadian northwest. Both Palliser and Hector suggested that this be addressed as rapidly as possible to prevent future problems, and Hector urged that the interests of the First Nations be addressed as well as that of the settlers.

*I*n 1859, at much the same time that Dr. James Hector had been in the region of Pipestone Creek and Siffleur River, another Scot, the Earl of Southesk, was probing from the north into the same general territory of the Rockies. Southesk and his men rode west from Edmonton, intending to go to Jasper House, then south to Kootenay Plains. This was not a trip of exploration or mapping, but a hunting expedition.

Upon learning that game was scarce in the Jasper valley, the Southesk party turned southwest near present Edson, intending eventually to reach the Kootenay Plains. They then travelled southwest, along a river valley. This took the Southesk party into the general region which later became Alberta's Coal Branch, where a number of coal mining towns were constructed.

By September 4, 1859, Southesk and his party were in territory which now is located in south-eastern Jasper National Park. They climbed to the top of a mountain at the end of a valley. This was on the present Southesk Cairn Mountain, located north of the Cairn River, in southeast Jasper National Park.

Southesk's hunting party followed Cairn River into the large, wide valley where it joins the present Southesk River. Shortly afterward the group appear to have become lost. Finally, coming to a valley which appeared to be entirely enclosed by mountains, they made their way up a steep ridge, and were overjoyed to see both a well-defined trail and a river on the other side.[5] By evening they were camped beside a stream where there were several very old remains of an Indian encampment. From there the party travelled southeast toward the Kootenay Plains, which they reached by following along "the bed of a torrent so stony as to hurt the horses' feet." They reached the North Saskatchewan after passing through a canyon "where the water escaped through a long, narrow, deep gorge of rock" extending "about ten miles, its height perhaps two thousand feet above the stream: in many places . . . nearly perpendicular."[6]

There still is speculation about the exact location of this torrent and canyon described in Southesk's journal. He states that "our direction tended always to the south-east," to the valley of the Saskatchewan.[7] Coral Creek, shown as Corral Creek on early maps of the area, is a good possibility, but it is a tributary of the Cline (formerly Whitegoat) River, and no mention is made of the river they were following having emptied into a larger river. As well, the Cline River once flowed directly onto the Plains, where it formed part of the North Saskatchewan River system; it now flows into Lake Abraham. Southesk's journal states that the following day, they followed the North Saskatchewan River southwest to the Kootenay Plains. If they had followed Coral Creek and Cline

The Bighorn River is a good possibility for the "stony torrent" followed by Southesk and party to the valley of the Saskatchewan. A. Belliveau collection.

River to the Saskatchewan, they would have been on the Kootenay Plains by the time they reached the North Saskatchewan River.

Another possibility is the Bighorn River, although this river flows more directly east than it does southeast. However, if they had followed this river to the North Saskatchewan, it would necessitate following the Saskatchewan River southwest to reach the Plains. The Bighorn River also fits the description given regarding the torrent with a bed so stony that it hurt the horses feet, as well as the description of the lower reaches of the river, and what might have been Bighorn Canyon, "where the water escaped through a long, narrow, deep gorge of rock." However, no mention is made of any of the falls along the Bighorn River, in particular the spectacular Crescent (Bighorn) Falls, thus leaving this river as another questionable route.

When the Southesk party reached the Kootenay Plains, Southesk dismissed the Plains as "merely an inconsiderable enlargement of the valley." He was more impressed with the size of the North Saskatchewan, which he estimated as 40 yards (37m) wide, and so deep that they had to cross on rafts, despite the lateness of the season and the close proximity to the source of the river.[8] After crossing the North Saskatchewan they followed the Siffleur River to Pipestone Pass, along the same general route by which, the previous month, Hector had arrived at the Plains from the south.

Although relatively few Europeans ventured into the Upper Saskatchewan River Corridor until late in the 19th century, the Stoney (Nakoda) presence remained evident throughout this area. This was pointed out during the December 1870 visit to Rocky Mountain House of Sir William Francis Butler, who stated that "the Mountain House stands within the limits of the Rocky Mountain Assiniboines." Butler had been requested by the Lieutenant Governor of Manitoba to visit Saskatchewan country and give an independent report on affairs in the west. He cautioned against abandoning posts in the Saskatchewan region because he believed that American traders from the Missouri then would move in. Butler recommended that a position of Commissioner of the Peace be instituted, and one of the individuals he suggested for this position was Joseph Brazeau.[9]

While visiting Rocky Mountain House, Butler took note of the presence of prospectors in the Upper North Saskatchewan River Corridor, and he commented upon the constant search for gold along the rivers and in the mountains of the west. He mentioned that gold had been discovered along a number of the rivers, including the North Saskatchewan, but prospectors had been able to make only a partial examination of the country because of the impossibility of obtaining supplies and provisions. However, Butler expected a determined effort would be made during the summer of 1871 to prospect and examine the headwaters of the North Saskatchewan. Butler fully expected gold to be discovered along the North Saskatchewan, and he warned of the vast changes that would result from this find.

He was concerned about extermination of the First Nations people by a large influx of miners. Miners and Indians in the Pacific and Central regions of the United States were carrying on fierce wars. Butler recommended organizing a well-equipped force for service in the territory. He suggested these men serve for 2 or 3 years and then be

Butler was concerned for the survival of the First Nations people. A. Belliveau collection.

given a land grant, becoming military settlers. This would guarantee a reserve force in the new territory, in case their services were required at a later time.[10]

When the Hudson's Bay Company turned over control of their massive territories to the Canadian government in 1870, the necessity of building a transcontinental railway was apparent. The ribbon of steel was needed to bind together this vast dominion. The Canadian government had begun the process of controlling both the First Nations and the land by making treaties and, by 1874, the North West Mounted Police arrived in the west to maintain law and order. The way of life in the west was changing rapidly.

Constructing a railway that eventually would stretch from the Atlantic to the Pacific was a massive undertaking. Walter Moberly was appointed by Prime Minister John A. MacDonald to be the district engineer in charge of the mountain regions. Moberly, who began his explorations in July, 1871, had been instructed to find the best route across the mountains for the railway.[11] He had been thinking about the route for the railway ever since he had first explored through the mountain areas in 1858, and he had definite ideas and strong opinions on the route to be established. He wanted the railway to go through Howse Pass, follow the Columbia River around the Selkirk Mountains, go through the Gold Range via Eagle Pass, then on to Kamloops and the Fraser River.

Moberly located his headquarters 8 miles (12.9 km) north of present Golden, British Columbia, near the mouth of the Blaeberry River, on the west side of Howse Pass, at what became Moberly Siding, along the rail line to the west coast. This is where the early adventurers of the Upper North Saskatchewan River Corridor emerged from their trek through Howse Pass, down the Blaeberry into the valley of the Columbia.[12] Surveyors began examining this first route of David Thompson through the Rockies. The brush was thick, almost impassible in places, but the rate of climb and descent was relatively gentle. The North Saskatchewan River area was an extension of the fertile belt described by the Palliser Report, and seemed the logical choice for the route of the railway. Moberly was so certain this was the only conceivable route, he began locating the line through Howse Pass before he had received permission to go ahead. He received a rude shock in April 1872, when he was informed that this route was to be abandoned, and he was ordered to survey the Yellowhead Pass to the north.

By the end of the following year, seven alternative routes to the Pacific were under consideration, and further exploration and assessment was being done on at least six passes in the Rocky Mountains. By 1877, the year that the Stoney Indians were committed to Treaty 7, the route of the railway still was uncertain.

Railway surveying and construction had proceeded at a fairly leisurely pace during the 1870s, but by 1880 a private company had taken over. The Canadian Pacific Railway Company was formed, and the Canadian government embarked upon policies to settle the west. This railway company wanted the shortest route to the Pacific; Yellowhead Pass was too far north.

Railway construction was expected to take place within the area that Palliser had described as the fertile belt. However, there were questions as to whether the arid areas of Palliser's Triangle were as unsuitable for farming as first supposed. The Canadian Pacific Railway syndicate became convinced that a more southerly route was practical. One syndicate member, Jim Hill, had announced previously that, if it was possible to do so, the railway would cross the Rockies by way of Kicking Horse Pass. By 1881, the eastern syndicate that had taken over construction of the Canadian Pacific Railway had decided to cross the mountains by way of Kicking Horse Pass. In 1882 the engineer in charge of the Canadian Pacific Railway Mountain Division, Major Rogers, accompanied by Tom Wilson, did another survey on both Howse Pass and Kicking Horse Pass, and Rogers confirmed that the choice of Kicking Horse Pass was feasible. In 1883 the final decision was made to follow this route through the Rockies.[13]

Kicking Horse Pass delighted the tourists, but the grade of the climb required additional engines, double and triple train crews, considerable time loss, high expenditure of coal, and numerous railroad firemen rapidly shovelling coal to keep up a head of steam which allowed the train to climb at a snail's pace along the shelf of the mountain side. All this caused operating expenses to be extremely high. Early in the 20th century the slope of the grade was cut in two by "spending millions of dollars on great spiral tunnels and gigantic loops."[14] Despite these modifications, the gradient of Kicking Horse Pass still is three times that of either the Yellowhead or Howse Pass. The rail route of the CPR would have been a natural extension of the First Nations thoroughfare westward, which also had been followed by the fur trade adventurers. This route had been developed over many centuries of inter-mountain travel, and it afforded the least resistance.

With the Bow Corridor having been selected to carry the traffic of the nation, the Upper Saskatchewan Corridor disappeared into obscurity. It was only the occasional adventurer with a desire for exploration into the relative unknown, who looked to this region to test his skill. One such was Stanley Washburn, who made his first trip into the Upper Saskatchewan Corridor the summer prior to entering college. In 1898, he and two friends, accompanied by guide and outfitter Fred Stevens, travelled west along the south bank of the North Saskatchewan River, beyond the abandoned Rocky Mountain House fort. They had hoped to follow the Native trail on the north side of the river, but the waters were swift-flowing, and too high to ford at the usual place. They discovered, as had David Thompson and James Hughes in 1800, that the south bank of this river is far less hospitable to travellers than is the north bank. It took the Washburn party 10 days to get just beyond the mouth of the Shunda, to the mountain gap "where the river comes pouring out of a great wedge in the mountains" before they gave up their attempt and returned east.[15]

But this trip had captured Washburn, creating the love of the mountains and the west country that keeps calling people to return. In 1909, he took the same route from the east into the Upper North Saskatchewan River Corridor. He was astounded at the changes that had taken place in the territory between Lacombe and Rocky. On his last visit there had been no houses or people between the two locations; a decade later he found that during each day of travel they were in sight of farm buildings or a ranch house, and nearly every day they passed a post office. Instead of a trail westward there was a wagon road, and pack-trains were becoming a thing of the past in this part of the country. At Rocky Mountain House, the North Saskatchewan River, which they had been unable to cross in 1898, now boasted a ferry to take the pack-train across. Near the ruins of the old Hudson's Bay fort they saw a fine ranch house and the outbuildings of the rancher who ran the ferry, and they were told there was a post office across the river. A railroad was coming, but there was no definite plan for it as yet.

The party followed the First Nations/Fur Brigade trail, branched onto the Big Fish Trail, and eventually reached the main Brazeau River. During their travels they met a mining engineer who was prospecting the country for coal. He talked to them about the limitless amounts of coal in the region.[16] Washburn commented: "It seems hard to realize, . . . within a few years that whole valley, then so utterly destitute of any sign of man, will be alive with miners, tearing out the vitals of those mountains that for so many aeons of time have stood wrapped in the silence of isolation."[17]

All this exploration and settlement was a direct result of the Canadian Government's aggressive immigration policy, begun in 1896, to recruit immigrants to help settle the prairies. This was to establish an agricultural hinterland to supply central Canada, and to whom central Canada could sell manufactured goods. Since Canada was a British colony, the Canadian government conducted an extensive advertising campaign for British investment and British settlers, and many British emigrated to Canada, but not as many as expected or as needed to open the west. Advertising then was extended into Europe and the U.S.A., promising free land for those who cleared and settled it. This brought thousands of people from Europe and the United States to join those already in the west, the majority of whom were from Ontario, and had strong British ties.[18]

Although areas of the prairies had begun opening up rapidly, and immigration was in the process of permanently changing the face of the west, the Upper North Saskatchewan River Corridor continued to remain outside the mainstream of activity. During the last quarter of the 19th century and into the 20th, adventurers, prospectors, and surveyors continued to be the chief visitors to this region. During the years 1907-1911, one of the prospectors of the Upper Saskatchewan Corridor and areas to the north was German and Canadian investment representative Martin Cohn (Nordegg). Cohn was searching for the coal which frequently had been mentioned in surveys and journals during the early days of exploration in the Upper Corridor.

Nordegg and the Changing Face of the West

Martin Cohn (who later changed his name to Nordegg) was born in Reichenbach, Silesia, (now Dzierzoniow, Poland,) on July 18, 1868. Although of Jewish background, he considered himself to be first and foremost a German citizen. He studied engineering in Berlin and he also served for a time with the German Army, but he obtained his release in 1894 after severely fracturing his arm. After Cohn received his release from the military, he returned to Berlin where he studied photochemistry. One of Cohn's instructors in photochemistry was Hermann Vogel, who was responsible for developing a number of modern color photography techniques. When Martin Cohn finished his studies in photochemistry, he was hired by the Georg Buexenstein and Company Photochemigraphical Institute.[1] The owner of this establishment, Georg Wilhelm Buexenstein, German newspaper and book publisher, was a Royal Prussian Counsellor of Commerce, and President of the German Tariff Association.

Cohn was fluent in English, French, and German, and he frequently was called upon to do extensive travelling. In England, he met and married his first wife, French-woman Berthe Marie, but the marriage does not appear to have been a happy one and they spent little time together. In 1898, a daughter, Marcelle, was born.

In 1902, Buexenstein recalled Cohn from London to become manager of the Berlin printing plant. By 1906, Martin Cohn was directing this largest printing plant in the country and spending only one day a week in the Technical Academy laboratory. During one of Cohn's infrequent days in the laboratory in early 1906, he was called upon to escort an interested visitor through the Academy. The visitor, Onesiphore-Ernest Talbot, was a Liberal Member of the Canadian Parliament. The two men got along well, and Talbot invited Cohn to dine with him that evening. During the course of the evening, Talbot mentioned that Canada needed men of Cohn's type, suggesting that if he had some capital, there was tremendous opportunity in this new country. Canada was envisioned as becoming a nation of white, Anglo-Saxon, Protestant settlers, and German immigrants appeared to fit this pre-ordained mold.[2]

Colonel Talbot mentioned that Prime Minister Sir Wilfred Laurier was his personal friend, and promised to introduce Cohn to the Prime Minister, and to many other important people who could be of great use, should Cohn decide to come to Canada. Having no capital of his own, Cohn went to the only capitalist he knew at that time, Buexenstein. Buexenstein went to his club and challenged members, most of whom were bankers, to fund Cohn as their investment representative in Canada. Within one-half hour $60 000 had been pledged, and within a week the first meeting of the Deutsches Kanada Syndikat took place.[3] Martin Cohn was on his way to Canada, the representative of German investment funds.

Colonel Talbot, true to his word, acted as host to the newly-arrived Cohn, introducing him to the Prime Minister and other Members of Parliament. Cohn met with Prime Minister Wilfred Laurier to discuss what areas of development he should venture into.[4] The Prime Minister suggested mining as a possibility. Cohn decided that nickel would be his choice for investment.

Dr. Alfred E. Barlow of the Geological Survey of Canada was called upon for his expertise. During the summer of 1906, which the two men spent in northern Ontario, Barlow confessed to Cohn that he could not see a future for himself in working for the government. He stated that he would be pleased to accept an engagement with Cohn, should the latter feel the need for his (Barlow's) services.[5] Cohn began negotiations to hire Barlow to work for the Deutsches Kanada Syndikat, resulting in Cohn's introduction to Barlow's lawyer, Andrew Haydon. Haydon and Cohn were destined to become life-long friends.[6]

It was Haydon who suggested the Deutsches Kanada Syndikat should consider the formation of a limited liability company with a Dominion charter. Accordingly, on November 15th, 1906, the Deutsches Kanada Syndikat became part of the larger organization, the German Development Company Limited, which incorporated with the authorized capital of one million dollars. Three gentlemen from Berlin, including original financier Georg W. Buexenstein, were among the seven incorporators. Also included in this group were three gentlemen from Ottawa: Colonel Talbot, Member of Parliament from St. Michel, Quebec; Alfred E. Barlow, geologist with the Geological Survey of Canada; and Harold B. McGiverin, law partner of Andrew Haydon. The seventh incorporator was Martin Cohn, who was appointed the Managing Director of this Company.[7]

Cohn established an office in the same building as the law firm of McGiverin and Haydon, at 19 Elgin Street, across from the Parliament Buildings. During 1907, Barlow, now one of the directors of the German Development Company, retired from the Geological Survey and continued prospecting in Northern Ontario. By 1910, Barlow had become discouraged about his lack of success in locating any valuable mineral deposits in northern Ontario and he resigned his position as geologist with the eastern branch of the German Development Company. However, he retained his position as a director with this company.[8]

By early 1907, Cohn had lost much of his interest in the northern Ontario venture. The coal fields of the Rocky Mountains now excited his interest. Barlow introduced Cohn to D. B. Dowling, of the Dominion Geological Survey, and these men discussed the coal situation in western Canada.[9]

By 1907, Donaldson Bogart Dowling had been a member of the Geological Survey for 23 years. In 1906, he had located large quantities of coal strata in the Rocky Mountains, north of the regions then being mined in both the Crowsnest Pass and the Banff areas. The Geological Survey of Canada had been mapping mineral resources of the Rocky Mountains since 1881, but Dowling's work also included assessment of the commercial value of mineral seams and extremely detailed maps of the areas he had covered. For the remaining winter months of 1907, Martin Cohn continued to study maps and reports from the Geological Survey of Canada. Although he did not have any extensive coal mining experience, he was familiar with the commercial value of coal from mining activity in his native province of Silesia.[10]

Martin Cohn, now venturing into the realm of western coal-mining, knew relatively little about such operations. His training as a scientist had been in the properties of light and color, but he was eager to find out all he could about coal. He learned that coal strata runs parallel to mountain ranges, while the rivers and streams, angling across the coal strata, wear away the surface landscape. Coal normally is covered by earth, often to such a depth that the rivers cannot reach it, but coal-seams do outcrop (approach the surface) in some locations. The easiest method of prospecting for coal is to follow along the banks of rivers or streams, watching for the coal strata, or shale.[11] Dowling suggested that Cohn discuss with the Minister of the Interior, Frank Oliver, the idea of venturing into coal mining in western Canada.

After a long conversation with Oliver it became evident to Cohn that there were no coal mining regulations for the west, but he did learn that Oliver was strongly in favor of foreign capital investments, especially in the unknown and sparsely populated regions of the west.[12] Cohn, who had taken a great liking to Dowling, requested of Oliver that Dowling accompany the prospecting party into the west. Realizing his own lack of prospecting experience, Cohn clearly understood the wisdom of having along a coal expert.

The interest indicated by the Minister in the westward expedition being organized for the German Development Company convinced the Director of the Geological Survey to agree to Dowling's participation in the venture, subject to specific conditions, including access to, and some control of, information arising from this exploration and prospecting trip. Dowling, who was surprised at the turn of events, added the stipulation that his salary and benefits be continued by the Geological Survey, while all personal expenses be covered by Cohn.[13] Based on this agreement, Dowling became an active participant in the prospecting activities of the German Development Company.

During Martin Cohn's first year in Canada he had involved major governmental departments and numerous influential individuals, including the Canadian Prime Minister, in organizational procedures and prospects, both of the German Development Company and of the project which that company was about to undertake. In May, 1907, one year after Cohn's arrival in Canada, he and Dowling departed for the west. Their long train ride ended at Morley, the Stoney Reserve.

While spending time in Morley waiting for the pack-train to be readied, Martin Cohn met Stuart Kidd, factor of the Morley general store. It was obvious to Cohn that Stuart Kidd genuinely liked the Stoneys, a large number of whom were store customers. Kidd had learned to speak the Stoney language fluently, and he appeared well liked by the Natives as well as by the cowboys and ranchers who also purchased from the store. Cohn appreciated the way Kidd dealt with all his customers, including the difficult ones.

Born in 1883, Stuart Kidd had grown up on a farm near Ashton, Ontario. By the time he turned 20, he was homesteading north of Calgary on the west branch of Nose Creek in Simons Valley.[14] In 1907, Stuart moved to Morley to become the storekeeper, taking over the job which his brother, Fred, had held since 1902.[15] Martin Cohn and Stuart Kidd got along extremely well – these two men also were destined to become life-long friends.

When the prospecting party left, they travelled north from Morley and over Pipestone Pass. They forded the North Saskatchewan and continued their journey to the Bighorn River, where they set up camp beside the beautiful double waterfall of the Bighorn (Crescent) Falls. These historic Bighorn Falls have since been renamed Crescent Falls, as there is another Bighorn Falls on the Red Deer River, near the Yaha Tinda forestry ranch, west of Sundre.

The following day, Dowling pointed out coal strata as they walked along the Bighorn River, where this distinctive strata is plentiful. Digging a tunnel into the river bank every 100 yards, they were able to ascertain the location of the coal. Six workable coal seams were located in the Bighorn field.[16] Tunnels were driven into the seams and core samples taken from across the face. Once the location was established, the area was staked, using Bighorn Falls as a landmark. That summer a total of four coalfields were staked: the northern properties consisted of the South Brazeau, the Bighorn and the Saskatchewan fields. The Saskatchewan coalfield was located just south of the Saskatchewan River

Coal strata can be seen as dark bands of shale in the cliffs along the Bighorn River. A. Belliveau collection.

and slightly east of the Bighorn field. Also staked that year was the south property of the Kananaskis field, located on Mount Allan, southwest of Banff.

Although assigned to Martin Cohn for the 1907 summer of prospecting, Dowling also continued surveying and reporting to the Geological Survey. The prospecting party extended their explorations along areas of the McLeod, the Embarrass, and the Pembina rivers, the region where the Coal Branch later was developed. Dowling also established the boundaries for Jasper Park at this time.

Near the end of the 1907 prospecting season, Cohn decided that he would take a large chunk of coal to the shareholders in Germany, so a block of coal weighing at least 30 pounds was cut from the South Brazeau field and packed for the return trip. During the trip back to Morley, Dowling and Cohn speculated about the cost of establishing a mine and running a rail-line to it; their estimate of eight million dollars "gave [Cohn] a headache."[17]

Cohn, transporting the 30-pound coal block, returned to Europe. When he told German Development Company President, George Buexenstein, the extent of the funds required to develop the Alberta coalfields, Buexenstein stated that in order to raise funds it first would be necessary to have an opinion on the coal from Professor Potonie, who worked at the Berlin Academy of Mining and who was Germany's greatest authority on coal. The Professor immediately asked Cohn to indicate on the map where this coal had come from. When Cohn pointed to the area north of the Saskatchewan River, the Professor stated that it could not be so. He pointed out that the Rocky Mountains were Cretaceous, and it was stated very clearly in the textbook which he, Potonie, had written that there was no coal to be found in the Cretaceous.[18] Calling Cohn an impostor and a swindler, Potonie chased him from the office, throwing the 30-pound block of coal after him.

Even the always-supportive Georg Buexenstein indicated some doubt of Cohn's credibility when told the reaction of the Professor. Cohn suggested cabling the Geological Survey in Canada for confirmation of the facts, and Buexenstein insisted on sending the cable himself. When the reply vindicated Cohn, Buexenstein suggested that it be arranged for the Canadian government to issue Professor Potonie an official invitation to visit Canada.

Meanwhile, Buexenstein had encouraged one of the bankers of the original Syndikat to seek further financial support for the coalfields through London. The prominent English banking house of Lazard Brothers and Company were sold $20 000 in shares, and they were extremely interested in future financing. Cohn now had enough money to purchase outright the Bighorn and South Brazeau coalfields.

On his return to Ottawa, Cohn told the story of the Professor to his friend, Andy, and the two men went to see Liberal stalwart Charles Murphy. Murphy promptly decided that the reputation of Canada was at stake. Within a few days Cohn learned that the scope of the Canadian Mining Institute's international meeting and tour would be enlarged from covering only eastern Canada to include the western regions as well. A special invitation was sent to Professor Potonie. Since the Professor had never ridden a horse before, and since the coalfield at Mount Allan was nearest the railway, this was the chosen destination. The Professor later wrote a strongly supportive report on the coal in Canada's Rocky Mountains and this, largely, was responsible for building the reputation of Canada as a major coal source.[19]

When Cohn returned to Ottawa, Dowling informed him that a Toronto syndicate of considerable means had been formed, headed by an Alberta senator. They had engaged an Edmonton surveyor, Saunders, whose prospecting party had followed into the same territory, staking over the previous stakes. Cohn immediately called upon his friends and partners for assistance and advice. It finally became necessary to speak to Prime Minister Laurier, who then consulted privately with Frank Oliver, Minister of the Interior, before the decision was made that the purchase of coalfields must be done by describing land to be claimed according to the Section, Township, and Range. Dowling spoke to the Chief of the Geological Survey, who declared that their sketches would hold the territory for them during the winter, since winter surveying could not be done.[20]

Because of this sudden flurry of interest in Alberta coalfields, the Minister of the Interior immediately made a new ruling creating coal-mining regulations whereby coalfields no longer would be sold outright but would be leased on a 21-year renewable term. This ruling later was incorporated into the Dominion Lands Act by a special amendment.

The Geological Survey had assigned Dowling to another field for the summer of 1908, upsetting the plans Martin Cohn had made for that year. Dowling recommended that Cohn hire James McEvoy. McEvoy was well qualified, having previously worked with the Crowsnest Pass Coal Mining Company as Chief Engineer and Geologist, and also with the Geological Survey in the Yellowhead Pass area.[21]

Cohn instructed McEvoy to stake more fields to the north. The immigration and transportation policies of the Canadian government were creating an increased demand for coal as a heating fuel, as well as for railway purposes. Martin Cohn planned to stake enough coal fields to cover most of the territory between the Canadian Pacific Railway, which followed the Bow Valley, and the more northern route being constructed by the other two transcontinental railways. He was staking claims which would put the German Development Company "in a strategic position to command the supply for a great part of the prairie."[22]

During the summer of 1908, the new Race Creek coalfield was staked, part of the South Brazeau field was examined, and the existing fields of the Saskatchewan, the Kananaskis and the Bighorn were thoroughly prospected. McEvoy also built a small coke oven at the Bighorn property to assess the coking, or binding, properties of this coal.[23] The best heating coal binds to itself as it burns.

When the prospecting season was completed and claims filed, it was discovered that a rival prospecting group had filed for basically the same land in the South Brazeau field as had the German Development Company, but neither group had been able to connect their surveys with the nearest official survey post, as the regulations required. McEvoy wanted to make application immediately, according to his estimates. He had found an official post while riding along the Saskatchewan River during the summer and had made a superficial survey at that time. When the government survey was done two years later, it was found that McEvoy had been only 32 feet (9.75 meters) off the actual location. The South Brazeau field went to the German Development Company.

By 1909, the railroad west from Edmonton had moved closer to the Athabasca Valley and its newly developed coalfields of the Brule Lake/Hinton/Yellowhead areas, not far from Fitzhugh (Jasper). The presence of railroad survey teams was indicating where the northern transcontinental rail line would run. This railway expansion encouraged a few prospectors to look more closely at coalfields which lay near the proposed railway. Activity taking place in the northern coalfields lent some urgency to Cohn's plans to develop the fields already staked by the German Development Company.

Martin Cohn spent the first part of 1909 dealing with the organizational and promotional aspects of the German Development Company, and its Canadian coalfields. It was decided that, since Canada was a British Dominion, London should contribute a large part of the required funds. However, Lazard Brothers of London, who previously had purchased shares in the German Development Company, did not want to advance further monies unless there was an established long-term contract for the sale of the coal.

Returning to Canada, Cohn met with representatives from the Canadian Pacific Railway to see if interest could be established in building a railway to the German Development Company's mining project. However, the CPR already had sufficient contracts with coal companies in the west. The Grand Trunk Railway too, was not interested in funding a railway to the German Development Company coalfields. Cohn decided that the best solution would be for the German Development Company to construct their own railway, so he applied for, and received, a charter to do so. At this time the Canadian government was encouraging railway construction throughout the west, resulting in local railway companies being formed to bring branch lines into more remote areas. According to provincial law, bond-guarantees would be in effect only after newly formed railway companies amalgamated with the Canadian Northern Railway.[24] The federal government was prepared to provide up to $6400 per mile of railway construction if that railway was for the general benefit of Canada. To his dismay, Martin Cohn learned that his proposal for a railway did not qualify for this government subsidy.[25]

The German Development Company would have access to markets if they were able to develop a railroad but, as yet, there were no established markets for the coal that was to be mined. No more capital would be forthcoming from Lazard brothers of London unless they were able to see markets with firmly established, long-term coal orders. Mackenzie and Mann, and the Canadian Northern Railway, were the last hope for selling the German Development Company's coal to a railway.

Martin Cohn's friends and acquaintances in Ottawa warned him to handle William Mackenzie and Donald Mann with extreme caution. The reputation of these two men for unorthodox business methods, combined with a hard-bargaining style, had caused people to be extremely wary of any dealings with them. But, despite the warnings, Martin Cohn knew he had no choice but to see if they would be interested in buying the coal which the German Development Company intended to produce.

An Unusual Alliance – Mackenzie and Mann, and Martin Nordegg

*T*he transportation difficulties with which Martin Cohn was grappling were mirrored throughout the Canadian northwest. Transportation was absolutely essential if settlers were to be attracted and development take place. The Canadian Pacific Railway had opened the prairies with its main line, but the service provided was not satisfactory. Expansion of the more northern prairies had been brought to a halt; Palliser's fertile belt had been left without the tentacles of transportation needed to open up the region.

There was an evident need for government assistance to encourage building more rail lines and, in 1895, Clifford Sifton, Minister of the Interior, initiated a plan whereby local government would issue bonds to guarantee payment of railway construction in case the railway was unable to do so. However, none of the existing railway contractors showed much interest in taking advantage of this plan until an unemployed railway contractor, Donald Mann, became interested in the idea. He soon was joined by another contractor, William Mackenzie. The opportunity to both develop and use the resources of the west made sense to these two men and the idea of building something permanent and worthwhile appealed to them.[1] Although there would be numerous delays and difficulties, the west was about to be opened with one of Canada's most aggressive and unusual partnerships. Between 1896 and 1918, when the system was nationalized, Mackenzie and Mann were responsible for the building of almost 10 000 miles of railway, an average of approximately one and one-quarter miles per day.[2] These two men made a considerable contribution to the settlement and development of Canada.

Since railways used coal to power their locomotives, there was much interest in the development of western Canada's coal resources. Rail lines being constructed in regions north of the Canadian Pacific's routes began offering transportation services that would allow development in areas previously isolated. It was expected that the Canadian Northern Railway eventually would become fully transcontinental by way of Edmonton, but coalfields were essential to the success of this operation. Costs would be too high to ship coal from the south to the more northerly regions of Edmonton, Jasper and the Yellowhead Pass. In 1906, the Canadian Northern Railway, wanting to assure themselves of an adequate, long term, and relatively inexpensive coal supply, had hired Thomas Russell as surveyor and prospector to stake coal lands west of Edmonton, near the proposed route for their transcontinental railway.[3]

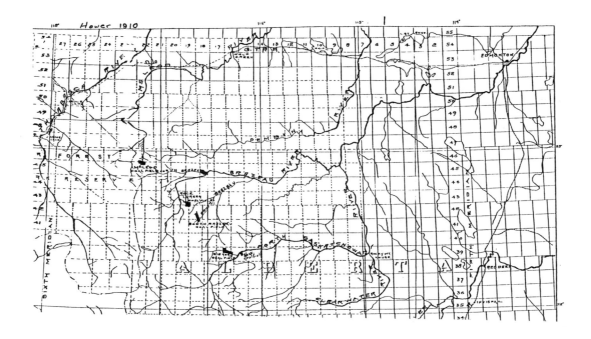

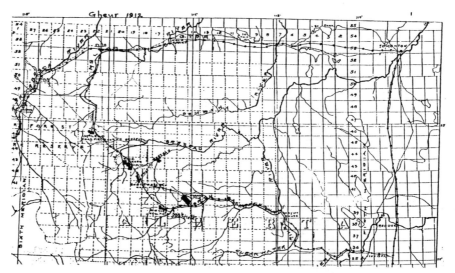

Above: Hower's 1910 map showing Brazeau Collieries coal holdings which, at that time, totalled 51.5 sq. mi. (133.4 sq. km). Below: Gheur's 1912 map shows coal holdings and rail lines (both proposed and actual). Brazeau now controlled 59.5 sq. mi. (154.1 sq. km).

*D*uring the time that Martin Cohn had been attempting to interest rail companies in building a line into the German Development Company's coalfields and buying some of the coal, a financial transaction between Mackenzie and Mann and Lazard Brothers also was underway. The Canadian Bank of Commerce and Lazard Brothers of London, who were major financial powers behind Mackenzie and Mann, later had considerable influence upon activities and commercial development within the Upper North Saskatchewan River Corridor. In particular, the backing of Mackenzie and Mann by Lazard Brothers, a firm who also had invested in the German Development Company and who, later, would invest in the Canadian Northern Western Railway into the Brazeau coalfields, eventually resulted in a multi-directional hold on the area by these financiers.

Canadian Northern Railways had evolved into a major organization run by two shrewd businessmen with a reputation for being rather unorthodox in their dealings. In looking for railway connections for the German Development Company's coalfields, Martin Cohn approached these men as a last resort. Much to his surprise, he found that he liked both men, especially the hard-driving Mackenzie. Despite later adverse times, the two men continued to remain friends.[4]

The Canadian Northern previously had obtained their coal from Pennsylvania fields. Since this had proven to be very expensive, Mackenzie and Mann planned to develop their own coalfields, which had been staked a few years earlier by Thomas Russell, and they also had federal guarantees for rail construction into these fields.[5] But Mackenzie did not want his competitors from the Grand Trunk or the Canadian Pacific railways to have access to all the coalfields belonging to the German Development Company. Accordingly, Mackenzie proposed that the Canadian Northern Railway and the German Development Company amalgamate their coalfields to form one large coal company.

A long negotiating session resulted in the informal creation of two new companies. The coal holdings of Mackenzie and Mann, and of the German Development Company now were to be jointly owned. The Brazeau Collieries would comprise all the northern coal territories of both. The fields that had been staked by Thomas Russell for use by the Canadian Northern Railway were the Main Brazeau field, located where the North Brazeau flows into the Brazeau River immediately west of the present Forestry Trunk Road, and the McLeod field at the headwaters of the McLeod River, an area which, in later years, lay just southeast of Coal Branch country. Canadian Northern coal also included the Sixth Meridian Coalfields, consisting of five claims on the headwaters of the Muskeg and Baptiste rivers, in the vicinity of the present location of Grand Cache,[6] northwest of Jasper.

The German Development Company's coalfields, which also had become part of the Brazeau Collieries, consisted of the Bighorn field, the South Brazeau field, the Race Creek field, and the Saskatchewan field, while the Rocky Mountain Collieries was formed to cover the German Development Company's Kananaskis field on Mount Allan. The Nordegg coalfields, where the town of Nordegg later was constructed, did not figure in the negotiations since they had not yet been discovered. Other than the Kananaskis, all coal areas involved were west and north of the eventual Nordegg site and in the vicinity of the Brazeau rivers. Because of this the new coal company was given the name Brazeau Collieries.

The combined total of all holdings, including surface, owned, leased, and pending at this time, amounted to 32 960 acres (13 339 hectares) or 51.5 square miles (133.4 sq. km) with the German Development Company having brought approximately 2/3 of this amount into the amalgamation. Later, when the Nordegg coal holdings were added, the Brazeau Collieries' total became 59.5 square miles (154.1 sq. km).[7] The coal claims brought to the partnership by Mackenzie and Mann fit well with Cohn's previous plans of claiming and developing territory between the north and south routes of the transcontinental rail lines. This empire-building was also the type of venture that appealed to the entrepreneurial spirit of both Mackenzie and Mann, and it fit well with many of their previous plans for railway construction.[8]

Negotiations were long and arduous, and not all of the conditions were to Cohn's liking. When the agreement appeared to be nearly hammered out, Cohn explained to Mackenzie that it would be necessary to have the signature of Georg Buexenstein, President of the Deutches Kanada Syndikat and a director of the German Development Company. As much as anything, this was a stalling tactic on Cohn's part. Not being totally happy with all the conditions outlined by the wily Mackenzie, Cohn was not willing to finalize the deal, but did not want to risk losing it either. He suggested that Mackenzie accompany him to Berlin to obtain the President's signature.

When the two men arrived in Berlin, the President made every effort to entertain and impress William Mackenzie. According to Martin Nordegg's memoirs, it was just prior to the return of Cohn and Mackenzie to Canada, and almost as an after-thought, that the agreement between the two business organizations was ratified, with conditions for the German Development Company being "all that could be desired."[9] In mid-June 1909, two new companies, the Brazeau Collieries and the Rocky Mountain Collieries, formally came into existence;[10] William Mackenzie was to be the President and Martin Cohn the Vice-President of both companies. On August 17, 1909, Brazeau Collieries Limited was officially incorporated by Letters Patent. Operation of these newly formed Collieries was based out of Toronto, where Mackenzie and Mann also had their headquarters.

In April 1909, the same year that Brazeau Collieries was formed, and prior to his and Mackenzie's trip to Europe, Martin Cohn became Martin Nordegg. This name change included, as well, the names of his wife and daughter.[11] A possible explanation of the significance of this name dates back to Cohn/Nordegg's great interest in the work of G. M. Dawson of the Geological Survey. During the 1870s, Dawson had located "practically unlimited" coal deposits in the north corner of an area west of Edmonton that was being surveyed and mapped.

It has been suggested that the German-sounding name "Nordegg" might be translated to mean "north corner." The German language has numerous dialects, varying almost from village to village, from one area to another, and from one German-speaking country to another. The term "north" translates to the German "Nord" in all dialects, while the German word "Ecke," meaning corner, could be pronounced as Ecke, Ekke, Ekka, Ache, Acke and Egge, according to the dialect used. The European place name which comes closest to the name Nordegg is that of Westegg, a town located in the northwestern region of Austria. Martin Nordegg had found his dream in the north corner of North America and his new name might indicate the extent of his commitment to it. During the few years he had been in Canada, Nordegg had accomplished what he had set out to do. He had both leased and purchased coalfields in an area which had drawn him since 1907. He had joined forces with a dynamic Canadian organization, and was now on the threshold of creating a mining empire which had an excellent opportunity to control much of the prairie markets for coal. He was at a turning point in his life and it appears he may have been celebrating this fact by adopting a personal name which combined both German and Canadian elements.

Later in the year, Nordegg received word from Berlin to return to Europe to organize the financial aspects of equipping and opening a mine. Banker Eugene de Wassermann of Brussels was selected to aid with the financial arrangements on the basis of his reputation as the shrewdest negotiator in Europe. The first decision that needed to be made was the selection of the coalfield to be developed. Nordegg and Mackenzie both favored development of the Kananaskis field first.[12]

Wassermann, who was to receive a percentage commission of all funds raised, refused to consider the Kananaskis, making his decision in favor of the northern fields because they were the most expensive to construct, being the furthest from a rail line. This would provide Wassermann with a considerably higher commission on the raising of needed funds. Martin Nordegg suggested that Mackenzie should be consulted prior to making such a decision, since the two men had come to a joint decision to open the Kananaskis field first. Wassermann refused, stating that it was simpler and more profitable for him to find millions of dollars rather than to find a few hundred thousand, and if the Brazeau Collieries did not agree with his decision they could look elsewhere for a financial negotiator. In a Brussels apartment, far from the Canadian Rocky Mountains, the final decision was made to develop one of the Brazeau coalfields and leave the Rocky Mountain Collieries' Kananaskis field until a later date. This decision by a European financier would have far reaching effects upon Alberta settlement, especially throughout the central regions.

Through Wassermann's skilful negotiation and manipulation, funds soon were pledged from firms in Belgium, England, France, and Germany. Ten percent of total Brazeau Collieries shares had been pledged to these financiers in return for their financial backing. The Lazard Brothers, who were already share-holders in the German Development Company, and who had considerable interests in the Canadian Northern Railway, now also became leaders of this new European financial syndicate by obtaining over one-fifth of the bond issue.

Later, the European investors also elected to share in the financing of the Canadian Northern Western Railway, and they purchased the Alberta-guaranteed bonds for this rail line. Since Mackenzie and Mann were now part of the same coal organization as the German Development Company, construction of the railway was assured. This European funding made the Brazeau rail line the only Alberta branch line in which Continental financiers were investors.[13]

Martin Nordegg returned to Canada with instructions to select the location from within the Brazeau Collieries coalfields where the first mine should be developed. Cohn cabled Stuart Kidd in Morley with the offer of a job as Purchasing Agent for the Brazeau Collieries, and he instructed Kidd to form an organization to begin development of one of the coalfields, the specific field to be selected later in the season. Brewster and Moore, a recently formed contract packing and freighting company, was hired, and they did a considerable amount of the trail work and packing required by the Brazeau Collieries over the next few years. This company of Brewster and Moore, which had chosen to operate in the territory of the Brazeau and Saskatchewan Rivers, was one of many ventures undertaken by members of the Brewster family of Banff.

Prior to Mackenzie and Mann joining forces with Martin Nordegg and the German Development Company in 1909, the plan for developing the Canadian Northern coalfields had called for a branch line of the Canadian Northern Pacific Railway to extend south from Wolf Creek into their McLeod coalfields.[14] When the German Development Company and Canadian Northern coalfields amalgamated in 1909, the originally planned line could become the main route into Brazeau River territory, with the addition of a southern extension through all the coal lands of the newly-formed Brazeau Collieries. This would create an important rail link among the various settlements that were to be created. The town of Tollerton, to be constructed a few miles south of Edson on the McLeod River, would become the northern terminus for this branch line.

As well as Canadian Northern activities in the area, the Grand Trunk Pacific Railway was making rapid progress west of Edmonton toward the Jasper region. By summer 1909, activity showed a marked increase in the area of Wolf Creek/Edson, and the territory to the south which soon would become the Coal Branch. Prospectors were rapidly claiming numerous coal lands located in the general area into which the railway was extending.[15] In April 1910, Mackenzie and Mann had a guarantee of bonds to build from Edmonton to the headwaters of the McLeod and Brazeau Rivers.[16] However, with rapid development underway in the area soon to become the Coal Branch, competition for markets could prove to be fierce.

Mackenzie and Mann, looking for what would give them the best advantage for profit making, elected to cover all possibilities. Thus they chose to create the infrastructure to build both south from the Edmonton/Jasper Park rail line into the Brazeau River region, and also to build west from the Calgary/Edmonton line into Brazeau River. Later, they could decide which route into the coal fields would be most to their advantage. By July 28, 1910, there was public notification of intention to build a rail line west from Stewartwyn (near Stettler) through Rocky Mountain House to the Brazeau River.[17] On December 5, 1910, the Canadian Northern Western Railway was chartered. It was to serve, among other areas, a line from the Canadian Northern's east/west line, south to Brazeau River and adjacent coal mining areas.[18]

After careful and shrewd consideration of the situation, Mackenzie and Mann elected to begin construction of the Canadian Northern's branch line into the Brazeau coalfields from the southeast terminus on the Calgary/Edmonton line instead of coming into the coal holdings from the northwest.[19] By May 1911, even before the Nordegg coal lands were part of the Brazeau Collieries' organization, the Canadian Northern Railway had bond guarantees to build a line from the Calgary/Edmonton rail line to the Brazeau coalfields in the district of the Big Horn and Brazeau Rivers.[20] This cut down, at least temporarily, on the competition from the coal mines being developed in the same general region as those of the Brazeau Collieries. It would give the advantage of time to establish markets for Brazeau coal.

It was decided that the Canadian Northern Western Railway's proposed new route into the Brazeau fields would begin east of Innisfail, along the Canadian Northern line which stretched between the Calgary and Edmonton regions. The Canadian Northern Western route would cross the Canadian Pacific line at Innisfail, and proceed westward. For many years Innisfail had been a starting point for trips into areas of the west country.[21] The Canadian Northern Western Railway planned to follow this same general trail west from Innisfail to the east side of the Clearwater River, passing between present day Caroline and Stauffer before turning north-northwest, following the Clearwater to its confluence with the North Saskatchewan near the old Rocky Mountain House fort.

A train-bridge would be constructed across the Saskatchewan and, west of Rocky Mountain House, the railway would follow the general route of the old First Nations/Fur Brigade Trail into the Upper North Saskatchewan River Corridor. However, it was planned that the rail line, on reaching the mouth of the Shunda, would follow along the North Saskatchewan River all the way to the Bighorn field instead of branching off to follow the trail along Shunda Creek. After reaching the Bighorn area it would swing north toward the South Brazeau coal lands and the other fields belonging to the Brazeau Collieries.[22] This first proposed route, following the Saskatchewan River west of the Shunda, soon was modified and, over the next two years, a number of possibilities and variations of rail routings to connect Brazeau Collieries coal holdings were suggested.

With the revised plan for construction of the Canadian Northern Western Railway to extend west from the Calgary/Edmonton line into west-central Alberta, it appeared that the eastern portion of this route was going to be served by two different rail lines. The Alberta Central Railway Company had been granted a federal charter in 1901, and they had received approval of their route map west from Red Deer, through Rocky Mountain House, then northwest toward the Yellowhead Pass area.[23]

Alan Rowbotham, topographer and surveyor for the Alberta Central Railway, was one of the early representatives of this commercial interest in the Upper North Saskatchewan River Corridor. He reported, in 1909, that a bank and a post office, known as Prairie Grange, were located not far from the old Hudson's Bay fort on the North Saskatchewan River. Rowbotham also reported that Leslieville was the largest settlement of the area. Exploring and assessing this country for the Alberta Central's rail route, Rowbotham had pushed west of the Saskatchewan from Rocky Mountain House. The previous year, a ferry across the Saskatchewan had become operational and homesteaders had advanced as far as 3 or 4 miles west of this ferry. Rowbotham's reports also indicate the ruggedness of the country. He commented upon the steepness of Jackfish Hill and the difficulty in getting up this hill while hauling equipment. He also reported a mixture of burned trees and dead windfall to a depth of as much as 4 feet in places as he advanced westward into the Nordegg area.[24]

The Alberta Central Railway planned to construct a train bridge across the Saskatchewan. From there they would follow near the river to just east of Horburg, approximately 15 rail miles (25 km) from Rocky Mountain House, before turning toward the northwest and Yellowhead Pass. Canadian Northern's plan of intrusion into the same general territory was not well received.[25]

The steel for the two rail lines followed the same general route for both and, in some cases, the 2 sets of tracks were very close to each other. Canadian Northern reached Rocky first, but not without a number of incidents of barricades, fences, and spiked rails. In 1911, the Alberta Central charter into the west country was purchased by Canadian Pacific Railways and, in 1912, their surveyors selected the best site for a bridge across the North Saskatchewan. Canadian Northern Western Railway either would have to build their bridge next to the Canadian Pacific Railway bridge, or reroute their rail line to another suitable location to cross the river. Martin Nordegg suggested collaboration between the two railway companies for the bridge to cross the Saskatchewan. William Mackenzie considered it a ridiculous idea. He told Nordegg to try if he wished, but it would be without Mackenzie's authorization. Sir George Bury, Vice President of Canadian Pacific at Winnipeg, was a personal acquaintance of Martin Nordegg and it was this man whom Nordegg approached with the idea. Negotiations between the Canadian Pacific Railway and the Canadian Northern Western Railway eventually resulted in the CNWR being granted running rights for the CPR bridge across the North Saskatchewan. These running rights continued in effect during the more than one-half century of rail service into the Upper North Saskatchewan River Corridor.

*I*n the years following formation of the Brazeau and the Rocky Mountain Collieries, Mackenzie and Mann expanded upon the idea of a western-based coal mining empire. They became involved in development of the Drumheller mines in southeast Alberta and the Dunsmuir Collieries on Vancouver Island. Drumheller was a complementary venture to Brazeau, but without the participation or influence of Martin Nordegg. However, Drumheller coal was lignite, and it proved to be too soft for any extensive railway use. The coal would not coke (clump together) when burning, and the resulting hot, burning matter escaped through the locomotive smoke stack, frequently setting the landscape on fire. These stack-losses of the coal also made it an inefficient and costly fuel for railway use. Instead, Drumheller coal built an extensive market as domestic fuel for prairie settlers.

Mackenzie and Mann were well aware that the idea of creating a mining empire to control prairie coal markets would be strengthened with the construction of rail routes in strategic places. Building westward into Brazeau Collieries territory from a junction on the Canadian Northern's north/south railway would give the coal company quick access to the prairies and all Canadian Northern's inter-connecting rail lines. Such a rail line from the Brazeau coalfields would create a coal funnel into the large triangle bordered by the Canadian Northern's lines connecting Saskatoon, Calgary and Edmonton, as well as the rail markets which the Collieries hoped to establish in the territory between the major railways which extended along the Bow and the Athabasca corridors. These rail lines would serve to expand markets of the Brazeau Collieries mining empire throughout the prairie provinces, and beyond.

The Canadian Northern Western Railway also had authority to build in eastern Alberta, to the Peace or Pine River passes, and to Alberta's eastern boundary north of the North Saskatchewan River. These lines would increase the range of Canadian

Northern, and introduce possible markets for Brazeau coal into more northerly areas of Alberta, including the Peace River district.[26] A strong network of steel was being created.

This network of steel, radiating outward from the core of the funnel, would be used to disperse coal out of the western wilderness. It would bring numerous spin-off benefits to Central Alberta, including access to an area which had remained isolated from mainstream activities despite previous use as a fur trade route, its consideration as a supply route through the mountains, and its obvious suitability as a transcontinental rail route. It also would help open the way to development of other mineral treasures to be found along the eastern slopes of the Rocky Mountains.

While the coal mines of the Nordegg Field were being developed and mined, a different type of mineral development was progressing into Alberta regions. Exploration for oil took place along the foothills, in Big West Country, the Red Deer River area, and southward from 1914 onward. Oil companies interested in the geological formations of the area did considerable field work around Nordegg during the late 1920s. By 1937, Home Oil (Brazeau) Limited was formed as a subsidiary of Home Oil Company and that same year a road was built to the well site on Chungo Creek, north and west of Nordegg. In the late 1940s and early 1950s, numerous seismic crews were based out of Nordegg, and exploration activity took place throughout this whole region of the west country. Oil exploration based out of Nordegg is still taking place, but now the vehicle of choice often is the helicopter. Since 1937, more than 100 wells have been drilled in the Nordegg-Brazeau area, with the majority of these since 1960. Many of these drillings have resulted in gas finds along the porous formations but, to date, the search for oil in this area has been nowhere near as successful as was the search for coal.[27]

*D*uring the first two decades of the 20th century, central Alberta and west-central Alberta grew very rapidly. It was difficult to determine which settlements might continue to grow and become influential centres in this new land. Red Deer and Lacombe competed for the status of divisional point and major centre. Meanwhile, the approved route of the Canadian Northern Western Railway west from Sylvan Lake had been located well to the south of both Eckville and Leslieville before reaching the Rocky Mountain House district.[28] By March 25, 1911, a revised route, reaching both settlements, had been approved. Rocky Mountain House had been included in all of the proposed routes into the Brazeau coalfields; it was expected to become a rail and supply centre.

By May 26th, 1911, the route was shown as travelling from Stettler, through Alix and Blackfalds to Sylvan Lake, Rocky Mountain House, and westward into the Brazeau coalfields.[29] Although there had already been numerous changes of the rail route into the Brazeau coalfields, still more would take place before the route was finalized. Once the Nordegg coalfields were discovered and absorbed into the Brazeau Collieries chain, the railway into the Upper North Saskatchewan River Corridor would be rerouted at Shunda Gap. Instead of following along the foot of the mountains bordering the north side of Shunda Basin, a wooden train trestle, which became known as The Five-Mile Bridge, was constructed to span Shunda Creek at Shunda Gap. This would bring the railroad into the town of Nordegg along the southern up-slope of Shunda Basin.

Unfolding the Dream

*E*nough prospecting and planning had taken place during the three years since Martin Nordegg first had come to the Canadian west; now it was time to develop the mining operation. His plan was beginning to take shape whereby Brazeau Collieries would control the majority of the coalfields between the Yellowhead and the Bow, becoming a major coal supplier for the Canadian prairies. The powerful and adventurous owners of the Canadian Northern Railway were his partners in the venture. The uncertainty seemed over.

Based upon the recommendation of a New York banking firm, and upon a reputation as the best-known coal-mining engineer in the country, Charles Hower was hired by Lazard Brothers early in the spring of 1910.[1] He was to assess the Brazeau Collieries' properties and help plan the stages of development. Hower was to explore and prospect the Race Creek, Main Brazeau, and McLeod fields, since information already was reasonably complete on the other coalfields, although only the Bighorn field data was complete enough for development planning. Later, he was to form an organization to begin development of one of the fields, location to be decided upon later in the season.

Hower was impressed with both the quality and location of the coalfields he was helping to ready for development. The official party inspected both the McLeod and Race Creek coalfields, and they made the decision that the South Brazeau field would be the first of the properties developed. The men were sent in relays to the South Brazeau and work was begun immediately on gathering construction data, building a permanent camp, and developing the area.[2]

In early fall, the prospecting party and their packtrain left the South Brazeau, heading south toward the Bighorn properties, which they planned to visit before turning eastward toward Shunda Basin, the North Saskatchewan River, and Rocky Mountain House. It had been a cool, wet summer, and the occasional frost and early snow, which can occur in some of the mountainous regions of the Upper North Saskatchewan Corridor, had given previous indication that the season was well advanced. Hower commented in his notes that when they left the Brazeau field for the Bighorn on October 12, 1910, they had to walk through 18 inches (45.7 cm) of snow. It also was snowing when the field party departed the Bighorn area, but it turned to rain as they rode further east. Everyone was cold and wet as they rode into Shunda Basin. The group, with their large pack train, made camp at the traditional Stoney campsite. It had been a long and tiring day, accompanied by miserable weather. Everyone, it seemed, was in a foul mood and each one had complaints to air. The entire party all had a good grouch session, tension was relieved, and everyone felt better for it.[3] From that time onward, this location was known by the nickname of Grouch Camp.

The following day dawned bright and sunny. After they left Grouch Camp, Martin Nordegg rode ahead of the pack train; he stated in his memoirs that he followed what appeared to be an old hunting trail near a mountain which looked like an extinct volcano.[4] He stopped to shoot at some geese on the lake to the south. At that point Martin Nordegg was looking across the valley to where the Brazeau Collieries mining complex and the town of Nordegg later would be constructed.

Knowing that the slow-moving pack train would take about 30 minutes to catch up, Nordegg sat down to wait for them. Ahead of him to the south was the lake, reflecting the clear blue sky and a few soft clouds. Beyond the lake lay gently rounded mountains covered in varying shades where forests covered the hilly landscape. From this angle the only mountain that appeared craggy and contained little growth was one lying to the southeast, forming part of the southern arm of Shunda Gap through the Brazeau Range. Idly gazing at this mountain, Martin Nordegg noticed the horizontal dark streaks with which he had become familiar throughout the coal lands of the Brazeau Collieries. He wondered if he might be looking at coal strata.

When the pack train finally reached him, Nordegg borrowed Hower's binoculars, supposedly to see if he could locate the geese at which he had fired. After the pack train had passed, he carefully studied the rocky side of this mountain on the south rampart of Shunda Gap.[5]

He was sure of it! It was coal strata.

Hurriedly he sketched the lake, the gap, and the mountain. Nordegg began to feel a certain pride and possessiveness about what he had just seen, as well as some sense of uncertainty. He decided to keep his observations to himself until he had had an opportunity to look over the maps and information available at the Geological Survey offices in Ottawa, to see if similar occurrences in nearby areas might be on record.

*M*eanwhile, development was well underway at the South Brazeau coalfield. In late August, 1910, Brazeau Collieries offices had been established in Edmonton. This was to be the headquarters of the Brazeau Collieries until such time as they could be relocated to the new town of Brazeau, which was to be built at the South Brazeau fields. A work schedule had been planned, extending from Nov. 1st, 1910, to April 1st, 1911. Hower was laying plans to simplify active development taking place well before the railway was expected to arrive at the South Brazeau coalfields in 1912.[6]

The location on the South Brazeau had been established as the future headquarters and major mining centre of the Brazeau Collieries coal empire. During the 1910 summer's work, all the Brazeau coal lands had been assessed to some extent. Hower had spent considerable time and effort organizing plans and blueprints for future construction, including plans for new towns, as well as for mining development for the coalfields. The South Brazeau field took in a considerable amount of territory through the George Creek valley, the Blackstone River area, and a northern tributary, shown on Hower's blueprint as Cabin Creek.[7] About 20 seams had been uncovered, of which at least 8 were of workable thickness. During the summer, an airway had been started on one seam that advanced toward the north. Hower organized a detailed, four year plan for development of this mining complex. He felt that this site afforded "one of the best plant and town sites in the Rocky Mountain fields."[8] As events transpired, this town did not materialize, and plans to develop these fields as the first of many, subsequently were changed.

To the south of the South Brazeau fields lay the Bighorn coal lands, one of the first fields staked and purchased by Martin Nordegg.[9] There were six workable seams located along the Bighorn River. The eastern end of this claim along the Bighorn River began approximately one mile northwest of the North Saskatchewan River. It followed along the southwest side of the Bighorn until it reached the 85 foot (26 meter) double waterfall now known as Crescent Falls.[10] At the base of the falls the claims reached across the river to include land on the northeast side as well, extending for a distance of one mile upstream. Below the falls, the river, for the most part, was outside the coal claim, but the falls, and the river above the falls, ran through the Brazeau property. The town was to be constructed on the northeast side of the river just above the falls, with the plant a short distance up the river.[11] An estimated 200 employee houses were contemplated, to be built over the years, as needed.

To the south and east of the Bighorn coal lands was the small Saskatchewan claim. It was south of, and adjacent to, the North Saskatchewan River, just east from where the Bighorn River flows into the Saskatchewan. Hower assessed the Saskatchewan coalfield as having no immediate mining possibilities. However, he noted that the field had value as an access control to coal south of the river, and he stated that its greatest value might prove to be as a shipping point for river coal "in case the Government's policy of making the Saskatchewan navigable is ever accomplished."[12]

In the more northern region, near Chungo, and lying approximately eight miles northwest of the South Brazeau field, was the Race Creek coal lands, a leased area located at the intersection of what now is the Rocky-Clearwater forest, the Edson forest, and Jasper National Park. Hower suggested that the plant and town be located at the northwest end of the coal claim, just downstream from the confluence of the Southesk and Brazeau rivers.

Northwest of Race Creek lay the McLeod field, on the headwaters of the east branch of the McLeod River, now known as Mackenzie Creek. In 1909, Gregg and Jones staked the northwest extension of these coal measures, and Mountain Park, the most southerly location of the area eventually known as the Coal Branch, came into existence.

Exploration and assessment of the other two Brazeau coalfields were incomplete when Hower was working on the master plan for Brazeau Collieries development in 1910. The Sixth Meridian fields were located north of the Athabasca River, near the headwaters of the Muskeg river. They were less than 20 miles southeast of the mining centre of Grand Cache, which began operations on September 1st, 1966.[13] The other unassessed field, the Main Brazeau, was situated at the confluence of the (present) Cardinal River and the Main Brazeau River, east of the McLeod field and northeast of both Race Creek and the South Brazeau fields. Not much prospecting was done on the Main Brazeau seam but tests had indicated it would provide a good domestic coal.

Hower was in complete agreement with the choice of coalfield to be developed. He stated that if he had to choose only one field, it would be the South Brazeau. However, he foresaw the expense and work involved in getting the field operational and he suggested that it might be wise to "place an operation on the easily accessible Kananaskis field" to create a coal supply and generate some cash flow while the northern properties were in the developmental stages.[14]

By October 12, 1910, when the prospecting party and their packtrain had left the south Brazeau coalfields, Hower had completed his field work and planning for the coming year. His report, completed in Johnstown, Pennsylvania, by December 31st, 1910, included an assessment of markets for Brazeau fuel. He summed up the situation with the comment:

> *Situated just south of the centre of Alberta, the Brazeau fields hold a position of advantage on the available mining territory that will in time afford almost a monopoly of the trade east and west across the central part of the Provinces. The demand for the product will increase as rapidly as it is possible to develop these fields, and ... the railway affiliations of the Collieries will help to bridge the dull season and place it in a position of advantage over other operations who must meet the market demands.*[15]

Meanwhile, although Hower's winter work schedule for 1910-11 was in place, and the South Brazeau field was being readied for active development during the summer of 1911, Martin Nordegg continued to think of the coal strata he had seen just west of the Shunda Gap. Hower's report, suggesting the need for an interim coal supply, held special significance for him.

During the 1910 season, Mining Engineer Charles Hower had accomplished a great deal of prospecting, planning, and preparation, and his schedule for the winter, if completed, would have allowed the south Brazeau coal lands virtually to be ready to begin producing during the summer of 1911. Available records do not indicate if Martin Nordegg chose to cut back on preparations for the South Brazeau because of the possibility of developing the new field he believed to be in the Shunda Basin. Although Martin Nordegg's memoirs state that he decided to keep his observations to himself about the possibility of coal strata in the Shunda Basin until he had an opportunity to look over maps and information available, he may have commented about this find, and he also may have begun to plan that, if coal was there, this field should be the first to be developed.

In any case, by March 7, 1911, just 2 months after Hower's report was completed, Hower, in a letter to Stuart Kidd, indicated extreme annoyance with, and lack of confidence in, Martin Nordegg, as well as disillusionment with the Brazeau Collieries. Hower stated that if he was to have any future connection with Martin Nordegg it would be in an advisory capacity only, and not in a situation where he (Hower) was responsible for results. He believed he could not do himself justice by working under Brazeau Collieries conditions. Hower further stated that he expected it to be several years before the northern property was developed, and he (Hower) imagined that Martin Nordegg would have very little to do with the real development. Hower also stated that Brazeau

Collieries either would have to change policy or they would become another northwestern mining failure.[16]

Nordegg spent time in the Geological Survey offices, researching information on coal deposits and claims in areas near the Shunda Gap. He found nothing. He began to have doubts about what he had seen so he decided to confide in his friend at the Geological Survey, D. B. Dowling. In Dowling's opinion, it was possible for coal to be present at that location but he expected it would be an inferior type to the other fields, since the location was further east and the coal would have been subjected to less pressures.[17] Dowling agreed to look at the area the following summer, after completing his 1911 season's field work in areas to the south.

Nordegg was concerned that this would be too late, as the Brazeau Collieries would be spending thousands of dollars on the South Brazeau field during the coming season. If coal was available just inside Shunda Gap, this would mean a saving of 40 miles of the most rugged section of railway construction, through the Bighorn Mountains into Brazeau coalfields, since the coalfields he now believed existed west of Shunda Gap were close to the route already decided upon for the railway. It was exactly the sort of plan Hower had suggested as a sound financial step while developing the other fields. If there really was coal inside Shunda Gap, it could not be in a more perfect location.

However, despite what appears to be Martin Nordegg's determination to do something about his suspicion regarding the presence of coal in the Shunda Basin, the field season for summer 1911 began as previously planned. Three parties were organized: one was to do developmental work into the Kananaskis seam, as Hower had suggested in his report, another group was to prospect for more coal along the Lusk Creek area of the Kananaskis, while the large main party, consisting mostly of miners, would begin development of the South Brazeau field. Nordegg planned to travel alone to the Shunda Basin area where he had shot at the geese the previous summer.

To Nordegg's consternation, he was unable to leave for the field immediately. A cable from Berlin requested that he meet, and act as an escort for, a director of the German banking firm that was a financial agent of the Canadian Pacific Railway. Frantic that someone else might stake the field just inside Shunda Gap before he could do so, Nordegg cabled from Winnipeg to have Fraser, the mining engineer in charge of the Kananaskis/Lusk Creek prospecting party, meet with him in Calgary. He had never met Fraser and knew little about him. Nordegg would be asking Fraser to go to an unknown district to stake a coalfield in Fraser's own name, according to the required regulations. Nordegg then would have to depend upon the man's honesty to transfer the lease into the name of the German Development Company.

By the time Nordegg managed to reach the Shunda Basin region later in the season, the claim had been staked and two coal seams uncovered. When Dowling arrived, he examined the field and became very enthusiastic, stating that it was a very large coal deposit.[18] Dowling named the fields the Nordegg Coal Basin, submitting this name to both the federal and provincial governments for their records. While Fraser and the survey party had been staking this new claim, work had progressed at the South Brazeau fields, and the railway line already had been cut by the rail gang. Nordegg ordered work stopped, and men and equipment were instructed to move to the new field. The South Brazeau field was put on hold; it now was expected to become the second field to be developed within the Brazeau Collieries coal chain, rather than the first.

During the second half of the 20th century, after the Brazeau Collieries mining operation at Nordegg had ceased, road and seismic crews, hunters, and tourists travelling in the region between Nordegg and the Coal Branch occasionally came upon various pieces of machinery and some buildings which appeared to have been abandoned. The theory advanced was that a second group of German investors were responsible for these and that they had been recalled to Germany when the war started, leaving all their equipment behind.

This is not so.

Martin Nordegg was the only representative of German interests involved in prospecting and mining in these areas, although during some of that time he went by the name Cohn. A number of items were simply left in place until such time as the railway expanded throughout the Brazeau Collieries coal holdings, and mining centres were developed at each of these Brazeau locations. Since this was expected to be a fairly rapid development, and since bringing the machinery in over such rugged country was both costly and difficult, it was deemed easier to come back to it than to take it with them when the Nordegg field was selected to be developed first.[19]

Since the German Development Company, represented by Martin Nordegg, had hired and paid the prospecting party to stake and claim the Nordegg coal lands, Nordegg was surprised to learn that Mackenzie expected to share in this new field. However, Mackenzie reminded Nordegg that German Development Company director, Georg Buexenstein, had said the two organizations would do business half-and-half. Nordegg had a vague recollection of this, but he reminded Mackenzie that it was the German Development Company that had done all the work and paid for the exploration and staking.

Mackenzie contacted Georg Buexenstein, and these two men held discussions with the Brazeau financiers, offering to sell the Nordegg claims to the Brazeau Collieries. Martin Nordegg considered this unethical, but commented that he "had yet to learn a lesson of high finance."[20] Discussions were heated, and it created some bitterness among Brazeau Collieries Company members. At one point Mackenzie stated that if the Nordegg claim was not purchased by the Brazeau Collieries, the Nordegg claims would be opened anyway, and would compete with the Brazeau Collieries. Martin Nordegg wondered how it was possible "for the new claims, belonging to us, to compete with Brazeau Collieries, which also belonged to us."[21] Eventually, it was agreed that Brazeau Collieries would buy the Nordegg coal claim for cash and bonds. It now was official – the Nordegg claims were part of the Brazeau Collieries mining empire and would become the first of many to be developed.

During the fall of 1911, two log bunkhouses and a cook house/dining room/assembly room had been built near the future minesite at the Nordegg claim. The townsite location was established east of the mine, along the southern up-slope of Shunda Basin,

During the fall of 1911, log buildings were constructed at the minesite. A. Belliveau collection.

approximately one mile distant from the minesite. The two were separated by dense bush and a wide, gently-sloped gully along which flowed a small creek which was given the name Cabin Creek, but which also became known as Mine Creek. The townsite would be situated directly in the path of a First Nations connector trail which joined their more northern routes with their Saskatchewan River routes and which passed out of Shunda Basin after crossing above (south) of the minesite.[22]

Plans were organized for the winter months. Very heavy sleighs would be built to carry machinery and supplies along the ice of the frozen Saskatchewan River to the mouth of the Shunda, then along the old trail where the rail line soon was to be constructed. Until the railway reached the mine, it was considered necessary to devise some method of transmitting information to personnel developing the site. Fred and Jack Brewster knew that their Uncle George had experience with stage lines in British Columbia, and they recommended he be hired.[23] George Brewster organized a stage line which covered the territory between Red Deer and Rocky Mountain House in one day, bringing communication and passengers half the distance that lay between the Calgary/Edmonton rail line and the Nordegg minesite. Tom McKenzie then freighted the mail and supplies to the Brazeau Collieries by packtrain.[24]

Late in 1911, Martin Nordegg returned to Toronto and opened an office in the building where Mackenzie and Mann and the Canadian Northern were located. A fairly large staff, including Ernest Gheur, a Belgian coal mining engineer, was hired to organize plans for the mining and construction activities. Martin Nordegg set to work to create an outstanding centre, an example of what coal mining establishments might be. He visualized a town of which he could be proud, a town unlike any mining town then in existence. This would be a totally planned community, with modern and pretty houses in the valley; hundreds of men would find work here. The turn of events had him in a state of high excitement. He imagined how happy he would be to live in this new town just inside the Shunda Gap; this would become his home.[25]

The townsite was built east of the mine, along the southern up-slope of Shunda Basin. Provincial Archives of Alberta, A.20, 064.

Packtrain fording the turbulent river at Saskatchewan Flats. Anne Belliveau collection.

Brewster's Flats

Stories about the Brewster family of Banff have become part of the pioneer folklore of the Canadian Rockies. The youngest Brewster boy who came west, and probably the least known, was George Brewster, who lived the later years of his life in the Nordegg area.

The Brewsters, long established in the Banff area, are descended from Irish immigrants who settled in Ontario. Of the nine children in this family, all four boys moved west during the latter part of the 19th century. George, born in 1866, came west as a scout for General Middleton's army, dispatched to quell the Riel Rebellion in 1885. Later, George was one of the prospectors who panned the North Saskatchewan for gold.

For a time, he and Tom Wilson lived in a cabin in Silver City, located near the base of Castle Mountain, north of Banff. These two bachelors began courting two young relatives of Reverend John McDougall, and Tom Wilson later married one of them. The father of the girl that George was seeing sent his daughter away to boarding school in eastern Canada, effectively separating this young couple. Although over the years George developed something of a reputation as a "ladies man," this appears to have been the only serious romantic venture during his lifetime.[i]

George went on to become an expert canoe man and, later, he worked at packing and hauling for mining companies in the Columbia Valley region. But his greatest interest was in prospecting for gold. He firmly believed that there was gold in the upper regions of the North Saskatchewan, and he had a number of stories related to gold and to the prospectors of the West Country.

In 1910, Brewster and Moore had been hired by Brazeau Collieries. Because of the time and distance involved in building the railway to the mines, it was necessary to institute some method of transmitting messages, and hauling mail and small items from Brazeau Collieries' head office in Red Deer.[ii]

When the railway was completed into Nordegg this service was no longer needed; Tom began farming in the Stauffer area, while George decided to make his home near the North Saskatchewan River, which had drawn him so strongly in previous years. He chose to settle in the wide, flat valley formed by the Saskatchewan River south of Nordegg.

These Flats also were used by Brewster and Moore Freighting and Packing as a winter range for their horses.[iii] George Brewster spent the rest of his life along the river he loved, within easy riding distance of Nordegg.

These flats, west of where the Bighorn Highway (Trunk Road) now crosses the river, are known as Brewster's Flats. This is the area where the short arm of the Indian/Fur Brigade Trail returned to the river. Alexander Henry the Younger commented in his journals that the meadows here along the river provided excellent grass for horses.

George Brewster made many friends among the Stoneys, and they often visited with George, making camp near his cabins. Eventually George built up a small ranch and grew hay for his horses. He also kept a few cattle and goats, and operated a small dairy. At irregular intervals, he took milk into Nordegg to be sold.[iv] Later he expanded his cabin into a log house with a kitchen/sitting room and smaller sized bedrooms. The building was chinked with moss, and tanned hides hung on the walls. A niece and her two children lived with George for awhile, but later moved into Nordegg so the children could attend school.[v]

During the 1930s, a trapper named Jock Richardson stayed with George Brewster. When George fell ill, Jock brought him into Nordegg for medical attention, turning the $200 which George had saved over the years over to Stuart Kidd so that George's financial needs would be looked after.[vi] For over two years, George remained a patient in the Nordegg hospital, where he died on July 15, 1937.[vii]

[i] Brewster, p.32

[ii] Brewster, p.40

[iii] PAA, Ira Gray notes, pp.9-10

[iv] Martha Fallow-McMullen, oral.

[v] Nellie Letcher, oral

[vi] Fred Kidd, oral... Aug.10/93

[vii] Records of Rene Wilson, Postmistress. T. E. Wilson Scrapbook #4

98　*Small Moments in Time*

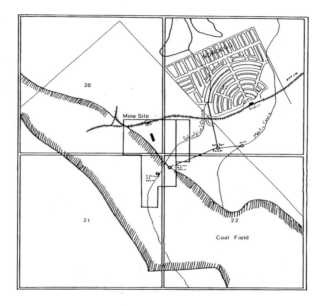

Township 40, Range 15, W5, Detail of a Mining Map in Provincial Archives of Alberta 76.507/138 MC. The grid extension beyond the semi-circle was not used until the 1940s, when new construction took place.

Nordegg – A Town is Born

Development of the Nordegg coalfield was well underway, manned by a skilled and competent staff who already had begun working the coal seams. Although Martin Nordegg's business sense had helped establish this nucleus of a mining empire, professional mining men now were collaborating on the needs of the mine. The driving interest of Martin Nordegg became construction of the mine's surface features and the town, which he planned with loving care. Towns constructed on Crown land, such as the one now to be built for the Brazeau Collieries, were known as "closed" camps. Long-term leases could be obtained by companies and the lease-holder became the proprietor. Such communities were operated by the parent company, giving this company almost total control of living conditions.

View of the timber yard and boiler house. A. Belliveau collection.

While the focus of Martin Nordegg's existence had become development of the Brazeau Collieries' mining establishment and townsite, this venture was only one of many projects in which his partners, Mackenzie and Mann, were involved at this time. These two men, who seemed to be riding a shooting-star to success, were well on their way to expanding throughout Canada. In 1911, while Martin Nordegg was dreaming about creating a mining town that would be a model for all others, Mackenzie and Mann had begun creating a plan that would incorporate a model community into a distant area of the nation; Montreal was the focus of their efforts.

Mackenzie and Mann, convinced their railway would be transcontinental by 1914, bought property in various cities and began constructing terminal buildings. They came up with a totally different and wildly expensive plan to bring their railway into the heart of Montreal. They would tunnel underneath the mountain, coming into the harbor area and Montreal's core from the north. The two men purchased choice commercial property in downtown Montreal, as well as farm land to the north. A tunnel would provide fast commuter service to areas north of the mountain, thus creating a highly desirable location, and the choice residential land would return tremendous profits to the company. On October 20, 1911, the two men filed plans for this huge project, which included a "model city," the new town of Mount Royal, to be created out of a large tract of farmland.[1]

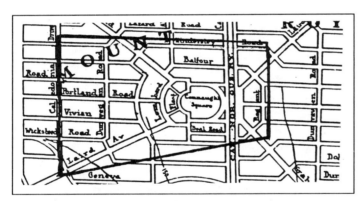

Mount Royal in 1913, after some changes to the original plan. Incorporated as a town by December, 1913. Map courtesy of Peter Heiler.

The plan of the Canadian Northern Railway's model city was ready to go into production in the fall of 1911; Martin Nordegg, who was planning his town in the same office building as his partners during late 1911 and early 1912, saw and liked this plan. Using the western portion of the Model City plan as a basis, Martin Nordegg drew up plans for the new mining town by elaborating upon this one section of the Mount Royal street plan.[2] The Canadian Northern Railway ran into serious financial trouble later in 1912, and some of their ambitious plans were changed, but the Montreal tunnel still had to be built for the railway to get into the heart of the city. Construction of the Mount Royal area went ahead and, by December, 1913, it was incorporated as a town.

The April 1914 blueprint of Nordegg indicates a strong connection to the May 1913 blueprint copy of the Mount Royal model city. However, the present-day Montreal street map shows some changes were made from the original Mackenzie and Mann town plan for Mount Royal. The original Mount Royal hub, the railway station from which everything was to radiate, is now Parc Connaught. Parc Connaught, when adapted to the topography of the Nordegg area, would correspond to Nordegg's railway station, the station platform and the crest of the hill upon which Main Street was built. As in the 1913 blueprint of Montreal's model city, the Nordegg rail terminal would be located at the hub of the semi-circular pattern, cut across by diagonal streets for easy access to the town centre. Although the topography and vegetation are markedly different, the similarity of street structure is noticeable. The rectangular grid extension beyond the last circular avenue, as seen on the original Nordegg blueprint, also is shown on the plan for Mount Royal. The rectangular formations were not utilized during early construction of the mining town, since the size of the town at that time did not warrant this construction.[3]

Martin Nordegg spent the winter of 1912 working in the Brazeau Collieries' Toronto office, planning the buildings for the mine and town soon to be constructed in the Upper North Saskatchewan River Corridor. The plans and sketches formed a booklet which he "looked at with greatest pleasure over and over again."[4] Also at this time, Nordegg consulted with University of Toronto medical authorities about setting up a fully-equipped modern hospital at the mining site; this hospital later became one of the best in Central Alberta. The hospital was a two-story building somewhat similar to a very large house. The front of the hospital faced north, overlooking a large terraced lawn and flower gardens. Because the timber growth was much less dense than at present, both the upper and the lower verandah afforded a good view across the valley. The main floor of the building held a patient waiting room, a consulting room, an examining room, a small dispensary, an operating room, a kitchen, and a men's ward. Upstairs there were private and semi-private rooms. The in-patient capacity was 19 beds.

The well-equipped Nordegg hospital had an in-patient capacity of 19 beds. Maggie Morris collection.

Once the hospital became operational, each employee of the Brazeau Collieries had a deduction of one dollar taken from his/her pay in order to maintain the hospital and pay the doctor a salary. By the 1950s, this medical deduction, which was like an early variant of Medicare, had risen to four dollars per month. The doctor was guaranteed an ample minimum wage, but the doctor's earnings usually were well in excess of this minimum. This monthly medical fee covered all medical, surgical and hospital services, bandages and dressings, X-rays, and some prescription drugs for every member of the contributor's family, but it did not cover childbirth. In turn, the doctor was held responsible for rent and utilities, the salaries of nurses, and for all supplies and maintenance required by the hospital. If a patient had to be sent to Edmonton or Calgary for specialized medical attention, the Nordegg doctor was financially responsible for the cost of transportation. The well-equipped Nordegg hospital soon developed a reputation for excellence, and patients were brought into Nordegg from outside locations when there was room to accommodate them.[5] When the doctor treated individuals from outside, he could set his own fee.

When the first coalfield to be opened was the South Brazeau field, Edmonton had been selected as the centre from where operations would be based until the office at the new town of Brazeau was ready to assume this responsibility. With the Nordegg coalfield now the choice for Brazeau Collieries' main centre of operations, the headquarters would now be based out of the Nordegg locality. Therefore, in 1912, Red Deer was selected as a convenient location in which to established the Brazeau Collieries office until it could be relocated to the new mining town when the mining operation went into full production.[6]

Construction at the mine was going well. A number of mule teams were brought from Texas to help haul the heavy equipment. Corduroy roads were built, with logs laid across the trail in areas of muskeg or soft spots, to simplify this job of hauling supplies and equipment to the mine.[7] That summer, Gheur wrote his Report on Nordegg Coal Claims (August 1912). He found definite advantages to the Nordegg fields over any of the other fields, remarking that the location was exceptional, being at the eastern entrance to the Brazeau's field of operations. The coal basin, being further east than the South Brazeau and other of the Brazeau Collieries fields, had less geological disturbance, resulting in more regularity in seam thickness as well as a more gentle angle or "dip" to the coal bearing measures. The dip at the South Brazeau basin is about 35 degrees; at the Nordegg basin it is 12 degrees. Gheur reported that five seams were known, but only two were workable, number 2 seam at 7 feet 9 inches (2.36 meters) in thickness, and number 3 seam at 15 feet 11 inches (4.87 meters).[8] The Nordegg field covered an 8 square mile (20.72 square km) area, situated between the North Saskatchewan River and Shunda Creek. At the northwest limit the surface altitude is 4330 feet (1319.78 meters), while the highest surface point within the claim is 5580 feet (1700.78 meters). This coalfield stretched southeast from Nordegg until it reached the North Saskatchewan River.

When Gheur was writing his report (prior to August 1912), tunnels were being driven into the seams at Nordegg, and temporary log buildings were in place. These buildings consisted of a boarding house to accommodate 36 men, an office, and a cookhouse which also contained a dining room and a store. Gheur stated that the houses and boarding

By 1912, tunnels were being driven into coal seams, and temporary log buildings were in place. A. Belliveau collection.

houses of the new town must be ready before hiring the full complement of men to work the mines. However, these structures would not be completed prior to the railway reaching the town, thus allowing easy transportation of required materials and equipment for construction. Gheur estimated that the total work force needed would be approximately 475 men, and he recommended that number be used as a basis for housing.[9]

Staffing the collieries was not considered a problem. Gheur stated that there were many mine workers around the western mine areas. The availability of men to work the mines had been stressed by Frank Oliver in the Commons debates in the spring of 1907, when he commented that it was more difficult to locate an empty boxcar for the coal than to find workers for the mines. This comment also is a succinct summary of many of the problems faced by the Brazeau Collieries over the years. New mines drew workmen easily because they liked to try new places. The men liked to see if the wages and conditions were better than previous locations.

Railway construction continued to proceed rapidly westward but the bridge over the North Saskatchewan was not yet underway. Meanwhile, work at the mine had progressed to the point that it was necessary to institute ventilation into the tunnels. The Chicago engineering firm of Roberts and Schaefer was contracted to build the complete mining installation, which was to have a capacity of 2000 tons per day. Until such time as the railroad was built to the colliery, the coal was dumped on the eastern side of Cabin Creek Hill, into which the mine seams were being dug.

Gilbert McKenzie of Rocky Mountain House was hired by the railway to work on construction of the numerous wooden trestles needed to span the valleys along the route chosen to bring the rail line into Nordegg and, when this work for the railway was completed, he was hired by Martin Nordegg to work for Brazeau Collieries. He set up a lumber mill, building it in a little ravine near where the Nordegg butcher shop and the Lakeview Hotel later were constructed.[10] More log buildings were constructed at the mine and the work force began to increase rapidly.

The first train crossed the newly constructed metal bridge over the North Saskatchewan River, just west of Rocky, in the spring of 1913. This removed a major obstacle, both for hauling heavy mine equipment to the mine site and in transporting construction materials and equipment for the town. The policy of MacKenzie and Mann in construction of their rail lines was to equip the lines according to immediate traffic requirements, with improvements to be made if increased traffic so warranted. Accordingly, the rail line to Nordegg was first of a light construction standard, with the consequences being that the tracks frequently spread under the weight of the train. Rail cars often jumped the tracks at curves or bumpy stretches. The engineer, fireman and crew became adept at getting the car back on the tracks through the use of heavy bars and considerable effort, but the uncertainty of travel meant that it was totally impossible to have these early trains run on any type of reliable schedule. The unballasted rail line reached the mine in late 1913.

The rail line was light construction standard, and trains often jumped the tracks. A. Belliveau collection.

*B*y January 1914 the townsite was to have been surveyed, the ground levelled, the lots laid out, and the street locations cleared. Construction of the townsite was to take place on the lower up-slope of Shunda Basin's southern edge. This location was raised land that was relatively muskeg free, and which the First Nations people had used previously for one of the connecting arms between the Big Fish Trail and the Saskatchewan River routes. Trees and brush were noticeably smaller in stature, and considerably less dense than they became in later years. Obviously, fire, which is Nature's way of forest conservation and renewal, had cleared the area of overgrowth. According to Peter Murphy of the Forest Service, the years 1889 to 1891 were particularly significant for fires throughout the west country, from the United States border, north as far as Grand Prairie.

The construction firm of William Baird and Alan McKenzie of Red Deer was hired to begin construction of the town's first 50 homes, the boarding house, and the necessary support buildings needed to maintain this new community. The town's roads, which followed the semi circular design of Martin Nordegg's town plan, were built to a 12-15 foot width (3.66-4.57 meters).[11] The March 3, 1914, *Red Deer Advocate* reported that the carpenters would be leaving for the mining area almost immediately. Soon a large work crew began construction of this new town. Men and machines worked from the first light of morning until darkness invaded the evening sky, creating a model town amidst the beautiful wilderness of the Shunda Basin.

Although it would be another 20 years before Nordegg would be connected to the outside world by any means other than the railway, in the vicinity of the town some of the roads that were used and later improved upon for vehicular traffic were those previously established by the Natives for whom this area had been an intersection of various trails. To the north was the Big Fish Trail, which later became much of the route to Blackstone, where the first flurry of Brazeau Collieries activity took place, and along which were located the two prehistoric Native sites, now the Shunda Creek Recreational Area and the Shunda Creek Hostel. From the east came another of the trails that merged with the network, and which later became part of the original road from the east into Nordegg. Another of the trails which intersected in the Nordegg area, and which passed just north of Nordegg's two lakes, was that from the west – the Bighorn/Kootenay Plains region. It is this inland trail which, in part, has become the David Thompson Highway west of Nordegg. The southern arm of this trail network passed through Nordegg townsite, angling to the southwest toward the Saskatchewan River. These four different routes, from four different directions, intersected by way of a short connector trail. This connector trail later became the road that ran between Nordegg's golf course and the original forestry buildings, located on a small rise just north of the golf course. The Nordegg Recreation buildings now are located just south and east of this connector trail and of the original forestry station.

The majority of the roads within the town itself were carved out of the bush. However, Stuart Road, which became the main entrance from the lower valley, was constructed on a diagonal toward the southwest, directly over the established First Nations connector trail to the North Saskatchewan River.[12] Stuart Road ended at its intersection with Elizabeth Avenue, but the Native trail continued toward higher elevations, climbing the south slope against which Nordegg was built.

Although the newly constructed roads and buildings obliterated much of this trail extending through the town of Nordegg, this approximately six to eight foot (two to two and one-half meters) wide Native thoroughfare could be seen clearly along its route through the trees above the railway tracks where comparatively little Nordegg foot traffic took place. The first indication of the section of this well worn trail that had not been obscured by construction was found south of the railway line, and was directly east of where a set of covered wooden steps, topped by an extended platform-bridge, was built to assist Nordeggers in climbing the embankment which rose from the railway terrace to the slope above. The well-worn pathway angled southwest up the slope of this terrace, passing under the upper edge of the wooden structure, and continuing up the hill in a south-westerly direction.[13] This clearly defined section of the trail above the railway tracks was a deeply embedded pathway, so well carved into the ground that no foliage grew where it passed. Many exposed, smoothly-worn, and well-polished tree roots laced their way across this path; these exposed roots often extended as high as 4 inches (10 cm) above the well trod earth. Although this pathway above the railroad tracks has had no use in over 40 years, it is still clearly visible. However, its borders are less distinct and the once bare ground now is green with low-level, mossy overgrowth.

This trail crossed through the terrace where Marcelle Avenue later was constructed, and continued up the southern slopes of Shunda Basin, constantly angling southwest and upward until, east of the mine and near the area where the water tower was constructed, it was joined by another trail from the east which had followed a higher terrace along the southern slopes of Shunda Basin. This second trail was less well defined, and narrower than the main one. After the two trails intersected near the water storage tower, the joint trail continued westward above the minesite, then turned south, passing through a gap in the mountains en route to the North Saskatchewan River. This trail angled southwest until reaching The Forks. From The Forks the short route to the river continued southward, soon descending the mountain slopes to the North Saskatchewan River valley (in the area between Gap Cabin and Brewster's Flats). The longer arm of the trail, when travelling by land along the north bank of the Saskatchewan River, passed through Black Canyon and over Teepee Creek before joining the river near the mouth of Tershishner Creek.

*I*n Nordegg, Marcelle Avenue was constructed on a terraced level above the railway line. On the western end of this street the hospital was built, and the water dam and reservoir were located on the eastern end. This eastern extension of Marcelle Avenue sloped downhill past a small pump house, then curved back to the southeast toward the small lake which was formed by the dam placed across Martin Creek. In the arm of this curve, and near this lake, Martin Nordegg had planned to build a Swiss Chalet type of home.[14] The blueprint for this Swiss Chalet-type structure showed six rooms, with an elevated deck area. This deck area would afford the occupants a panoramic view extending over the quiet expanse of the reservoir created by the water dam and spillway to the east, part of the town of Nordegg and the distinctive mountains to the north, the train station, the tracks to the distant mine, and the Bighorn Mountain Range along the far horizon to the west. The present view from this location is much more restricted; the growth of trees and underbrush was much less during the first half of the 20th century than it is now.

The hospital was located on the edge of the hill which marked the western end of Marcelle Avenue. East from the hospital, five larger, two-story homes were constructed for senior management personnel. Nearest the hospital was the home of the general manager. This is where Martin Nordegg lived during the short time he was a resident in the town. Next door was an identical home to that of the general manager, except for a reversed floor plan. For many years this was the residence of the town's doctor. These two homes and the hospital were separated from the remaining three houses by a stretch of trees and bush. East of the stretch of trees and bush was the home allocated to the manager of the Bighorn Trading Company. Next to this was the home of the mining engineer and surveyor, and the easternmost of the five two-story homes was that of the chief accountant for the Brazeau Collieries. South of the general manager's house, and further up the mountain, in a large clearing where fresh-water springs were located, the home of the pump house operator was constructed.

Plans originally had called for other management homes to be built further east along Marcelle Avenue, between the five two-story homes and Martin Nordegg's Swiss chalet, but members of management helping to ready the town had other ideas. They felt it was necessary to have supervisory personnel available in the immediate vicinity of the mine at all times, and they were uncomfortable with the idea of all management living at such a distance from the mining operation.[15] Accordingly, for 30 years, the only buildings located along Marcelle Avenue were the hospital and the five two-story homes; it was not until the building boom of the 1940s that other residences were constructed in this area. Other of the original homes for management personnel, such

APP Constable Norman McDonald, wife and family, with family friend Mattie Fallow (centre rear). McDonald said his main duty was flushing out moonshine stills during Prohibition. A. Belliveau collection.

as mine manager, pit boss, foreman, and fire boss, instead of being constructed on Marcelle Avenue, were built on a ridge overlooking the mine site. At the mine, one of the original log buildings, dating from the earliest days of the Brazeau Collieries operation, continued to function as a home during the lifetime of the town.

Homes built at the mine site included not only these mine officials' residences, but a few other residences as well. These were constructed on the eastern side of the mine site, directly below the crest of the hill upon which the mine office was located. Situated just east of the briquetting complex, which is now being preserved as a historic site, two residences also are expected to be preserved and restored. The closest of these buildings to the mining complex was turned into an officials' club early in the town's history, but this was a short-lived institution; by 1918 this building had become a residence.[16] Barn Boss Jack Constable and his family lived in this home until they left Nordegg in 1939. Also in this same area below the mine office was the first of three locations for the police office. One side of this duplex contained the jail cells and a security office. A connecting door joined this office area to the living quarters of the police constable and his family. The majority of police officers stationed at Nordegg throughout the years were members of Canada's national police force, although the Alberta Provincial Police also played a role in area law enforcement prior to being disbanded in 1932.[17] Later in the town's history, the duplex which had been constructed as a teacherage to house unmarried female teachers, and which was located just west of the butcher shop near the bottom end of the business district, was converted into the jail and police living quarters. The original police duplex at the mine then became The Batch, a building set aside as a residence for the single working girls of Nordegg.[18] During the construction boom of the 1940s, the jail/living quarters duplex was relocated once again when a new police establishment was constructed near the east end of South Marcelle Avenue.

The semi-circular pattern of the main portion of the town housed most of the population along three streets, named (from south to north) Elizabeth, Lily, and Marthe. During the building boom of the early 1940s, more streets were created, extending northward onto the valley floor in a grid pattern, as shown on the original blueprints for the town.

*B*y March 1914, the railway was operating into the new coalfield, although 40 miles of track still remained to be ballasted. Officials of the Canadian Northern Railway, of Robertson Schaefer and Company, and of the Brazeau Collieries travelled into the new mining area aboard a special train in early March 1914, and the new rail line was taken over officially from the contractors.[19]

Sir William Mackenzie was well pleased with the state of both the coal and the mine in this new field, including the fact that the promised 100 000 tons of coal had been mined and was ready to be moved. As a gesture of appreciation, Mackenzie announced that the new town would be named after Martin Nordegg. The name was painted on the railway station and application was made to Ottawa for a post office for the town. On April 1st, 1914, the post office was established and Stuart Kidd, along with his other duties, was appointed postmaster.[20] The town of Nordegg officially had come into existence.

By the summer of 1914, the new town of Nordegg was developing into an attractive community with an entire mountain playground at its doorstep. The Upper North Saskatchewan River Corridor had been a land of plenty for centuries, providing for the Native population that had chosen this land as their own. Now a new breed of people had become part of this land, and the Corridor would provide for them as well.

Shortly after the railway became fully operational into Nordegg in 1914, women and children began to arrive, travelling in by boxcar. By the fall of 1914, rail coaches had taken the place of boxcars. Early residents who travelled into Nordegg on the passenger train commented on how slowly it moved. One story recounts a passenger jumping off the train to pick wild strawberries growing along the tracks, and then running along the tracks to catch up to the train. The Rocky Mountain House newspaper reported on March 27, 1914, that nine houses were completed. The first construction of the town took place west of Main Street and, except for the teacherage which was a duplex located just west of Main, construction took place to the southwest, on Lily Street, near the diagonal extension of Ernest Street (Dewdney Hill). Ernest Street was named for engineer Ernest Gheur. The hill at the east end of Ernest Street was known as Dewdney Hill and, eventually, this name became the more common term for this diagonal extension. These early buildings included the first home of the doctor and a temporary hospital. The nurse and mid-wife, Helen Duncan, delivered any babies born in the new town.

Also among the first buildings constructed were four single family residences and a four-room boarding house with a lean-to built onto the back to serve as a kitchen and fifth bedroom. Before the Bighorn Trading Company opened its doors to the public, all groceries and other essential items were purchased from the store that was operated as an extension of the cookhouse at the mine. A 16-bedroom boarding house on Main Street was operational by July 21, and three weeks later a second set of 50 homes had been completed. The lots were wedge shaped, with 28 feet (8.53 meters) of space separating one house from another.[21] The town of Nordegg now had over 120 buildings, including an ice cream parlor and a theatre.[22] The theatre also served Nordegg as a dance hall, a general meeting hall, a banquet hall, and a gymnasium. Before long the business district also included a bakery, a butcher shop, and a miner's club.

Later, after prohibition was repealed in 1923, and public drinking establishments became operational, Nordegg also had three beer parlors as well as a liquor store. Two of the houses constructed across Stuart Road from the designated site for the school became the temporary school.[23] Plans were made for a Protestant church to be built on the hill to the south.[24] The first dairy was located northwest of the town; later a dairy was constructed below the hill north of the original school site. Cows were kept in the area where the Sports Complex later was built, and where condominiums now are located, across from the Tourist Office and Nordegg Historical Society Heritage Centre.

Martin Nordegg wanted this to be the most modern and attractive mining town of the time-period. He was determined that the dreadful living conditions prevalent in many Alberta mining towns would not be a part of this new town on the eastern slopes of the Rocky Mountains. Although not all Alberta mining towns had terrible environments, some unbelievable housing conditions were reported in Alberta Coal Mining Industry Commissions. Miners' houses in Alberta coalfields could be as crude as a dug-out. In 1919, the Drumheller Valley was described by a Calgary newspaper as a desolate, wretched, and godforsaken slum, the worst in all Canada. In 1928, the newspaper of the Communist Party stated that housing at Wayne was no more than rabbit hutches constructed from old grain doors. Two mining communities were considered model communities – Brule and Nordegg. In Brule, force had been used to keep organized labor away until the Blue Diamond Coal Company, in 1919, created a model town to see if management concern for environment and worker welfare would help to settle labor unrest. (It did.) Nordegg was an example of a more genuine employer concern for the workers.[25]

As a scientist, Martin Nordegg had spent much of his earlier career pioneering in the field of color reproduction and printing; he called upon his artistic sense, his knowledge of color, and his humanitarian instincts to create an outstanding town – a model for all others. Along with keeping close watch on construction, he also selected the colors to paint the houses. He refused to use "the crude colours which the superintendent liked," instead selecting gentle pastel shades which would blend with the landscape and be pleasing to the eye.[26]

He found his most difficult task to be selection of colors for service buildings such as the water tank, located high on the mountain south of town. Martin Nordegg considered this an ugly building and he wanted it hidden from view. He experimented with various shades of green until he found one that allowed this structure to blend with the surrounding foliage. The color choice for this water tank succeeded in so completely concealing it among the surrounding trees that it became almost invisible until passing directly below and beside it along the trail above the mine. During the decade of the 1940s, when a great deal of construction and repair was taking place, the water tank was repainted a cream color, making it instantly visible from almost anywhere in the Shunda Valley. This water tower, although in a state of disrepair, is still standing. The cream color now has faded to a dull buff, but it is no longer visible on the side of the mountain, due to the heavy growth of the trees and the underbrush which now conceals it from view.

The town of Nordegg had both four and five room homes for the labor force. Although by today's standards of house construction, the Nordegg homes would appear small, they were similar in external size and appearance to many homes still occupied in older areas of both Calgary and Edmonton. In present day Nordegg, the two miner's cottages that have been relocated to the minesite from the lower flats near the miner's graveyard were part of construction done in the 1940s. These buildings are of different design, and smaller in size than the original homes built in 1914. The house at the minesite, directly below the previous location of the mine office, is more typical of original construction. All Nordegg homes were expected to contain indoor plumbing, as well as electricity powered by the mine generators. The electrical generators constructed at the mine were built to handle requirements of the business district and residential buildings, as well as the Brazeau Collieries industrial complex.[27] All Nordegg buildings had electricity from earliest construction, well before this was a common occurrence throughout Alberta. By the fall of 1937, a 33 000 volt transmission power line had been constructed west from Red Deer to the Brazeau Collieries, and the electrical source for the mine and town then became Calgary Power Ltd. The April 1, 1914, newspaper issue of *The Rocky Mountain House Guide* commented upon all Nordegg houses being supplied with electric light; by 1932, Rocky began planning to have the business section wired for electrical service.[28] When the Calgary Power line was constructed to the Brazeau Collieries in 1936/37, Rocky Mountain House had a sub-station built, and by 1939 Rocky had 164 customers connected to Calgary Power.[29] Calgary Power, now TransAlta Utilities, also instituted a tie-in to the Brazeau Collieries generators and a long-standing deal was set up between the two companies. The Brazeau Collieries contracted to supply "make-up" power to areas west of Red Deer in times of need. When Calgary Power was making changes to power transmission supplies in 1951, they called upon the Brazeau Collieries to supply reduced electrical power to all areas extending from Nordegg to Red Deer, including Red Deer itself.[30]

Martin Nordegg also intended to have every home supplied with water and sewer. Pipes for this purpose were shipped into the town by rail. These pipes were stacked in areas near the railway tracks. This unheard of idea of equipping all workers' homes with water and sewer facilities was not well received by members of the Brazeau staff who felt it would be a waste of time, effort, and money. Mass indoor plumbing was not a widespread service in Alberta at this time, and was not considered to be an essential utility. In 1914 just over 9000 buildings had water connections to accommodate Calgary's approximately 81 000 population.[31] After Martin Nordegg discovered that a few families were using the white enamel bathtub to store coal, and the toilet was being used for bathing the babies, he decided there was no point in forcing the issue. The decision was made to have all five-roomed homes equipped with water and sewer while all four-roomed homes would be without. Instead, each street of four-roomed homes was equipped with a stand-pipe for the water supply.[32] Many mining areas of the day had no running water available for their population, and in some locations water had to be hauled in by wagons or taken from unsanitary wells.[33] The stand-pipe system used in Nordegg tapped into underground pipes carrying water from the local reservoir, created by building a concrete dam and spillway across the mountain stream of Martin Creek. The water and sewer pipes that were not used during early construction were left in readiness for the time when the rest of the town's buildings would acquire indoor plumbing, and they remained stacked against the sides of the hills near the railway tracks throughout the lifetime of the town.[34]

Since first coming to Canada in 1906, Martin Nordegg had worked hard and accomplished a great deal. Now his dream was progressing according to plan, with the creation of a model town to house and support the workers of the mining complex which he had been instrumental in developing. In addition, his honesty, diplomacy, and determination had secured for him the friendship and respect of people from all walks of life. Within Canadian Government circles he had made good friends and excellent contacts which would serve him well during the troubled times ahead, and for the rest of his life.

Dreams and Reality

*I*n September 1912 it was reported in the *Rocky Mountain House Guide* that Martin Nordegg had announced only English-speaking men should be employed at Brazeau Collieries. The first workers hired for the mine probably were British, as well as those European immigrants who had been in Canada for sufficient years to have become comfortable with the language. By February 1913, two-thirds of the work force were European immigrants, and by early 1914 there was a fairly large group of Italian mine workers located at Nordegg.[1] It was necessary to have experienced men to mine the coal and a large number of the mine workers who came to Nordegg had been recruited from the Fernie and Crowsnest Pass areas. When the Brazeau mining operation was in early production, prior to spring of the year 1913, Martin Nordegg was the General Manager and Ernest Gheur was Consulting Mining Engineer in charge of the Western Office of Brazeau Collieries. The Western Office consisted of three departments: the Operating Department, controlled by Superintendent Cory Weatherbee, incorporated all men and operations at the mine, including the Bookkeeping Department;[2] the Provisions and Supply Department, controlled by Stuart Kidd, incorporated all men employed by this department, including the clerk at Rocky Mountain House; the Accounting Department, controlled by Mr. Perry, was based in Red Deer at this time.

These three departments worked independently from each other, and the person in charge of each was answerable only to the company officials. Also, at this time the Board of Directors of Brazeau Collieries consisted of President: Sir William Mackenzie; Vice President: Martin Nordegg; Secretary-Treasurer: H. Prud'homme; Assistant Secretary-Treasurer: R. P. Ormsby; Directors: Sir Donald Mann, Georg W. Buexenstein, Emil Baerwald, A. J. Mitchell, L. Jadot.[3]

Other personnel who were hired for the fledgling operation of the Brazeau Collieries were William Stevenson, who was the Assistant General Manager, Engineer, and Surveyor. However, the Mines Act did not recognize the term "Assistant Manager" as signed on a report by Stevenson.[4] After this, the individual who filled the position designated as Brazeau Collieries Assistant General Manager was classified as the Mining Engineer, Technical Operations. The mine managers of the two mines were Norman Fraser and Andrew Millar. Names of some of the men already working at Brazeau mines at this time were Blasetti, Morris, Hale, Janigo, Luyckfassel, McKelvie, Armstrong, Hall, and McDougall. Some of these men arrived prior to railroad completion by following the river and walking into the new mining area.

Aside from Martin Nordegg himself, two individuals who were associated with Nordegg even before the mines were begun or log cabins constructed, and who

Early Brazeau Collieries personnel (r. to l.): Dunc Stewart (Bighorn Accountant), Stuart Kidd (Provisions and Supply), Martin Nordegg (General Manager), Gilbert McKenzie (timber boss). A. Belliveau collection.

remained at Nordegg for many years, were Stuart Kidd and Jack (Johnny) Constable. Stuart Kidd, hired as Purchasing Agent in the spring of 1910, was the first employee of the Brazeau Collieries after funding was arranged. When The Bighorn Trading Company became operational in 1914, Kidd became Manager. He also became the first Postmaster, the Justice of the Peace, and the Undertaker. In June 1915 Stuart married Robina McKelvie.

Johnny (Jack) Constable appeared on the scene shortly after Norman Fraser had staked the Nordegg coal lands for the German Development Company. Constable, a small boy at this time, was brought into the Nordegg area by Stuart Kidd during the summer of 1911.[5] Young Johnny Constable went to work in the kitchen of the log messroom, and when this was phased out after the boarding house became fully operational, he became stable boy at the mine horse barns, located south and up the hill from the mining complex. Eventually, he became Barn Supervisor, in charge of caring for the mine work horses. When he married he took up residence in the house which first had been the Officials' Club, located just east of and below the mine office. This house and the original police duplex are expected to be stabilized, preserved, and protected by the historic interests involved with the Brazeau Collieries historic site.

Belgian Consulting Mining Engineer Ernest Gheur, who had come to the coal fields with Martin Nordegg in 1912, brought his wife over from Belgium and they made their home in Red Deer for four years, until Gheur died in a Calgary hospital while being treated for cancer. Mrs. Gheur then returned to Europe. In 1914, Andrew Millar left his position as Mine Manager at Nordegg; in later years he became the Chief Mines Inspector for the Province of Alberta. When Millar left Nordegg, Martin Nordegg contacted Johnny Shanks, then at Fernie Mines, to see if he was interested in hiring on as Millar's replacement. Shanks was becoming well known in the Crowsnest/Fernie area as a competent mining man, and one who was well respected by the miners. He commanded considerable loyalty from the men who worked under him. Shanks sent Jimmy Stewart, a fire-boss at Fernie Mines, to look things over. Both Shanks and Stewart decided to relocate from Fernie, bringing with them some of the Fernie miners. Among those who followed from Fernie to Nordegg were D'Amico, Ambrosie, Duncan, Crockett, France, and McQueen.

Johnny Shanks had emigrated to Canada from the mining area of Whitehaven, in northwestern England, and he continued to maintain contact with that area, resulting in a somewhat nebulous connection between the two locations. This caused the Brazeau Collieries' name to be known at Whitehaven Collieries, resulting in some later migration from Whitehaven to Nordegg over a lengthy period. Immigrants from Whitehaven included G. Batty, G. Fitzsimmons, W. J. Hall, and A. "Mac" McMullen. Shanks also recruited his brother Dave from Scotland; Dave Shanks became Under Manager of Number 2 Mine in the spring of 1916. Another new resident who arrived in Nordegg during 1914 was Archie Sturrock, who had worked with the Canadian Bank of Commerce, Montreal, before transferring to Edmonton. In 1910, he joined the financial branch of the mining community in the Jasper Park/Coal Branch region and, in 1914, he came to Nordegg to work with the accounting department. Some of these same family names that were part of the Nordegg fabric during the early years of the Brazeau Collieries were still part of Nordegg when the town closed.

The Red Deer Office of Brazeau Collieries was closed in February of 1915 and, from that time until the Brazeau Collieries ceased operations in 1955, the mine office at Brazeau Collieries minesite became the nucleus of the operation, answerable only to the Toronto head office.[6]

Miners recruited for Brazeau Collieries from the established mining areas were joined by European immigrants answering the call of the Canadian government to help populate and open up the Canadian west. Language and nationality differences, along with the tremendous adjustment problems faced in coming to a new country, were difficult obstacles for these immigrants to overcome. This was especially true of first generation women who had much less contact with the English language, and with other people, than did their husbands. Some women never really adjusted to their new life. Their own language was always spoken in their homes, although family members who attended school, or worked outside the home, soon learned to speak English.[7] However, in subsequent generations it was the acceptance and melding of these differences which helped create the unique blend of society which is to be found in western Canada today.

Originally, all of the homes for management personnel had been located south of the railway tracks, although they were divided into two widely separated areas located on two different ridges of this hilly countryside. All other homes were constructed north of the tracks and further down the slope upon which the town was built. Martin

Nordegg began to feel uncomfortable with this division of housing, wondering if it might create both a physical and mental division between management and labor in the town.

This segregation by class, which Martin Nordegg had hoped to avoid, soon became evident in the new town. Wives of personnel living south of the tracks refused to mix socially with those living north of the tracks.[8] However, this type of segregation by class was accepted practice in Canada at this time. In any given community, whether a company town or a city, there was job-related social structure as well as an ethnic-based class consciousness, based upon attitudes and theories of the times. This rapidly became evident in Nordegg as well.

During the early years of the Brazeau Collieries, managerial positions were held nearly exclusively by the British. Canada was part of the British Empire, giving rise to the attitude that the British were not immigrants like those from other nations. By the time the second wave of settlers began responding to advertisements for free land in the "Last, Best West," bringing immigrants from European nations, the WASP structure was firmly in place in the west. British institutions, traditions, and culture were considered the norm, and immigrants were expected to conform to these standards. This guaranteed almost complete control and a strongly British flavor to the institutions of politics, religion, education, and culture. Schools were expected to be the tool by which immigrants from other nations would learn the acceptable attitudes and customs.

People of American, German, and Scandinavian backgrounds were welcomed as immigrants, as they were easily assimilated into a British-type society. The suitability of immigrants for Canadian settlement appeared to vary according to the geographical and cultural distance from London, England, as well as how light-skinned they were. Central and eastern Europeans were considered less desirable but acceptable, but Asian immigration was severely restricted.

Such attitudes were widespread at the turn of the century, and government immigration policy indicated their conformity to these theories and ideas. The people coming into the new town of Nordegg from other mining camps, from other areas of Canada, and from overseas, brought with them the attitudes, beliefs, and ideas of that time. The wives of Nordegg's management personnel soon made it quite clear that they too

A two-sheet, outdoor curling rink was built just north of the railway tracks. Maggie Morris collection.

intended to maintain class distinction. Tennis courts were constructed along southeast Marcelle Avenue, a two-sheet, outdoor curling rink with an enclosed warm-up room was established just north of the tracks along southwest Cherie Avenue and, later, a nine-hole golf course was laid out on the Flats north of town. Specific days and hours were organized for management wives living south of the tracks, which included those living at the minesite, while different days and hours were assigned to those living north of the tracks. The facilities would be shared between upper and lower town, but socializing with each other was considered out of the question during the very early years.

Martin Nordegg, who had not yet begun construction on his Swiss chalet, moved into the General Manager's allocated home, east of the hospital. He settled happily into the life of the town which now bore his name. His dream had just begun to flower and bear fruit when, on August 4, 1914, Great Britain entered World War I. This meant that Canada, as part of the British Empire, also was at war. Martin Nordegg, still a German citizen at this time, suddenly had become an enemy alien.

The large payment due from the bankers syndicate in London was needed to pay Roberts and Schaeffer, of Chicago, for installation of the mine's surface features, but Martin Nordegg was informed that the London banking establishment was unable to collect payments from the continental financiers of the German Development Company. During a hurried trip to the Toronto office of the Canadian Northern Railway, he learned from Sir Donald Mann that if the German Development Company went into bankruptcy the Canadian Northern Railway would take full control of the Brazeau Collieries mining operation. Martin Nordegg rushed to Andrew Haydon, in Ottawa, and the two men discussed the situation with Canadian Government Ministers, followed later by a discussion with Sir William Mackenzie. It was arranged by Mackenzie that the mine would be kept going, under condition that Martin Nordegg run the mine and be responsible for all going well. Martin Nordegg would be allowed to draw on the Canadian Northern for payrolls and expenses, and they also would pay any Brazeau Collieries monetary notes that came due.[9] The next nine months were very difficult ones for Martin Nordegg. The majority of the townspeople remained friendly, but some of the senior officials began to show hostility. This hostility gradually became more widespread, developing into animosity and bitterness as casualty reports were published. Martin Nordegg began to live the life of a recluse.

When hostilities first had surfaced, Martin Nordegg, fearing what the future might hold for him, had made preparations to protect himself by calling upon his many contacts in Ottawa. Sam Hughes, Minister of Militia and Defence, was prevailed upon to provide a protective letter.[10] In his memoirs, Martin Nordegg relates both events of the war and local incidents which occurred during the spring of 1915; he began to feel more and more uncomfortable in what was becoming a hostile environment. The Italian community celebrated entry into the war with the Allies by having a parade. They requested Martin Nordegg's permission to fly the Italian flag from the town's only high flagpole, which was located outside Nordegg's house. On two separate occasions, the flag went missing at night. Martin Nordegg believed that such incidents, and the resultant complaints, hastened his departure from Nordegg.[11] During the late spring of 1915, his papers were confiscated, although they later were returned to him, and he received notification to return to Ottawa. With a heavy heart, Martin Nordegg boarded the train for Ottawa on June 4th, 1915, leaving the town of which he was so proud and which meant so much to him. The majority of Martin Nordegg's plans already were solidly in place by the time he had to leave Nordegg in June 1915. Through subsequent years, new development or construction within the town generally followed the 1914 blueprint which had symbolized Martin Nordegg's dream of a new kind of mining community. The mining operation was working smoothly; development of the remaining Brazeau Collieries coalfields, as well as other planned developments, would have to wait until the world situation returned to normal.

In Ottawa, Martin Nordegg met with his friend, Andy Haydon, to discuss the situation in which Nordegg now found himself. Haydon suggested that naturalization would be a logical step to take, but Nordegg refused to follow this route because he believed he would feel like a traitor to his country of origin. Martin Nordegg had very strong feelings for the Canadian west and for the town that bore his name, but he also had a very strong loyalty to Germany and the German people who had first commissioned him to invest in the development of Canadian minerals. This decision, made at this particular time, changed the course of his entire life. So, despite the numerous influential friends Martin Nordegg had made in Ottawa, the fact remained that he now was classed as an enemy alien. He did, however, avoid persecution or detention. After arriving in Ottawa he was subjected to an intensive oral investigation which lasted two days, and which consisted of numerous questions concerning various and diverse areas of his life, especially those areas which involved any contact with Germany or with citizens of German extraction. The following day Martin Nordegg discovered that, rather than being detained in an internment camp, as was happening to most individuals classified as enemy aliens, his case had been dismissed. He had been given permission to leave Canada and take up residence in the United States, and a letter had been issued by the Chief Immigration Officer granting Martin Nordegg permission both to leave and to re-enter Canada as needed. One week after leaving the town of Nordegg, Martin Nordegg departed for New York.

When Nordegg contacted William Mackenzie to inform the latter about these developments he received word that Mackenzie considered Nordegg essential for the progress of the mining development and instructions had been given for Nordegg to receive regular reports and statements which were then to be returned with Nordegg's remarks. All correspondence was to funnel through the head office of Brazeau Collieries in Toronto, but Martin Nordegg, in absentia, was to continue as general manager of the operation. For a time, and according to William Mackenzie's wishes, decisions continued to be made by Martin Nordegg, with correspondence and records funnelling through the Toronto office of Brazeau Collieries. However, as time went by, Nordegg began to feel that he had less and less control over what was happening at Brazeau Collieries. He still had every hope of returning to his former position of general manager of Brazeau Collieries in Nordegg after hostilities had ceased.

On May 22, 1917, while Martin Nordegg was still exiled from Canada, he received permission, through Andrew Haydon, from Canada's Chief Commissioner of Police, to accompany Marcelle and Mrs. Nordegg to Holland. Berthe-Marie, his first wife who had been residing in the United States, had become ill and wished to return to Europe.

This trip, however, did not take place; early in 1918, Martin Nordegg posted a bond for Marcelle and Mrs. Nordegg to travel to China where Marcelle was to be married to L. E. May, a representative of the interests of Standard Oil in a large American colony located northwest of Shanghai. Nordegg himself was denied permission to leave the United States at this time. However, as a result of wartime bureaucracy, Marcelle's marriage did not take place until 1919.[12]

At much the same time that the course of Martin Nordegg's life changed direction through the intervention of World War I, operating costs for the massive and far reaching Canadian Northern Railway had increased rapidly: Mackenzie and Mann found themselves in serious financial difficulties. As early as 1912, Mackenzie and Mann had experienced financial problems. These problems now had intensified. In 1918, Brazeau Collieries shares held by Mackenzie, Mann, and Company were used as collateral with the Canadian Bank of Commerce, thus giving this bank control of the voting rights.[13] The financial house of Lazard Brothers of London, who had invested in both the Canadian Northern Railway and the Brazeau Collieries, now had a strong grasp on the Brazeau mining operation and on the transportation facilities which served it. The company of Lazard Brothers had purchased or underwritten a large part of the Brazeau Collieries bonds and, in 1917, they pushed for a parliamentary bill to cancel the entire original bond issue of Brazeau Collieries. They requested legislation to permit these bonds to be exchanged for a new issue. Holders of old bonds could exchange them for the new stock if the holder could prove, among other things, that he was not an enemy alien. This bill was defeated. As a precautionary measure, Nordegg transferred all shares of his own, and of the Deutsches Kanada Syndicat, to his friend Andy Haydon. Brazeau Collieries had continued to flourish under the regime set in place after Martin Nordegg had been forced to leave the west, but as time passed with still no end to the war in sight, and with the Canadian Northern Railway and its founders in a precarious position, far reaching changes were beginning to take place. Martin Nordegg's correspondence with the Brazeau Collieries became less and less. When he drew this to the attention of the Toronto Office, he was told that it slowed things down by the length of time it took to contact him and then wait for his reply. On instructions by Sir William Mackenzie, the policy now was that information dealing only with important matters would be sent to Martin Nordegg.

On April 13, 1917, John Shanks, Interim Manager of Brazeau Mines, met with the Advisory Committee of the Brazeau Collieries in their Toronto office where he was officially appointed Manager of the Company and placed in full charge of operations at the mines. This was a three year appointment, with a clause allowing termination by either side after a period of three months notice. It was directed that all communication between the mining operation and the head office was to be through Shanks. Thus Martin Nordegg no longer was fully responsible for decisions affecting the Brazeau Collieries mining operation, although Shanks was ordered to submit all reports in duplicate "as on account of war conditions any communications between Mr. Nordegg and the Company's officials are to be through the Head Office."[14]

By 1918, the Canadian government had taken over the capital stock of, and the shares held by, the German Development Company. This was done to property of all enemy aliens in order to ensure that no assets could be used to aid the enemy. G. T. Clarkson, Mulvey, and Haydon, who now controlled and administered the shares owned by the German Development Company, were elected directors of the Brazeau Collieries. To his dismay, Martin Nordegg discovered that, as an enemy alien, he was ineligible for the Board of Directors and he had no voting rights.

On December 20, 1919, by Order-in-Council, the Canadian government nationalized a number of railroads that were having severe financial problems, thus creating the government-owned Canadian National Railways Corporation. This action combined the railways of the Canadian Northern, the Grand Trunk, the Grand Trunk Pacific, and the Intercolonial into one unit. Both Mackenzie and Mann remained active in other businesses until their deaths, but their financial support of, and influence in, the affairs of Brazeau Collieries were drawing to a close. The dream of a mining conglomerate in west-central Alberta was not to be, although subsequent Brazeau Collieries management never fully gave up the idea of further development of Brazeau properties. For almost the next half century, and for almost the entire lifetime of the coal mining settlement, the Canadian Northern Western Railway continued to serve both Rocky and Nordegg. This railway had not been amalgamated with the Canadian Northern Railway even though it was a wholly owned property. Therefore, it came under the banner of the Canadian government as a subsidiary of the Canadian National Railway. On June 8, 1954, the Canadian Northern Western Railway was absorbed by Canadian Northern Consolidated Railways which, in 1956, then amalgamated with Canadian National Railways, one year after the Brazeau Collieries mining operation had ceased to function.[15]

There was no further attempt to carry out the extensive original plans for northwest expansion of the Canadian Northern Western Railway, which had been expected to continue beyond Nordegg, connecting all the Brazeau coal lands with the Canadian National Railway's transcontinental rail line. The most northerly portion of this route would have brought the Canadian Northern Western Railway past areas where the Coal Branch developed. This land, through which the rail line was to extend, has remained undeveloped wilderness territory. The area now has a few access roads, but no rail-line ever has penetrated into the region.

During the First World War (1914-1918), when anti-German sentiment was running high, German place-names became a ready target for patriotism. The first rumor of a name change for Nordegg surfaced as early as 1916; the reply to a query by Stuart Kidd stated there had been talk of changing the name, but Mackenzie had given instructions to the contrary so nothing further was expected to be done. However, in November, 1919, a four-page letter was sent from Martin Nordegg to D. B. Hanna, who had become President of Canadian National Railways when the Canadian Northern Railway was nationalized.[16] Nordegg tried to dissuade him from allowing the name change to take place. Nonetheless, in 1919, almost a year after the end of the war, the railway station was renamed Brazeau. In 1923, the Secretary of the Nordegg Branch of District 18, United Mine Workers of America, on behalf of the Nordegg miners wrote to Sir Henry Thornton, a Director of Canadian National Railways, requesting that the station revert to the name of Nordegg.[17] The station remained Brazeau.

Helen (Letcher) Ross collection.

According to railway maps and schedules, the settlement was Brazeau, as proclaimed by the sign on the railway station building from 1919 onward, but less than 350 yards (320 meters) north, and downhill from the station, was the post-office, known throughout the town's entire history as the Nordegg Post Office. The town itself was known as Nordegg, but the mine, which was the reason for the town's existence, was usually referred to as the Brazeau Collieries or Brazeau Mines. The coal field from which the coal was extracted was the Nordegg Coal Lands but the Company doing the mining was the Brazeau Collieries Limited. For anyone wanting to travel to Nordegg by train, no such settlement appeared to exist; for anyone wanting to send mail to the town of Brazeau, no such post office existed. And this is the way it remained for the lifetime of the town.

Shortly after the war had ended, when consideration was being given to the future of the German Development Company as a major shareholder of Brazeau Collieries, Martin Nordegg suggested selling the Rocky Mountain Collieries (the Kananaskis field) to the Brazeau Collieries. Ottawa accepted this suggestion, as it would help to simplify the upcoming settlement with the bankers. Thus the Rocky Mountain Collieries ceased to exist as a separate company, and the Kananaskis coalfields on Mount Allan were brought under the blanket of the Brazeau Collieries.

As time distanced the world from the horror and upheaval of the war years, Martin Nordegg once again began to long for the day when circumstances would allow his return to the land he had adopted as his own many years before. He awaited the 1921 Canadian elections in a state of mounting excitement, believing that if his friends (of the Liberal Party) were elected he would have a much greater opportunity to re-establish himself in Canada. The Conservative Party had come into power in 1911. Nordegg's long-time friend, Andrew Haydon, was involved in the organization of the Liberals for this 1921 election, which they hoped to win under the leadership of William Lyon Mackenzie King.

In a letter to Stuart Kidd, written in early summer of 1921, Martin Nordegg commented, among other news, that he now was the grandfather of a one year old; Marcelle had given birth to a boy in October, 1919. At this time Nordegg was contemplating taking a holiday trip to an area near the Athabasca River, northwest of the major coal holdings of Brazeau Collieries. In this letter he suggested to Kidd that "next time you have an opportunity, just say to Johnny [Shanks] you hear that I am coming out west shortly and report to me every word he says."[18]

The Canadian election of late 1921 returned the Liberal Party to office; Martin Nordegg was elated. A few weeks later, when Nordegg and Haydon visited a number of the new Cabinet Ministers, Nordegg found the hoped-for support in regaining his former position. In a letter to Stuart Kidd, Martin Nordegg stated that Clarkson would be resigning and he (Nordegg) would be re-instated as Vice President of Brazeau Collieries. He stated that he would have to wait for the settlement of complicated legal affairs connected with this, as well as for an Order-in-Council. In this letter he asked Kidd if there was an official's cottage available for him or, if not, was there a five room cottage with bath. He cautioned Kidd that he did not want anyone to know he was coming, stating further:

> *Maybe that Shanks will find it necessary to resign. In that case I have to see that the entire organisation does not quit with him. If he is clever, he will try to apologise to me for past behaviour. I was the man who started the whole business.... If Shanks goes, the business will still go under a different man. Rely on it.*[19]

On May 22, 1922, he received a telegram recalling him to Canada. He was informed that the only condition prior to re-instatement with the Brazeau Collieries was that he be naturalized, so on June 8, 1922, he became a British Subject (equivalent to present-day Canadian citizenship). However, despite Martin Nordegg's optimism and high hopes of returning to his former position, he ran into difficulties with the officials of the new interests now controlling Brazeau Collieries. The representative of Lazard Brothers stated that his firm intended to eliminate all German interests in the Brazeau Coal Company. Although Martin Nordegg had strong support from the government, the Company was privately owned, subject only to shareholders' decisions, and immune to government intervention. Reluctantly, Martin Nordegg was forced to accept the fact that he would not be resuming his former position with the Brazeau Collieries and that part of his life now was over. However, he had one last duty to perform for the shareholders of the German Development Company – to sell their shares at the greatest possible monetary advantage.

He decided to visit the town of Nordegg, and to see for himself what progress had taken place since his departure seven years previously. Mulvey and Haydon felt it was a good plan because the three of them then could estimate the value of their holdings, apart from the reports they received from the head office of the Collieries. In November 1922, Martin Nordegg returned to visit the town which bore his name. He made it a point to tour the mine site and to look at the Company's records in the mine office. He expressed great disappointment that there had not been any move to enlarge the scope of the mining operations into other Brazeau Collieries coalfields and, in particular, he was upset that no move had taken place to develop the Kananaskis coalfield which was situated so close to a profitable market in the Canadian Pacific Railway. While visiting the Brazeau office, he examined the variations in the demand for coal by the railway. He was aware that the railway could absorb more coal from the Brazeau Mines. After Martin Nordegg returned to Ottawa, he held a meeting with Mulvey and Haydon. Nordegg proposed that they sell their interests in the coalfields since they now had relatively little influence upon the decisions made by the Brazeau Collieries organization. However, Nordegg suggested they wait until it could be seen if the coal output could be raised, thus increasing profits for the Collieries and, in turn, creating a favorable climate to sell their shares in the German Development Company at a greater profit.

Charles Vaughan, who was Vice President of the Canadian National Railway, was an individual Martin Nordegg had known for some time. Nordegg visited Vaughan to

Brazeau Collieries' lower tipple. Maggie Morris collection.

explain how he was being forced out of the company that he (Nordegg) had helped create, and that he had decided it would be best to sell the interests of the German Development Company in the Brazeau Collieries. He requested that Vaughan see if purchases of Brazeau coal by the Canadian National Railway could be increased. Vaughan promised to see what he could do.[20]

During the following year (1923) the Brazeau Collieries' mines reached peak production, becoming one of the highest producing mines in the province of Alberta, in an attempt to fill all the coal orders received. Never again in the history of the Brazeau Mines did their coal production approach the level reached in 1923. During this year of peak production, the labor force climbed to over 800 men, causing considerable strain upon living conditions in the town. Health and sanitation became a growing concern. The boarding houses were forced to go to double-shifting to accommodate the require-

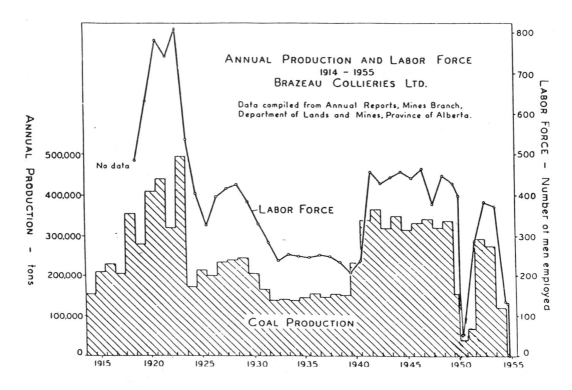

The chart shows mining was more labor intensive in earlier years. Data for labor force are number of men employed on December 31st of each year, except 1950 (ends of June and July), 1951 (ends of February, March, and December), and 1955 (ends of January and February). Data for 1950/51 indicates Brazeau's Nordegg and Kananaskis operations. Courtesy Nordegg Historical Society.

ment for lodging. This double-shifting meant that two workers, working opposite shifts, were assigned to one bed. When one of the men got out of bed in preparation for going to work, his bed was turned over to another man who had recently finished his shift and now was ready to sleep.[21] This double-shifting eased the plight of accommodation for single men, but for married workers there was no easy solution, as there were no additional houses available.

Even in 1922, when coal production was climbing, two families had made their homes in tents located east of Main Street, behind the bank building, in a grove of trees that separated Main from the residential areas. When accommodation became even more strained in the peak year of 1923, a small tent town of four or five families sprang up east of town. Some tents were situated on both sides of Martin Creek, east of the intersection of Stuart Road and Elizabeth Avenue, and near the first school. Others were located beyond the second rail trestle east of the railway station. The occupants equipped their tents with heaters, coal/wood stoves, and essential furniture such as tables and beds. Water was carried from the nearest standpipe on the street, or from nearby creeks, while washing could be done in the creeks when they weren't frozen. Winter weather did not pose a major problem as the tents were warm and comfortable, but severe hailstorms were a major hazard because they caused the tents to leak.[22] Another phase of construction was begun to provide homes for those who came to work in the Nordegg coalfields. The prospects for the mining centre of Nordegg and for the Brazeau Collieries appeared to be extremely positive. However, in 1924, there was a distinct drop in coal orders as well as a general strike. For both the Brazeau Collieries and the town of Nordegg, this effectively removed the pressure of too much growth in too little time.

Martin Nordegg had bided his time until Brazeau stock had climbed before selling the shares of the German Development Company to Lazard Brothers for cash, which Nordegg then distributed to the shareholders of the Company. Although this signalled the end of Martin Nordegg's influence upon, and involvement in, the Brazeau Collieries and the town of Nordegg, he never lost his interest in them, and in the coal industry in general.

When Martin Nordegg returned for a visit to the west in 1923, he was accompanied by Sonia Marcelle, the woman who was destined to become the second Mrs. Nordegg. Sonia was an accomplished actress whom Martin Nordegg had met when, with his wife Berthe-Marie and his daughter, he had attended the theatre in Atlantic City in July 1917.[23] The two were drawn to each other and, before long, Sonia became Martin Nordegg's constant companion. Coincidentally, Martin Nordegg's daughter and his second wife both carried the name of Marcelle, although this was simply a stage name for Sonia. Old timers of Nordegg were not always in agreement as to whether Marcelle Avenue was named for Martin Nordegg's daughter, his lady-friend, or his wife. The conviction held usually depended upon the age of the individual and the time period in which he/she had come to Nordegg town. However, the street was named for Martin Nordegg's daughter, and was assigned at the town's inception, well before Martin Nordegg had met the lady who would become his second wife.

*I*n Ottawa, during previous years, Nordegg had helped Mulvey in administering sequestered German and Austrian property and, gradually, Nordegg's assistance had come to be depended upon. After the German Development Company had been dissolved, Mulvey suggested that Nordegg remain in Canada, assisting Mulvey in his work as Secretary of State. Martin Nordegg made the decision to remain in Ottawa. He worked closely with the Canadian Government on various assignments, maintaining a special interest in matters which assisted political refugees and displaced persons.

In July, 1924, Berthe-Marie Nordegg died while in temporary residence in Switzerland; she had been in ill health for years. In November of that year, Martin married his long-time companion, Sonia Marcelle. In late 1928, they bought a large home in Ottawa, located at 28 Range Road. This home now has become the official residence of the Sri Lankan High Commissioner.

In 1930, Martin Nordegg's book, *The Fuel Problems of Canada*, was published; it received mixed, although generally good, reviews. The main thrust of the book dealt with coal as Canada's major fuel source and in this book he discussed the difficulties which were facing the industry. He emphasized the extreme importance of the railways to the survival and success of the Canadian coal industry which had to contend, among other things, with massive haulage distances to distribute the coal, and with Canadian purchases of American, rather than Canadian, coal. He pointed out the need for Canada to have a national fuel policy, organizing the railways and the coalfields to work together very closely in the interests of success for both.

In 1936, when Martin Nordegg had reached the age of 68, the Nordeggs sold their Ottawa home and, by late 1937, they had taken up permanent residence in New York City. During the following years, Sonia urged Nordegg to write his memoirs.

Martin Nordegg's life was punctuated with both triumph and tragedy. His correspondence with Stuart Kidd allows the reader brief glimpses into Nordegg's private life and gives small amounts of information regarding the people about whom he cared. In a 1928 letter from Martin Nordegg to Stuart Kidd, Nordegg mentioned that Marcelle was better than she had been previously, but she wanted to divorce her husband, who was having an affair with a married woman. Nordegg expressed the belief that this was a result of Marcelle frequently leaving him alone. In 1929, Marcelle and her son spent some time with Sonia and Martin in Ottawa. Marcelle's mental health seemed to be deteriorating by this time. With her son, she returned to China, but not long afterward she left there to take up residence in Germany, leaving her husband and her 10-year-old son in China.[24] In 1931, she was placed in a private psychiatric sanitarium for disturbed individuals, in Bonn, Germany. When the heavy Allied bombing of Germany took place, Nordegg contacted the State Department in Washington to obtain information about her. Each month, Nordegg was informed that they had been unable to locate her. Finally, in early September, 1945, he cabled one of his Ottawa contacts, George E. Beament, who by this time had become a Brigadier General. Nordegg received word approximately 2 weeks later that the sanitarium had been repeatedly hit by bombs during the previous December and had been partially destroyed. Marcelle had been taken to an air raid shelter where she had lived for a few weeks. Near the end of January, 1945, she had died from shock and exposure. Nordegg's letter informing Kidd of Marcelle's death included the comment:

> You knew her well – she was such a delightful and clever girl, and she had to end that way. We had hopes of her recovery as long as she lived and now she is gone![25]

Martin Nordegg's health began to deteriorate during the last few years of his life. In letters to his friends in the west he often spoke of returning to visit the areas he had known so well during the early years of the 20th century and, on occasion, plans were made to do just that. In 1947, he had reservations at the Jasper Park Lodge, which had to be cancelled due to many weeks of illness and a frightening session during which he nearly lost an eye when it became contaminated with smallpox vaccine. This was followed, in 1948, by a heart attack. By that summer he was weak, frail of health, and nearly blind.[26] Martin Nordegg died in New York City on September 13, 1948, at the age of 80.

Nordegg – Its People

*D*uring the first half of the 20th century, the town of Nordegg began to take its own unique place in the colorful pattern of early Alberta development; in many ways it continued to follow the plans and dreams of its founder, Martin Nordegg, even after he had been forced to depart. According to C.A. Seager, who has done extensive research on Alberta coal mining, very little is known about the actual character of the various communities in which miners lived and worked. He states that "all of Alberta's coal communities experienced periods of growth, development, and maturation, but not, however, in the same way and to the same degree.[1]

The overall ethnic structure of Nordegg was different from that of other Alberta mining towns and this had a direct and early influence upon the development of town identity. According to the 1925 study done by the Royal Commission on Coal, ethnic distribution in the majority of Alberta mines showed the British as the largest group in all the mining areas, the Slavic population as the second largest, usually followed by a considerably smaller Italian population. However, the source-countries of Nordegg's immigrants were largely British and Italian, since a disproportionately high number of Italian workmen had followed Johnny Shanks from Fernie to Nordegg, but Central European immigration after World War I created more diversity in Nordegg's ethnic structure. However, the 1925 Coal Commission report indicates that Nordegg's population distribution of that time still did not follow the established pattern of a large Slavic population. This same Coal Commission indicates that Nordegg had the highest percentage of Italian workmen of any mining area in Alberta.[2] This departure from the norm in ethnic composition of Nordegg's townspeople was one of a number of factors which helped shape the character of the maturing town.

The British were the largest ethnic group in coal mining. British immigration to Canada has been relatively constant during the 20th century. Coal is, by far, the leading mineral product of the British Isles, and this meant that people with appropriate technical expertise were available for recruitment. Since Canada was part of the British Empire, the government made a special effort to encourage their immigration. This resulted in a domination of management positions by the British. Immigrants from other countries were expected to conform to the standard of established British culture, society, and traditions.

The Nordegg Italian population was drawn from specific locations within certain Italian provinces, but the provinces from which they came were widely scattered. Approximately 30% came from Sicily and Calabria, the most southern provinces. The original homeland of these Italians was one of the poorest in Italy. About 30% of

Nordegg's Italian population had come from the province of Abruzzi in the mid-regions of Italy, along the Adriatic Coast southeast of Rome, while the remaining 40% came from the northern areas of Veneto, Friuli, and Liguria.[3]

Some immigrants from southern Italy to Nordegg had to leave behind wives and small children, and the amount needed to bring them all to Canada seemed unreachable. In one instance, in 1922, Stuart Kidd wrote a letter recommending a specific Italian immigrant's family be allowed to come, stating that repayment for the fare would be guaranteed because the miner had a good job and was earning a steady income. Some of these immigrants to Canada never were reunited with their families in Italy. One father brought his eldest son, aged 11 years, and many years later brought a second son. His wife never did come, and she never again saw her boys after they left Italy. Two others who had left families behind in the 1930s were able to bring them to Canada after World War II. One wife sent the couple's 15-year-old daughter to her father in Nordegg during the late 1940s, but was unwilling to make the trip herself. Too much time had passed and she no longer was willing to give up her life in Italy to venture to a new country. Another wife took the chance, and made it to Nordegg in the early 1950s.[4]

Among working class Italians there was a great deal of solidarity, as might be expected from people who understand strong ties to family and town. This loyalty to kin creates a support system of values, customs, and attitudes which kept them independent of Canadian support institutions, other than those created among the immigrants themselves. This extended form of self-help resulted in the formation of Italian Societies. Many central and eastern European miners who worked in Nordegg hired on for only a season or two before leaving, but a core group remained there permanently. For the most part, the eastern Europeans were extensive readers, vitally interested in schools and in higher education. There was a tremendous development of technical education in these eastern European countries during the late 19th and early 20th centuries and, as a result, many eastern and central European immigrants were skilled workers. Under good management they were excellent laborers – hard workers who were capable of surviving great hardships, and often they were preferred for the heavy manual work of coal mining.[5]

As the workforce settled in at Nordegg, the European immigrants soon became aware that the British miners seemed to be getting all the good jobs. There was a definite ethnic distinction which resulted in a certain amount of friction. After the Officials' Club had been done away with in 1918, all Brazeau employees, whether management or labor, became members of the Miners' Club, and each man had membership fees deducted from his pay. Class distinction, which had been based upon the hierarchy created by divisions between labor and management, had begun to give way to stratification following ethnic lines. Ethnic societies and mutual aid organizations began appearing.

The Nordegg Italian Society was an active group during the history of the town, and even afterwards. The Grand Lodge of this society was located at Fernie, but there was not a great deal of contact between Lodges. A per capita assessment was sent from the local Lodge to the Grand Lodge and this covered long-term problems. If a member was sick and unable to work, the local Lodge paid $1.00 per day to a maximum number of days, after which the Grand Lodge took on the responsibility. Upon death of a member, $100.00 was given to the family. Meetings were held on a regular basis and this acted as a sounding board for members to help each other look for solutions to problems.[6] The Nordegg Slavic Society, which operated along the same lines but on a smaller scale, was active in Nordegg for a few years but disbanded in the mid-30s due to lack of both interest and funds.[7]

Relatively early in the town's history a major activity of the British, following the pattern set in England and in eastern Canada, was the formation of the Nordegg Dramatic Society which, by the 20s and early 30s, was performing very demanding musical productions, complete with elaborate sets and props. These were usually organized and produced under the direction of Kate Shanks, wife of general manager Johnny Shanks, along with their school-teacher daughter, Margaret. Participation in these activities was based upon ethnic category. British officials, shop-keepers, teachers, miners, and wives worked together to create dramatic evenings to be presented to the general population of Nordegg.[8] Robbie Burns night also was a big event for the British group, for which they organized an elaborate dinner and entertainment, both of which were strongly tied to British traditional practices. British immigrants had looked to Canadian open spaces to make their dreams come true, and in a land as small and densely populated as Britain, it was not possible to imagine the emptiness and loneliness they would find in the Canadian west. The various activities they organized were how they held onto their homeland.

Tables set up for a banquet in the theatre/show hall. Maggie Morris collection.

An extremely strong influence upon development of the collective identity of Nordegg was the almost total isolation of the town from the outside world, and from other mining centres of Alberta. The Crowsnest Pass and Coal Branch areas both were made up of a series of mining towns, affording interaction and companionship through their close proximity to each other. Still other Alberta mining centres, such as Canmore, Lethbridge, and Edmonton, were on, or near, mainline rail or road traffic routes. Nordegg's nearest neighbor of comparable size was Rocky Mountain House, lying 60 miles to the east by railway.[9] For over 20 years this thin band of steel was Nordegg's only connection to the outside world. Although freight trains for the coal usually came once a day, or more often when coal orders were sufficient, they had no direct bearing on town life, so they were ignored as a link with the outside, except by the men at the mine who were dependent upon them for shipping out the coal. The "mixed" train, pulling both passenger and freight cars, came three times a week, bringing passengers, supplies, and news of the world beyond the Upper North Saskatchewan and the Shunda Basin.

This extreme isolation and dependency upon the rail line created a dangerous situation for Nordegg and its people during the forest fire of 1919. The two previously established timber camps, logically but unimaginatively named East Bush Camp and West Bush Camp, supplied most of the timber that was cut and hauled into Nordegg. In 1919, a raging forest fire broke out in the East Bush area, causing considerable panic among residents of the town. The railway tracks, the only exit from the town, followed the southern edge of Shunda Basin along the lower edge of the mountain upon which East Bush timber camp was located. It was quite conceivable that the only route out of Nordegg for mechanized travel could be cut off by this fire.

Box-cars were loaded and stood waiting in case of the need to evacuate the residents of the town. Because it would be impossible to haul much in the way of personal effects in the limited amount of space in the box-cars, some of the residents took to burying their valuables, with the hope they would be able to locate them once again if the town did burn.[10] Fortunately, the weather co-operated, with the wind pushing the fire further up the mountain and away from the town, rain removed the fury of the dry wood, and the town was able once again to get on with the job of developing into a major Canadian coal centre.

Although the title West Bush drifted into oblivion when that area was no longer used for cutting timber, the name East Bush became part of the folklore of the town. The remnants of an old rutted wagon road, which began just east of the town reservoir, joined up with the original hauling road from the mine on an upper level of the mountain south of Nordegg. This road, in turn, led to a subalpine meadow where East-Bush Falls is located. The mountain rising from this now fully-treed meadow became known locally as The Burned Patch. The Burned Patch, gradually renewing itself with new growth, was a constant reminder to the following generations that, although Nature is a gracious landlady, she can be an extremely powerful and dangerous one as well.

The second fire threatened the area during the summer of 1933 when a forest fire blazed to life in the general area of Susner's Valley and Box Canyon, southeast of Nordegg. This was not a great distance from the area of the previous fire which had threatened Nordegg in 1919. Eastbush Mountain to the west and the northern shoulder of Eagle Mountain to the east form Box Canyon at their juncture. The Box Canyon fire was lower in elevation, and closer to the train tracks which connected Nordegg with the world outside. The Box Canyon fire actually jumped the tracks, catching one trestle bridge on fire, before expanding to become a 10 mile (17 km) burning front. Despite the nearness of Box Canyon to Nordegg, the westerly winds that were blowing at the time caused it to be more dangerous to the Saunders/Alexo region to the east than it was to Nordegg. However, the same precautions were taken as with the Eastbush fire, with boxcars ready to attempt evacuation of Nordeggers, although getting anywhere by train became a doubtful proposition because of the location of the fire and the damaged train trestle. Other forest fires took place in this west country of Central Alberta during the years of Nordegg's existence, including a major bush fire in the Blackstone region in June, 1922. However, no other fire was as threatening to the town of Nordegg and the Brazeau Collieries organization as were the fires of 1919 and 1933.

One of the forces which helped unite the various ethnic groups in Alberta coal towns was interest and participation in various sporting activities. Through this active involvement in athletic pursuits the sharply drawn lines of ethnic divisions first began to blur. Early in Nordegg's history, horseshoe pits and bobolinko alleys were constructed in the central area of town. Bobolinko, also known as bocci, is an outdoor game played with heavy metal balls, and it is a cross between lawn bowling and pool. Eventually there were 3 bobolinko alleys available for recreational play.[11]

Over the years Nordegg developed a history of fielding strongly competitive teams in numerous activities, frequently winning, or being strong contenders for, regional championships. Team effort became town effort, and solidarity in the name of the town began to emerge. Soccer was the first team sport to become a part of life in the early days of Nordegg's history, but first it was necessary to have a playing field. The area at the foot of the town was soft muskeg, but it was really the only level place for competitive activities such as soccer, so a sports field was constructed through the efforts of all the townspeople. Branches were laid over soft areas, as needed, and ashes were hauled from the mine to create a build-up. Goal posts were erected, a bandstand platform constructed and a grandstand built, with soccer change rooms located underneath.[12] Nordegg was ready to enter the field of competitive sport. This soccer team, of championship calibre, succeeded in winning a major football trophy, as well as playing exhibition games in Calgary. Since there was no shortage of hills in the Nordegg area, skiing, bob-sledding, and sleigh riding were natural outcomes of Nordegg's winter environment. Hills were plentiful, while vehicles were not, so skiers and sled riders simply assumed that they owned the road until such time as they discovered something larger, or mechanized, approaching from the other direction, whereupon evasive action was taken into the nearest ditch. The approaching vehicle was usually the 5 ton coal truck, used to deliver coal orders to local homes. However, these particular sports usually were left to the young people who, from one generation to the next, are convinced that they are completely indestructible, and then try to prove it.

Early residents skated on the two lakes near the base of the south mountain upon which Nordegg was built, and also on Fish Lake, west of Nordegg. These were favorite spots for a favorite pastime, although many of the numerous nearby lakes or creeks were used at different times. When one of the lakes below the town was converted into a sewage dump, that area became much less popular for skating but still was used to some extent. A skating rink was opened in Nordegg on December 8th, 1922. Located just west of the curling rink, it was below the tracks, on the south side of Cherie Avenue. Hockey teams became the winter equivalent of the summer soccer and baseball teams. Any outdoor rink is completely at the mercy of the weather but, in Nordegg, as long as players and helpers were able to shovel snow faster than it fell, the game could go on.

In the years after the end of World War II, it was decided to erect a memorial to those who had died. This became the Memorial Sports Complex, which was constructed by the local branch of the United Mine Workers of America. The funding to build this complex was raised by deducting two percent from each worker's salary until sufficient funds were available for construction. All Nordegg working people agreed to contribute to this fund, whether a union member or not, since all would benefit by it. The Nordegg Literary and Athletic Association funded the necessary equipment to supply the Sports Complex. This complex included a hockey/skating arena, tennis courts, and a four-sheet indoor curling rink. When this complex had been in the planning stages, there was considerable discussion as to whether construction should include a swimming pool or tennis courts. It was decided to go with the tennis courts, because Fish Lake already provided the opportunity for swimming, at least during the summer months.

Residents skated on the lakes. A. Belliveau collection.

Once the indoor skating arena was constructed, outside area hockey teams became more willing to participate in games and tournaments. Nordegg hockey teams, at all age levels, soon became a force to be reckoned with. Every game played to packed stands. In the later years of the town's existence, one of the strongest driving forces behind the Nordegg hockey scene was Brian Shaw, who was born in Nordegg on November 8, 1930. Brian, who subsequently became part owner, president, and general manager of the Portland Winter Hawks of the Western Hockey League, was instrumental in getting Nordegg into the Highways 2-11 hockey league, as well as generally keeping Nordegg in a very high profile position in the Central Alberta hockey scene.

The nearest hockey rival town was Rocky Mountain House, 60 miles (97 km) east, while Carstairs, approximately 190 road miles (306 km) to the southeast, was one of the most distant. Nordegg's home games most often were scheduled on weekends to cut down on the travelling difficulties of the opposing teams. Because of the extreme isolation of the town in relation to the other hockey towns, trips out of Nordegg to compete against other teams became planned expeditions, an adventure embarked upon by competitors and fans alike. The roads, being frozen during winter, usually were more navigable than in summer, when rain could cause mud severe enough to make them impassable. Nordegg hockey teams usually were good enough to be serious challengers for league championships and, because of this high calibre of play, the other teams, often grudgingly, continued to make the long trek into Nordegg for return matches. The year that Nordegg won the 2-11 league championship, Brian Shaw was

Nordegg hockey teams always were serious challengers for league championships. John Janigo collection.

one of the goaltenders for the Nordegg team, while the other goaltender, Arnold Nylund, is the father of the NHL's Gary Nylund, ex-New York Islander.[13]

Baseball also was a sport of major interest and participation. The soccer field, created by Nordegg's early residents, also doubled as a ball field, and active competition took place. Soccer gradually lost its popular appeal and baseball became the major team sport of summer. In the late 1940s, the Nordegg baseball team advanced to the regional finals against Rocky Mountain House; they were scheduled to play in Rocky for the trophy. So many people wished to attend that particular game it became possible to charter a special train from the Railway. The Nordegg Literary and Athletic Association paid the guarantee price for the train and sold space to fans at cost. The train left Nordegg early in the morning, filled with fans carrying suitcases crammed with musical instruments and liquid refreshments. It was a party all the way, and an even more exuberant party on the way back, after the Nordegg team had won the hardball trophy cup. By the time Nordegg closed, the Miners Club had a series of trophies on display, testifying to the athletic capabilities of the town's population.

Annual Sports Days became Nordegg's main community-centred celebrations of the year. The first Sports Day to be held in the new town of Nordegg was scheduled for September 1, 1914; by the 1940s, Sports Days were being held on the weekends of May 24th, July 1st, and Labor Day, with Labor Day being the biggest of the three. The celebrations involved the entire town, as well as the Stoney Indians of the region. Resplendent in traditional costumes, the Stoneys were the most colorful part of the Sports Day Parade, which signalled the beginning of the day's activities. During the course of the day, various displays were put on by the Stoneys, including a tipi-raising race. Games, horse races and foot races, log-straddle pillow fights, bareback horse wrestling, and numerous other contests took place throughout the day.[14] In later years, a further attraction was added when a corral was constructed so that contests could include both riding and roping events. Spectators either peered through the gaps in the logs of this high and sturdy corral, or climbed up to perch on the top-most log rail. As part of the afternoon events, games of baseball and hardball often were arranged, usually against visiting teams. The Literary and Athletic Association organized these Nordegg Sports Days, also providing substantial cash prizes for competition winners. The event-filled day and evening finished with a dance held in the Community Hall/Empress Theatre. Involvement in these various sporting and community events gave townspeople a strong feeling of solidarity. Ethnicity, class, and religion played no part in such activities. Instead, strong ties to community were developed and fostered.

The Stoneys were the most colorful part of Sports Days. A. Belliveau collection.

Fish Lake, approximately 3 miles (4.8 km) west of town, emerged during the early years as the centre for water sports. Fish Lake, which drains into the Shunda system, occasionally has been known as Shunda Lake. However, no Nordegg resident referred to this as Shunda Lake; since the early years of Nordegg's history, when this lake became the summer place for the townspeople, it was known as Fish Lake. This lake became the place not only to swim, but also to camp, to have wiener roasts, and to gather for songfests around a campfire. The *Rocky Mountaineer* reported, on June 15, 1932, that large crowds were going to Fish Lake. By that time, a pier, with both low and high diving boards, had been constructed at the outlet (northern) end of the lake, along with change rooms for the swimmers. A picnic shelter also was erected, complete with a cooking stove. During summer months the Nordegg Literary and Athletic Association hired a lifeguard, part of whose duties was to teach local youngsters how to swim. Occasionally, the Association also organized community fun days to take place at Fish Lake. Later in the town's history, a concession stand was established from which ice cream, hotdogs, and cigarettes were sold.

Early access to Fish Lake had been by a walking trail westward from the mine. This trail was improved to the extent that some of the women pushed baby buggies from the town to the lake. Eventually, easier access to the lake came about because of the Great Depression, when road construction was undertaken by the government. This make-work program resulted in construction of improved earth roadways west from Rocky Mountain House. In the Nordegg area, this new road was built over part of the inland Indian trail from the Shunda, en route to the Saskatchewan River through Nordegg's townsite. It followed the Indians' original arc around the muskeg and onto the Flats below town where, in a swooping V-shape, it intersected with the route to the west. The road westward from Nordegg utilized the Indians' short connector trail, which had joined together a number of their routes throughout the area. This road west toward Bighorn, Windy Point, and Kootenay Plains began with the connector route which passed to the south, and just in front, of the numerous log buildings which made up the Forestry headquarters, barns, and corrals.[15]

Fish Lake emerged as the centre for water sports. Rose (Oblak) Gourlay collection.

Just beyond the forestry site and the short connector route, were two other major Indian trails which intersected with each other, and with the connector; these both were made suitable for vehicular travel. Angling north-northwest, the route of the Big Fish Trail became the road to Shunda Flats, Grouch Camp, and the Blackstone. The road westward, travelling further into the mountains, followed the Indians' overland route. At the mouth of Tershishner Creek it was reunited with the more southerly overland route which followed the North Saskatchewan River, as well as being reunited with the river, itself. This interior overland route passed just north of the two lakes lying in the valley below Nordegg, before turning west in what is now closely approximated by the David Thompson Highway.

During the first 20 years of the town's existence, the thrice-weekly train had remained the only method of travel into Nordegg. Although cars were not of much use in these very early days, some people had had them shipped into Nordegg so they could drive around locally. The numerous Native trails, which covered the entire Upper North Saskatchewan River Corridor, were more suitable for travel by horse than by motor vehicle, but occasionally a driver would attempted to follow the First Nations/Fur Brigade Trail, which followed close to the North Saskatchewan River, westward from the minesite through Black Canyon and toward Bighorn. But the trail was steep and rough, causing considerable difficulty for vehicles.

East of the Nordegg townsite there were extensive areas of muskeg, numerous hills, and heavily wooded countryside. During the first two decades of Nordegg's existence, construction of a connector road between this new settlement of Nordegg and Rocky Mountain House seemed almost beyond reach. Settlement west of Rocky was sparse; settlement west of Nordegg was non-existent. As in previous centuries, the nomadic Stoneys remained the only inhabitants of the western regions of the Upper North Saskatchewan River Corridor. At this time, there seemed to be little enticement for construction of a road west of Rocky.

Native trails were more suitable for horses, but some Nordeggers often used them as roads, fording rivers when necessary. John Janigo collection.

Rocky Mountain House resident Ernie Ross became a driving force in trying to get a road built westward. By 1928, an improved earth roadway extended approximately 20 miles (32.2 km) west, to the Horburg corner. Ross and Bill Bradshaw hacked through an equal distance further west, to the Saunders area. In 1931, Ross and four others took five days to force themselves through to Nordegg by car. However, it was not until depression era work crews were formed that a road westward became reality. Construction of the Nordegg-Rocky connector road began in July 1933, and the Fish Lake connector road was a later part of this construction. A year later the Rocky Mountain House ball team drove a convoy of cars to Nordegg. They reported the road was rough but open, even though the highway was not yet fully complete.[16]

Once Rocky Mountain House and Nordegg had been connected by the newly constructed road, cars became somewhat more common in Nordegg. However, this road did not provide constant and easy access to the outside world, since a heavy summer rainstorm could make the road impassable. After freeze-up in winter, when the road into Nordegg became solid and therefore passable, the ferry across the Saskatchewan River just west of Rocky Mountain House ceased to operate for the season. Some people did drive out during the winter by crossing on the ice or by taking their car over the railway bridge, but this was not common practice. It was not until 1946, when a traffic bridge was completed over the Saskatchewan River, that Nordegg had the capability for continuous vehicular contact with the world beyond the Shunda Basin.[17]

By 1940, Ernie Ross, who still held onto the dream of a highway which would follow David Thompson's general route westward through the mountains, had begun an organized trek from Rocky to the recently completed Banff/Jasper roadway. This first Cavalcade consisted of two vehicles which took ten days to forge through the wilds before returning eastward through Banff and Calgary. Each year that the Cavalcade journey took place, more adventurous individuals were attracted to it, including some interested Nordeggers who also wanted to promote the opening of a connector road to join with the Banff-Jasper route. By 1946, there was a reasonably good road as far west as Windy Point, where the Saskatchewan River passes through the Front Ranges of the Rocky Mountains and into the Bighorn Valley. However, block and tackle, shovels and axes were the required equipment for the rugged country beyond. Whirlpool Point, in particular, caused considerable difficulty. On one side there was the river, formed of a very large whirlpool, while on the other side loomed a huge mountain. By 1955, when Brazeau Collieries ceased operations and the town of Nordegg closed down, the road west, now known as the David Thompson Highway, was still only a dream.

The David Thompson Cavalcade became an annual event as of 1958. Publicity became more widespread and support increased for the idea of a link westward to the Banff-Jasper Highway. Hundreds of people began to participate, camping and visiting with each other on the Kootenay Plains, as had numerous First Nations people throughout countless previous centuries. Although the strongest proponent of the David Thompson Highway, Ernie Ross, died in 1963, his dream of a connector road was not forgotten, nor was he. A triple-peaked mountain near the usual Cavalcade campground on Kootenay Plains was dedicated to Ernest Ross in 1969, in honor of this trail-blazer.[18]

By the 1965 Cavalcade, the event was being sponsored by the Central Alberta Chambers of Commerce. In 1968, the David Thompson Highway was opened, although paving was not completed until 1974. The route westward which, for centuries, had been used by various First Nations people and later by the fur brigade, now had become fully accessible to the general public.

During the 1920s to the 1950s, music, which always had been popular with Nordegg's people, became even stronger as a unifying force. A multicultural Town Band was sponsored by the Literary and Athletic Association, and it became very popular among Nordegg immigrants of all ethnic groups, most of whom were interested in music. The Association bought instruments and saw that lessons were provided for those who wanted them. The participation-oriented Town Band took part in ethnic society celebrations and in the Sports Days Parades. Both the Catholic and the Protestant churches had good choirs, and works of four-part harmony often were presented. This interest in music of all Nordegg's ethnic groups extended to employing a full-time music teacher during the late 1930s and well into the 1940s.

Local musicians, beginning during the early years of the town's existence, had banded together to create dance bands who played for community dances held in the Empress Theatre, as well as for the locally produced musical entertainment performances. In later years, the school principal, Steve Hencley, who was an accomplished

Music was a unifying force. A. Belliveau collection.

Nordegg's music teacher began a rhythm band for youngsters. A. Belliveau collection.

musician, increased the scope of local musical experience for the young people of the town, not only through in-school instruction, choral classes, and private music lessons, but also by encouraging a few of the talented youngsters to participate in the dance band he organized. Hencley's popularity with the young people of Nordegg, along with the amount of music he brought into their lives, resulted in complete acceptance and keen interest in this art form. A major form of entertainment for young people of this era became a spontaneous trip to Fish Lake for an evening of singing around a campfire. Instrumental accompaniment usually was a harmonica, a guitar, or a violin.

Over the years, the British institution of drama productions and musicals gradually evolved into a variety-concert format. The prerequisite for performance was no longer ethnic background but interest and willingness to participate, combined with some form of talent. A community Christmas Concert was the norm, and spring concerts were organized on a semi-regular basis. For many years Mrs. Josephine Beveridge organized these programs, teaching the participants how to perform various dances and other musical numbers. Music, in all its forms, was an important part of life in Nordegg.[19]

In Nordegg, first and second generation Italian family size had tended to be larger than the British, with an Italian family averaging five children, as compared to two children for the British. Since Nordegg had a relatively high percentage of Italian families, as compared with other mining centres, this resulted in the overall population of the younger generations having an Italian predisposition. By the 30s, Italian influence was strong and, to many Nordegg residents, the Italians seemed to be the dominant society.[20] By the 1941 Census of Canada, there were over 20 different nationalities and eight different religions represented in Nordegg. In the years following World War II, a number of immigrants from various areas of Europe chose Nordegg to be their new home, again changing and enriching the ethnic mix. The immigration wave following the end of World War II saw a number of Dutch families move into the town, and homes were constructed to accommodate this influx. This became known as New Lane.

This early multi-culturalism in mining camps did not divide the working-class movement, as might have been expected, but actually enriched it. By the early 30s, the British-Canadians of the prairies were beginning to appreciate the immigrant groups that had settled in Canada, bringing their rich cultural heritages with them. As the years passed, Nordeggers got to know something of other cultures through friends they made, and through the friendly informality of isolated community living. It was this budding cohesion that became the nucleus of the tightly-knit community into which Nordegg evolved.

The Brazeau Collieries Mining Operation

By the time Martin Nordegg had departed the town of Nordegg on June 4th, 1915, en route to what he had hoped would be only a temporary exile from this area in which he planned to make his permanent home, the area was already humming with activity and people. It would remain this way for almost half a century. During 42 years of production, over 10 000 000 tons (10 160 000 000 kg) of coal were produced by Brazeau Collieries Limited. This amounted to approximately five per cent of the total coal production in Alberta during those same 42 years. However, the amount produced by Brazeau actually is less than one per cent of the total coal reserves of the Nordegg area.

The existence of the town of Nordegg depended solely upon the mining operations of the Brazeau Collieries. It was expected that a number of mining centres would develop under this banner, but Nordegg was expected to remain the centre for all such operations. Even when Martin Nordegg was no longer involved, and Mackenzie and Mann had lost control of the Canadian Northern Railway empire, the possibility of Brazeau Collieries expansion into their other coalfields continued to exist and frequently was discussed by management personnel.

Ernest Gheur, the Belgian engineer who had helped to establish the Brazeau Collieries in Nordegg, and who had written the Report on Nordegg Coal Claims in August 1912, continued to act as Consulting Engineer to the Brazeau Collieries until shortly before his death. In 1917, Johnny Shanks was appointed General Manager in Martin Nordegg's place, taking over responsibility for the operation. Doug Moore became Engineer and Surveyor in late 1919, when William Stevenson left. When Moore left the Collieries in 1928, Arthur McMullen was assigned to the position, and remained there until January, 1955. McMullen, born in Harrington, England, and trained at Nottingham University College, apprenticed at Whitehaven Collieries before immigrating to Nordegg in April 1926, where he started work for the Brazeau Collieries as a timberman's helper.

Access to a plentiful supply of timber is an essential element for a successful coal mining venture. The process of removing coal from under ground and processing it is hard manual labor and there can be danger involved in every step. An important area of the process is the cutting, gathering, and preparing of timber and lumber. Two timber camps, West Bush Camp and East Bush Camp, were established in the Nordegg area prior to 1920. From these camps, timber was cut and hauled into Nordegg on horse-drawn open wagons. The first timber camp, West Bush, was located near the mine, and supervised by Gilbert McKenzie. A second camp was begun at East Bush, and a logging road to the minesite was created. East Bush was a name still in use until the time of the town's closure. By that time, it was the name given to a general area dominated by the Burned Patch mountain, located east and slightly south of the town.

The unending requirement for timber for the mines, and the desire not to leave unsightly scars on the local landscape through stripping too many trees in one area, resulted in the need for a new timber camp by the 1930s. Johnny Shanks asked McMullen to survey and set out the area at Grouch Camp for a bush camp. The final result was a camp laid out in a U shape. One building was the cookhouse and the other three were bunkhouses, although one of the bunkhouses later was remodelled into a house for the Bush Supervisor and his family. Grouch Camp timber camp had a permanent cook assigned to it. Bush-camp workers, including those young fellows whose permanent home was with their parents in Nordegg, were required to live right at the camp in the bunkhouses. A number of young Brazeau Collieries employees began their mining career by working in these timber camps. These apprentice timbermen became assistant cutters, skidders, and brush burners, under the supervision of experienced bushmen.

After Grouch Camp was developed, logging roads were laid out, leading to a cutting area on the north side of the lower west slope of Shunda (Baldy) Mountain. By taking timber from along the back of Shunda mountain, the scar on the landscape from the stripped timber was not visible from the town.[1] A timber strip was worked in threes: two cutters and a skidder. Each group worked a strip, and in that strip everything of a certain size was cut. Most timber cutting began in the fall when the frozen muskeg created "winter roads," although constructed roadways were usable all year. The timbers were hauled from the cutting areas to the skid-way, just north-west of Shunda

East Bush lumber camp, 1926. A. Belliveau collection.

Mountain, where it then was loaded onto trucks which transported it to the timber yard at the mine.

Timber, as needed, was loaded onto trams and taken into the mine, or taken to the sawmill and cut to size for mine roof supports, as well as for other types of construction. The largest trees became sawmill timber; mine timbers were slightly smaller. Trimmed lumber was used in the mines as lagging. These were supports placed behind the timbers approximately every 4 feet (1.23 meters) to keep the loosened coal from sliding out of an area that had been mined. They also were used as part of the ceiling supports. The actual amount of coal taken from a mine is much smaller than the amount which is left behind. In the mined areas, if the remaining coal slides out, the roof then exposes and this puts more strain on the mine timbers and props, sometimes causing them to crack or break. Therefore, lagging was used to prevent this from happening. Lumber also was used as "stoppings" to close off underground rooms or levels where the coal had been mined, preventing precious air being wasted in areas where it wasn't needed.

Grouch Camp was considered an extension of Nordegg, part of the total picture. People who had never heard the story of Martin Nordegg and his 1910 prospecting party into the Shunda Basin, thought that the name Grouch Camp must be simply an error in pronunciation, with the correct name being Grouse Camp. This latter name also received considerable usage over the years. But it had been christened Grouch Camp, and Grouch Camp it remained, for those who knew the story behind the name. Grouch Camp was a favorite stopping-off spot for Nordeggers when either walking or riding north of town. Located in a secluded area where Shunda Creek runs through a small plain, it is easy to see why both the First Nations and the Europeans had favored this spot for a campsite.

The original Brazeau mining plant was designed by Roberts and Schaefer, an engineering firm based in Chicago. These original structures consisted of a boiler house, carpenter and blacksmith shops, a generator house and repair shop, a warehouse, a tipple with concrete foundation, two exhaust fans for the mines, a mine office, a wash house, track scales, and a temporary commissary. All buildings were made of wood, with the boiler house and tipple sheathed in corrugated metal siding. Many of the present Brazeau Collieries structures still standing, in particular those of the briquette plant, date from the massive rebuilding which took place after the disastrous 1950 fire which destroyed a large percentage of the surface works of the Brazeau Collieries operation and forced a 19 month shut-down of Brazeau operations at Nordegg. These, and some remaining structures from earlier years, have been declared part of this Alberta Historic Resource.[2]

When the Brazeau Collieries was first in the process of establishing itself at the Nordegg Coal Claim, five coal seams had been located along the side hills of Cabin Creek. After an analysis of the coal obtained from each seam, it had been decided that only seams number 2 and 3 were workable. These were both semi-bituminous coal, both containing over 17% volatile matter, both indicated less than 14% ash content, and both with a total combustible matter of over 85%.

Brazeau's Coal Seam Number 3, which measured 15 feet 11 inches in thickness (4.85 meters), was located 123 feet (37.5 meters) above Seam Number 2. At times it was possible to hear the rumble of mine cars from one mine to the other. The dip of the coal seams at Brazeau was 12 degrees, a relatively gentle angle or slope, which would help in preventing excessive breakage of coal when dumping it into chutes. Mining Engineer Ernest Gheur examined three methods of working these seams, settling upon the "room-and-pillar system, up the pitch" as being by far the best and the most economical method. This meant that the coal seams were cut so that, within each coal seam, rooms were created, with thick, rectangular pillars of coal left standing in order to support the roof and to separate the rooms. Within the rooms, wooden props, or timbers, were placed upright to support the roof.

Coal had to be transported from the coal face (where it was dug) to the mine entrance: a pulley relayed the full and empty cars along a narrow gauge track from where the coal was dug. Trips of coal were gathered on the levels and brought to the slopes by horse haulage; the coal cars then were brought to the surface by direct single drum hoists. A ten-ton trolley locomotive then took over haulage to the tipple where the coal cars were tipped by means of a rotary dump in order to load the coal into a chute. Through the use of various sized screens, the coal then was separated into its different sizes, cleaned, and placed upon a conveyor belt which transported the coal to the waiting railway boxcars. An Ottumwa gravity tipping cradle was used to tip railway boxcars in order to facilitate loading them with coal.[3]

Above: coal cars were brought above ground with a cable hoist. Below: a ten-ton trolley hauled coal to the tipple. G. Poscente collection.

Digging and loading the coal from underground was the responsibility of contract miners. Each miner was an independent employee, not paid a daily wage according to hours worked but paid by contracting for the going rate for coal, per ton. The more coal that contract miners could load and move in a day, the more money the miners made. To prevent having an excess amount of rock in a coal car, each car was weighed and checked for rock when it reached the surface. A standard deduction was taken off for expected amounts of rock but excess rock resulted in the miner losing additional money. In this way it was in the miner's best interests to have little amounts of rock and to mine as much coal as possible in a day. If too much rock was mixed with the coal and the total weight of the mine car included over 150 pounds

Coal cars were dumped at the original tipple by means of a double rotary dump. Courtesy Nordegg Historical Society.

(68 kg) of rock, the coal car was taken to the confiscate-shed where the coal was confiscated. To ensure fairness in this assessment, two men were assigned to work the Weigh Shed; one was a Brazeau Collieries employee and the other was a Union representative. The money earned through this confiscated coal then was placed in the Christmas Tree fund. This fund purchased gifts for all Nordegg children aged 16 years and under, and these gifts were distributed at the annual Children's Christmas Party put on by the Miners' Union.[4]

Contract miners always worked in pairs while loading the cars and they alternated between the two as to whose tag would be placed on the loaded car when it was taken to the surface. The miners had a small crew working in the same area with them, but this crew consisted of employees of the Brazeau Collieries, and they were paid a set hourly wage by the Company. However, if any such employee was inclined to move too slowly or shirk any of his responsibility, the contract miners, whose payment was not an hourly wage, soon would straighten out the individual as to what was expected of him. A pair of experienced and very hard working contract miners could load as much as 20 to 30 tons (approximately 20 320 kg to 30 480 kg) per work shift. Working in conjunction with the contract miners were timbermen who maintained the timber in the levels and slopes, as needed (the miners put up their own timbers as they removed the coal); track layers who lay the tracks and maintained them as the tunnels were dug; drivers, who acted as the supply lines by signalling miners when a car could be released to a level, thus seeing that the full coal cars were hauled away and a sufficient supply of empties were available; the rope rider, or traffic manager, who rode every trip and who would signal through an assigned number of bell rings that a

Morning shift going down #3 mine. G. Poscent collection.

hoist was needed on a specific level; and the hoist operator who organized the movement of the coal cars into and out of the mines. Miners worked in assigned tunnels on different levels, and doors were constructed to separate these levels. Everything was simple and very basic, but everything worked; each individual had his job to do and each depended upon the other to keep the operation moving smoothly.[5]

During the very early years of mining the Nordegg coal lands, very little gas was found.[6] However, methane gas (CH_4), also known as marsh gas and often called firedamp by miners, is always present when coal is mined, although the amounts vary from one location to another, even within the same mine. If ventilation is efficient, methane gas is given off too slowly to be dangerous. The greatest menace is gas trapped or stored in open crevices, in porous strata, in a broken roof, and in sealed old workings.[7] To circumvent the danger presented by the presence of methane gas in any mine, a powerful and efficient ventilation system is required; diffusion of gases is a fundamental principle of mine safety. A mine ventilation system includes air intake fans to move fresh air in and exhaust fans to move stale air out of the tunnels, as well as cross-cut tunnels created to enhance ventilation. The Brazeau Collieries' main intake and exhaust system was part of the surface complex of the mining operation, but fans also were installed whenever miners extended a tunnel into an outcrop, breaking through to the surface. When this happened, the outcrop tunnel was closed off for digging and an auxiliary fan was installed at the surface outcrop to assist with the ventilation of the mine.[8]

By hanging lengths of brattice cloth in strategic areas, the ventilation system of a mine was enhanced. Brattice, a fabric somewhat similar to burlap or potato sacking, was not penetrable by wind so was used to direct air currents created by the intake and the exhaust fans. These air currents were directed by the brattice being hung down the centre of the tunnels and in the 'rooms' where coal was mined. Brattice cloth was used in enormous quantities.

Methane gas is released from the solid coal face, and also as coal is dug from the bed where it has been lying for centuries, as the rotting vegetation becomes tightly compressed into coal. As a result, this gas usually is most plentiful nearest the coal face. Early regulations required that all rooms – small side-extensions of the main tunnel – in which pairs of miners worked at digging out the coal, be bratticed within 12 feet (3.66 meters) of the coal face. Smaller pieces of brattice were used to brush gas manually – to move and direct the gas by waving it away from areas or pockets where it collected. Despite all mining precautions, pockets of methane gas usually could be found near the roof of mine tunnels and rooms.

One of the safety features of the Brazeau Mines was the excessive dampness of the tunnels and rooms. The Shunda Basin area is characterized by considerable amounts of muskeg and sloughs. The seepage below ground of all this surface water is a continuous process, resulting in the miners often choosing to wear rain slickers underground in order to keep themselves dry. Electrical lines were extended into the mine, and electric pumps were used to pump out this drainage which pooled on the floors of the tunnels. This dampness acted as a safety feature in the presence of methane gas, as it prevented the dry conditions which create multiple sparks caused by a build up of static electricity,. This dampness also was beneficial in holding down the coal dust which usually runs rampant in any coal mine. Although anthracite coal dust does not have the same characteristic, bituminous and lignite coal dust both are explosive in nature, especially in the presence of methane gas.[9] At Brazeau Collieries, there was more coal dust in the environs of the tipple and the briquette plants than there was underground. One distinct disadvantage of the dampness below ground was found during the cold winter months. Miners leaving the warmer, damp environment below ground, found their clothes freezing into a stiff, uncomfortable envelope when they returned to the surface at the end of a shift.[10]

Mine horses wore protective gear. Smaller horses worked #2 mine. G. Poscent collection.

Horses were used to pull the mine cars on levels where coal was being dug. When they worked in the mine they wore protective head-gear consisting of a thick leather helmet with ear holes. This protected the horse's head if it bumped into the heavy timbers which were used to support the mine roof, or if any loose rock fell. Prior to the early 1940s, the horses were better protected than the men; until that time the men were not required to wear hard hats, and often wore canvas caps with a leather piece in front to hold the lamp. Horses were not allowed to work a double shift, although the men were permitted to do so. If a man chose to work a double shift, the horse had to be returned to the barn, located on the hill above, or south of, Number 2 mine entrance, and another horse assigned for the new shift.

Men who worked a double shift underground were required to return to the Lamp Cabin to obtain a newly-charged lamp. Another precaution to help prevent sparks anywhere below ground was in relation to the miner's lamp. It was not possible for the battery to be opened except by the use of a special magnet kept above ground in the Lamp Cabin where lamps were recharged for each shift. For each shift, lamps were issued to each individual going down the mine in exchange for the man's lamp-check, an oval metal tag which was stamped with the man's number. This, also, was a safety precaution as it was possible to tell if someone in the mine had not returned to the surface after the completion of his shift. Also part of the Lamp Cabin building were offices for the mine managers of each mine. These men were responsible for management of all underground work and personnel. Time sheets were controlled through these offices although the results would be sent to the Brazeau Central Office, a separate building located on the crest of the hill overlooking the Shunda Valley and the mountains to the north. In this main office building were the individual offices of the mining engineer, the chief accountant, the secretary/stenographer, and the general manager. There was also a larger, communal office for those workers who recorded all the various activities of the Company. On the south-east side of the building was an outside entrance to another room on a lower level, created by the slope of the hill upon which the office was constructed. This area was used for coal assaying and briquette testing.

Electricity was considered a normal part of life in Nordegg, both at the mine and in the town, although electricity was by no means an accepted part of everyday life in the world outside of Nordegg. The Collieries' Boiler House produced steam which was used to produce electricity and to heat the buildings at the minesite. The boilers were large metal cylinders which sat on top of a firebox filled with burning coal; pressure from the steam which was created ran the generators, which supplied electrical power to both the mine and the town. The whistle, which blasted signals of various types to the townspeople, including the times of day, was located on top of the Boiler House. The Boiler House created the steam which then was used by the Power House to generate electrical power. All the wiring, fuses, and switch boxes were housed in the Power House, as well as air compressors which were needed to run the air picks when the Collieries ceased blasting with dynamite after the 1941 mine disaster. Also part of the same building as the Power House was the Machine Shop, which contained many different types of equipment and which also contained the office of the Master Mechanic, who was responsible for all things mechanical at the minesite, including the boilers. He also managed the machinists, welders, and blacksmiths, and was responsible for the heating and water systems of the town.

Another surface installation at the Brazeau Collieries housed the Carpenters' and the Blacksmiths' Shops. At the Blacksmith Shop, mine car axles and wheels were repaired, miners' picks were sharpened, and axes were ground and sharpened. The Carpenter Boss, who had an office in the Carpenter Shop, was responsible for seeing that his crew dealt with mine repairs, as needed, including any necessary replacement of wooden planks on mine cars. The Carpenter Boss, who could have as many as ten men in his crew, also was responsible to see to repairs of homes, as needed, and to the construction of some new buildings, although the Brazeau Carpenter crew were not expected to take care of extensive new construction. When population increase warranted considerable construction, an outside company was hired to do this.

The Electrical and Locomotive Shop, known more often as the Battery Motor Shed, was used for the maintenance and repair of the battery motor locomotives and for the electrical trolleys used above ground. As well as a repair shop, this building also was used to store spare parts and any locomotives not currently in use. It also contained a still to make distilled water used in battery-driven locomotives and in the wet batteries for the lamps used by all the men who went down the mines.[11]

Another of the installations at the minesite was the Wash House. Working with coal, either in or around a mine, is a dirty job, so a separate building was designated for the use of Brazeau Collieries employees to shower and clean up prior to going home. The original Wash House was a wooden structure, which was replaced in August 1948. The new building was constructed of steel, concrete, and stucco. It had a large common room for showering, and a room with lockers where the men kept their change of clothes. Posted in this Wash House was a notice to workmen from the Workmen's Compensation Act with the information printed in seven different languages.

Railway companies depended upon coal supplies for fuel during the first half of the 20th century, but the large number of operational coal mines in Alberta, along with many built-in variables, all affected coal production in any one year. An erratic supply of boxcars had a great effect upon the success of any mine and upon the amount of work available for that mine's labor force. The tremendous dependency of the coal industry upon the railway was a deciding factor in nearly all of Brazeau's operational decisions. The amount of coal orders or lack thereof, the number of empty boxcars to be filled or lack thereof, often spelled the difference of whether the mine would work a full week or not. As early as May 1915 there had been a work stoppage for a week due to a boxcar shortage, and Inspector's Reports from later dates indicate that this was not an isolated incident.

In any given mining location, the extent of work available was subject not only to the accessibility of boxcars for shipping coal, but also to factors ranging from unseasonably warm weather to the uncertainty of labor unrest. Often the eastern-European immigrants were very militant in nature, but socialism or communism was not necessarily one of their characteristics. The Slavs were expected to have a socialist or communist outlook, while the Italians were not. Working class Italian immigrants to Canada were considered to be immune to communism, but actually this did not hold true in the coalfields. In actual fact, the ideological difference was much less than expected, and depended more upon individual leanings. Communism spoke strongly to labor problems, and there were many such problems in Alberta coalfields.[12]

For the most part, there was a lack of militant action on the part of the majority of immigrants to Nordegg. During the mid years of the Company's existence, District #18 Miners' Union, to which Brazeau Collieries workers belonged, participated in the strikes of 1917, 1919, 1922, and 1924. The Socialists had a following in Nordegg, but moderation prevailed in labor relations, and strikes generally were non-violent. In 1935, Canadian Communist Party leader Tim Buck visited Alberta coal camps; he was welcomed in Nordegg by a small group of supporters, but the policies of his party were not universally embraced. In Nordegg, the labor movement was strong but it was not overly radical in nature. Immigrants, including those who settled in Nordegg, had left their old country in search of a better life for themselves and their families. If they felt they had found what they had been searching for, they freely gave their full loyalty and support to their new country. If conditions showed little or no improvement upon those they had left behind, they were willing to do whatever was necessary to achieve the better conditions they were seeking.[13] The majority of immigrants seemed to be satisfied with what they had found at Nordegg.

The 1919 Alberta Coal Commission stated that the cost of living in Nordegg was not noticeably different from that of Calgary. The 1925 Report relates that a cost of living study of cities, put out by the Department of Labour, Ottawa, showed that United Mine Workers of America District 18 (of which Brazeau Collieries was a member) paid less than the cities for rent, fuel and light, but more for food staples. The average showed that Alberta Mining camp expenses, per week, were 95 cents higher than the average in Canadian cities. Another study found that Nordegg's food prices were 15 percent higher than Edmonton's, as opposed to those of the Coal Branch, which were 25 percent higher, even though Nordegg was more isolated.

A major point of contention for all miners was living conditions in Alberta mining camps and this issue, periodically, received considerable attention from coal commissions and humanitarians. Consideration of the squalid and even dangerous living conditions of many other mining towns of this time period indicates that Nordegg, from its inception, was an extreme departure from normal practice. Martin Nordegg's paternalism, in the form of a modern and pretty town, was to pay off, as in Brule, in the workers' response to labor problems. Nordeggers who had visited or lived in other Alberta mining towns were aware that their location had definite advantages over many of the other mining camps. Nordegg was a "smoothly functioning operation" with "stability of the labour force." There was very little disorder, but a great deal of "local pride and solidarity." Nordegg "was never noted for grievance strikes" and "government commissions and even Communists – when in a charitable mood – agreed that Nordegg was one of the best camps in all the West."[14]

Brazeau Collieries' daily output increased from 320 tons (325 120 kg) per day in March 1914 to 1500 tons (1 524 000 kgs) per day in February 1919. However, production stopped on May 24, 1919, when the Brazeau Collieries workers joined in the 1919 strike which involved all large mines in the province. Some additions to the town took place during the year 1919, and one of these changes came about as a result of the strike. During the time of the strike, the Company installed a sewer system for the town's use, and also enlarged the reservoir at the water dam to a capacity of 2 000 000 gallons (approximately 9 092 000 litres). This work employed approximately 30 men. Also during this strike period, the Nordegg Mine Rescue Team won first prize in a Rescue Teams competition held in Calgary.[15] That same year, the Canadian Bank of Commerce, which held shares that had been used as collateral for financial transactions by Mackenzie Mann and Company, opened a branch office in Nordegg.

In 1923, Brazeau Collieries had their best year ever, producing one-half million tons (508 000 000 kg) of coal. After the 1924 strike, which curtailed coal production throughout the province, many of Alberta's coal mines were able to recover production levels but the Brazeau Collieries did not. As well as the problems facing the whole coal industry in Alberta, Brazeau Mines had difficulties which were specific to their Collieries. By 1924, the mines had extended a good distance underground and the quality of the coal began to change. Coal taken from the Brazeau Mines always was friable (crumbled easily) by nature, but the further the mine extended the more evident and the more severe this became. More and more of the coal that was mined was very small in size, with as much as 46.5% being less than one-eighth of an inch (3 millimetres).[16]

Small coal was not as great a problem for the railways when locomotives had firemen shovelling the coal. These firemen could distribute the fine coal throughout the fire so that the smaller coal was mingled with the larger. Brazeau coal had the desirable characteristic of giving off a high heat (BTUs) which was a distinct advantage for any extra demands to create steam to run the locomotives. Good steam coal, when burned, would burn above 12 000 BTU. Brazeau coal, at this time, burned in the range of 14 200 BTUs.[17] However, introduction of the automatic stokers into locomotives caused a serious problem for the Brazeau Collieries. The fragile nature, or friability, of the larger lumps, combined with the large proportion of very tiny pieces of coal, called fines, when loaded with the force of an automatic stoker, along with the stoker's inability to place specific coal in specific spots, now made Brazeau coal much less desirable as a locomotive fuel. A great deal of the fines – sometime as much as one-half of the total – would be lost out of the smoke stack without being burned. These stack losses meant that Brazeau coal now gave considerably less value for money than it had previously.[18] By 1925, the Collieries' sales to the railway had dropped by over 50% from 1923, the year in which Canadian National Railway orders for Brazeau coal had reached their greatest heights, as had been requested by Martin Nordegg prior to his selling the shares held by the German Development Company.

An attempt was made to improve the coal quality in 1926, through installation of an air cleaning plant which would clean the coal. This air cleaning plant helped improve the coal quality, but not enough. With this equipment, the system was inefficient when the coal was less than one-eighth inch (3.2 mm).[19] A partial solution was to wet down the coal before it was burned, which helped solidify it. This improved it considerably but there was still too much stack loss of the fine coal. Officials of the Canadian National Railway frequently complained to Brazeau Collieries about the coal quality and, by the early 1930s, they were complaining constantly.[20] A second major problem for Brazeau Collieries was that expenses had increased due to the fact that the original mines had extended a considerable distance underground, creating longer hauling distances from the underground coal face to the tipple and processing plant above ground. To counteract this, in 1928 new slopes were begun within the original mines.

The early 1930s saw Brazeau Collieries at their lowest production level. This 1930s drop in production was not only a result of the problems specific to Brazeau Collieries but also was due to the Great Depression which caused, among other things, a lessening of railway traffic and a reduced demand for coal. This was a condition that affected all Alberta mines. By 1936, Nordegg's total population had shrunk to a size comparable to that of 1916. However, the majority of those who looked elsewhere for work were single individuals, young people looking for work wherever it could be found. A core group of families chose to remain in Nordegg, where they attempted to ride out the hard times. It was far from easy, but the location of the town was of benefit to those who stayed; the surrounding countryside supplied many of the necessities of life. The construction of an improved-earth road to connect Rocky Mountain House and Nordegg supplied some work to a number of the men who had chosen to remain in Nordegg.

It was during these difficult years that Brazeau Collieries, as a matter of survival, began to consider alternatives and to move in a different direction – a direction which, if coal had remained the fuel of choice, would have made this Collieries a world leader. In 1937, Brazeau Collieries began making briquettes. The decision to venture into making briquettes came about through the recommendation of Gus Vissac, of Blairmore Mines, in the Crowsnest Pass. Gustav Vissac was born in France; members of the French interests who had helped finance Blairmore Mines arranged to have Vissac appointed as general manager of these mines. Vissac had a degree in mathematics and was a very clever mathematician. Over the years, he developed a reputation as an extremely knowledgeable mining man and frequently he was called upon for advice relating to specific mining problems. He was looked upon, throughout the collective Alberta mining community, as the "Dean of Coal Mining" and as everyone's Consulting Mining Engineer; he was accorded a tremendous amount of respect from knowledgeable mining professionals.[21]

In the early 1930s, Vissac had invented a mechanically-pulsated coal cleaning jig which was adapted to the types of coal, and to the conditions found, in the mountains of Alberta and eastern British Columbia. After perfecting his coal cleaning jig, Vissac began to make the rounds of mining centres to see if the various collieries were interested in purchasing this jig.[22] When Vissac visited Brazeau Collieries in 1936, Johnny Shanks asked him what could be done to assist in solving the Brazeau Collieries' problem with their coal. Vissac, who still kept in touch with mining interests in Europe, was aware of briquetting practices taking place there. Briquetting is a process which binds fine coal into a larger form by using a heated binder such as petroleum asphalt. The hot mixture then is pressed into the desired shape before being cooled and the rough edges smoothed. At this time, both Germany and France were doing briquetting with their coal, creating blocks which were similar in shape to bricks used in construction. Also, experimental work on briquetting had been done by the Alberta Research Council in 1928, and additional testing done in following years. Vissac suggested that, considering the amount of "fines" with which Brazeau had to deal, briquetting might very well be the answer.

A second-hand briquetting plant was purchased by Brazeau Collieries from a firm in Seattle. Once it was assembled, Vissac, who had acted as go-between, notified Brazeau Collieries that the operator of the Seattle plant, MacMillan, would make himself available to help the Collieries begin their briquetting venture. MacMillan was brought to Nordegg where he ran practical training and maintenance sessions to instruct McMullen, who would be overseeing the briquetting operation for Brazeau Collieries. In January 1937, Brazeau Collieries' briquetting venture was launched. This move into briquetting required a considerably higher outlay of electrical power than previously. Prior to this time, all electrical power for the mining operation and for the needs of the town was supplied through the Brazeau generators, but it was felt that this additional requirement forced, to the limit, the ability of Brazeau Collieries to generate sufficient power. In 1936, it had been arranged with Calgary Power to extend their lines and take over the role of supplying power to the Collieries' Power House, which then distributed it to required locations.

The Canadian National Railway's fuel agent was pleased with the results of the Brazeau's move into briquetting, stating that, although the briquettes were poor in shape, their quality made them satisfactory for locomotive use.[23] The original Brazeau briquette was oval in shape but this was later changed into a square pillow-shape that was thicker and more rounded in the centre than at the perimeter. For home heating produced by coal, briquettes were definitely preferable to ordinary coal because they were much cleaner to handle, as the briquetting process eliminated much of the dust associated with coal. The method of construction created a sturdy, breakage-resistant, relatively clean, and easily handled briquette, suitable for the needs of the railway and also as a domestic fuel source. The Brazeau briquette became a relatively popular form of fuel. A reasonably good market began to develop as far east as Winnipeg and, in 1939, Brazeau made its first small sale in the Ontario market. It appeared that Brazeau's persistent problem of dealing with the large amounts of fine coal produced in their mines had been solved.

Challenge and Change

Brazeau Collieries had moved in the direction of briquetting in 1937; by the second half of the 1940s, the Company had established itself as a major player in the field of coal production. The Collieries had become the largest briquetting operation in Canada, and one of the largest briquette output locations on the North American continent. This had involved a process of experimentation and change, and the addition of more briquette plants as orders increased. The low volatile coking coal of Nordegg allowed a distinct advantage for briquetting in that it was non-smoky, which was a particularly

In January, 1937, Brazeau's briquetting venture was launched. A. Belliveau collection.

desirable property for the use of briquettes as a domestic fuel. Other desirable qualities included a relatively low ash content; a high fusion point of the ash, rendering it almost self-clearing; the consistent caloric value at which it burned, giving a steady heat; ability to withstand rough treatment in handling and to be stored in exposed places, due to its rigid, hard, and durable qualities; and the characteristic of bursting like popcorn during combustion, while maintaining strength without disintegrating. By 1948, there were five briquetting units installed at the Brazeau Collieries Surface Plant, although number 3 plant, a binderless operation, was not in use. A sixth plant was being considered for construction to supply local demands. The intention was to use the press from number 3 plant, which at that time was sitting idle. The working plants operated under controlled conditions 24 hours per day, with three shifts of operators per day, over a five day work week.[1]

Oval briquettes on Apron Pan Conveyor to the Storage Bins. A. Belliveau collection.

The change to briquetting by the Brazeau Collieries was not the only reason for the 1940s being a decade of greater prosperity. The coal requirements created by World War II reactivated the entire Alberta coal industry. Demands for industrial and agricultural products created a high level of railway activity throughout the country, and the demand for coal to fuel the railways exceeded Alberta's production ability. Part of the problem was a shortage of miners created through the slack years of the Depression and through the lower demands for coal.

During the early war years, an effort was made to conserve on United States currency exchange. Large consumers of coal, including the Canadian National Railway, used as much Canadian coal as possible, and this was assisted by the government's coal subventions of freight rates.[2] A fairly large market had been built up in Winnipeg and the surrounding area, and federal government coal orders resulted in a substantial supply of Brazeau briquettes being shipped to the military base, Camp Borden, near the Georgian Bay area of Ontario.[3] It was at this time that Brazeau began the expansion of its briquetting operation, as well as experimenting with improvements upon their original briquettes, toughening the finished product for the expanding markets.

Mining is dangerous work, and no mine ever is accident-free. The first fatality at Brazeau Collieries occurred on March 4, 1914, the result of an accident. The fatality rate, from the earliest years onward, averaged one per year. The usual cause appears to have been an individual laborer being struck by some form of work vehicle, ranging from a run-away coal car to a timber truck backing up, although the underground cave-in of rock or the breaking away of large chunks of coal also contributed to serious accident and fatality statistics.

The high demand for coal during the early years of the war brought, along with prosperity, the ingredients for danger and catastrophe. Bituminous mines are the most dangerous for gas being given off when coal is mined, and gas is a continuous presence in these mines. This is not considered dangerous under safe mining practices, and when there is proper underground ventilation maintained.

The demands for coal were never satisfied; there was too much rush to produce. This resulted in the Brazeau Collieries' mine tunnels being extended underground at a rapid pace, and ventilation requirements did not keep up. The mines gradually moved into the danger zone. Brattice cloth occasionally was in short supply because of shipping problems, but the greatest problem was the rush to remove the coal, combined with a disregard by officials, at various levels, about ensuring that ventilation standards remained high. Without the adequate time and care required to move ahead safely in the underground tunnels, and without brattice cloth being used to direct the ventilation system, gas build-up was inevitable but unpredictable, as Brazeau Mines were not viewed as gassy mines. However, any mine can become a gassy mine under the right conditions, and Brazeau Mines were well into the process of developing those conditions. On October 31, 1941, an underground explosion in Number 3 Mine took the lives of 29 men. This was not the first fatal accident of the Brazeau operation, nor was it the last, but it was, by far, the worst.

Number 3 Mine, while not as gassy as Number 2 Mine, was harder to monitor because of size and geological construction. Number 2 averaged a little over six feet (1.83 meters) in height, with five and one half feet of coal (1.68 meters), while Number 3 averaged 16 feet (4.9 meters) in height, with a coal seam average of 15 feet (4.6 meters). Number 2 also had a better roof than Number 3, as well as a good floor. This meant that ventilation was especially important to Number 3 Mine because of possible accumulation of methane at high points, and in the caves and crevices of the roof.[4]

When the explosion occurred, the day shift was working Number 3 Mine on the main fourth level, where the coal was being loosened in preparation for digging. This means that the slope of the mine had descended 2600 feet and, from there, levels ran both to the left and to the right of the slope. Fourth level had been driven a distance of 3900 feet (1188.7 meters) from the slope. At regular intervals the rooms had been driven up from fourth level to third level. From the slope, another level had been driven parallel to, and about 150 feet (45.7 meters) below, the fourth left level. This was known as the fourth left water level and was the lowest of the levels. It was in this lowest level that the explosion occurred. As the name indicates, this level was constructed for drainage purposes. All the water which collected in this part of the mine flowed down to this level, which had a slight gradient, causing the water to flow down to where the pumps were situated.[5]

Explosive shot was fired almost every shift by either the fire-boss or the pit-boss, and there always was a certain amount of resultant flame involved. When the shot was fired at 9:10 a.m., on the morning of October 31, 1941, the flame ignited gas that was present. The explosion travelled along the fourth water level, about 500 feet (152.4 meters) past the ventilating cross-cut and up to the main fourth level, penetrating into all the rooms as it went. A cave-in closed off the main level.

Explosion in Number 3 Mine, Brazeau Collieries, October 31, 1941 9:10 a.m.

V. Dibus, 43; wife and two sons, ages 17 and 8.

J. Goyda, 35; wife and son, age 6.

G. Halass, 45, wife (Mrs.Goyda), son (R.C.N.)

F. Zrubak, 35; wife and 3 sons, ages 10, 8, and 3.

P. Rezunik, 47; wife and two sons.

J. Oblak, 50; wife and 6 daughters (youngest - age 2)

P. Hindemarsh, 22.

S. Romanov, 45; wife.

E. McLean, 30; wife and daughter, age 2.

Roual Gervais, 35; wife (Roual and his brother, Raymond, had married two sisters just days before the explosion occurred*).

Raymond Gervais, 21; wife.

A. Pastashusak, wife and family.

J. Golyana.

P. Bifana, 51; wife and family in Italy.

P. Merlo, 52.

K. Czotter, 45; wife, two sons, ages 17 and 15, two daughters, ages 13 and 5.

A. Posz, 39.

J. Volko, 36; wife and son, age 7.

H. Mugleston, wife and family.

N. Omelusik, 58; wife, son age 12, step-son, and step-daughter.

R. D'Amico, 21.

J. Fejer, 45; wife and family.

F. Gejdos, 26.

W. Saxon, 37; wife and family in Czechoslovakia.

J. Bocko, 39; wife and family in Czechoslovakia.

W. Kempo, 38; wife, one son, two daughters (youngest – age 4).

J. Renchuk, 49; wife, daughter, and son.

W. Phillips, 28.

J. Armstrong, 47.**

*PAA:73.368. Wohlgemuth, Anton. Interview.

**Gilmour, Clyde. "Nordegg Disaster," *Canadian Mineworker*, December 1941, p. 15.

Requiescat in Pace;
May They Rest in Peace.

The Mine Rescue Station was situated by the Barns, and the Rescue and Recovery Team put on oxygen masks and went to work as quickly as possible, working night and day until the last of the bodies were removed from the mine on Thursday, November 6. The Empress Theatre was turned into an emergency morgue. On Monday, November 3, the first, and largest, of the burial services were held. Rev. Father Neil MacKenzie, Roman Catholic priest, and Rev. E. W. Kemp, Pastor of Nordegg United Church, conducted funeral services in their respective churches. A separate cemetery was set aside for the victims, and the United Mine Workers of America erected a memorial within the graveyard area for those men who had died that fateful day.

Twenty-nine men died in that explosion – a relatively small explosion when we consider mining history – but a disaster of catastrophic proportions to the town which looked upon all members as family.

An inquiry into the explosion was held in Nordegg from January 6th to 16th, 1942, presided over by Commissioner A. F. Ewing. The findings confirmed that it was an

Funeral services were conducted in both churches. A. Belliveau collection.

explosion of gas in the mine, not caused by any defects of apparatus or by the safety lamp of Pit-Boss Armstrong, who was killed while firing the shot in the fourth left water level. Prior to the explosion, rooms were being driven up from the fourth left water level to the fourth left level, and room 13 in the water level had extended about one-third of the way up to fourth left level. It was in room 13 that the explosion occurred.

A large number of witnesses testified to the previous presence of gas at the point of explosion and in nearby areas which were not in the main air current. This area was ventilated mainly through an eight inch (20.3 cm) vent tube extending from an auxiliary fan (small, movable and reasonably powerful fans) placed at room 12, located approx-

United Mine Workers of America erected a memorial within the special designated graveyard. John Janigo collection.

imately 150 feet (45.7 meters) from room 13. The tube ran along the water level from room 12, with a branch tube extending into room 13. However, according to witnesses' statements, the tubing extended only 15 to 20 feet (4.57 to 6.1 meters) into room 13, while the distance to the face was 40 feet (12.2 meters).[6] Explosive shots to loosen the coal were fired about 4:00 p.m., October 30, during the afternoon shift and, following the smoke being cleared from the point of firing, the two miners working in room 13 found gas at the coal face. By 9:30 p.m. these two miners decided to leave because of the presence of gas, and they told the shift pit-boss that more vent tubing was needed. When the two miners turned in their lamps and signed out, they reported that gas was present. One of the miners stated, during the inquiry, that he had heard a small "blower" of gas during his October 30 shift. This indicates a hissing or whistling sound of escaping gas which has been stored under pressure in an enclosed place within the solid coal seam.

Testimony of the fire-boss on the night shift prior to the explosion indicates that, at the beginning of his shift, he was made aware of gassy conditions in room 13. He sent a man to lay more tubing in the room. Testimony of the individual laying the tubing indicates he extended the tubing to within six to ten feet (1.8 to 3.05 meters) of the face, finishing about 1:30 a.m. He checked the tubing again at 6:30 a.m. and stated that it seemed to be working. At 6:00 a.m., the fire-boss also had checked room 13, and he testified that it was clear of gas.

Commissioner Ewing speculated that, if the room was clear of gas, as stated by the witnesses, the morning shot firing, which triggered the explosion, may have released a pocket of gas on the first or second shot, which was sufficiently large to have been ignited by the energy of the third shot. The final shot may have, due to some opening or weakness in the rock or coal, escaped in the direction of the open air rather than deep into the coal seam. This is known as a "windy" shot. An examination of the face of room 13 after the explosion indicated that three shots had been fired and that one of these was a windy shot.[7]

From all this evidence, Commissioner Ewing concluded that one of the first two shots suddenly released a quantity of gas so great that it overpowered, for the moment, the ventilating ability of the tubing, forming an explosive mixture which was ignited by the windy shot. There was speculation, and some controversy, about the range and spread of the explosion from its origins. One suggestion was that the explosion, which left Room 13 comparatively undamaged, was continuously fed by the ignition of small pockets of gas in intermittent cavities in the roof along the route travelled by the blast. A methane gas specialist from the University of Alberta, Dr. E. H. Boomer, declared that, in his opinion, the explosion in Room 13 was followed by a second explosion approximately 2000 feet (609.6 meters) distant, and in the 4th left level. John McAndrew, an Alberta Workmen's Compensation Board superintendent of mine rescue work, testified that, in his opinion, there were four or five explosions, or even more. According to witness testimony, numerous complaints of gassy conditions had been made by miners working in both fourth left and fourth left water levels during previous weeks, and considerable gas brushing was requested on both levels. One fire-boss testified that, in his opinion, the levels were moving too far ahead of the last clear channel. This opinion also was expressed by J. Stewart, Mine Manager of Number 3 Mine.[8]

While Mine Manager Stewart was on holidays from September 18 to 29, General Manager Johnny Shanks acted as Mine Manager of Number 3 Mine. A general manager, who acts as agent of the owners of the mining company, and who handles the business, financial, and organizational aspects of the mining venture, was not required to have mining papers; qualified individuals were hired to run the technical aspects of the mining operation. But Shanks, who had come to Nordegg as mine manager, was a qualified mining man and able to take on this role in the absence of the designated manager. Neither Martin Nordegg, the previous general manager, nor Archie Sturrock, the following general manager, would have been able to run any of the mining operations, as they were not qualified mining men.

General Manager Shanks, while Acting Mine Manager in Stewart's absence, had inspected number 3 mine. He found some traces of gas but found the ventilation adequate where ventilating cross-cuts had been put through. He stated, in a plan of development which he posted in the office of the fire-bosses, that he wanted to discontinue the method of driving levels far ahead of rooms and cross-cuts. This plan showed brattice close to the faces of the level and the rooms. A statement made by Shanks during the Provincial Court trial held the following year, indicated that there was no brattice in either the fourth left level or the fourth left water level at the time of the explosion.[9] On three occasions during 1941, a committee of union members complained to Mine Manager Stewart of gas conditions and, just prior to Stewart returning from holidays, the committee spoke to Shanks. Shanks wrote a letter to Stewart indicating he wanted to do away with the auxiliary fan system, using the more efficient system of brattice-directed ventilation to the coal face through the main intake/exhaust system.

Rule 30 of the Mines Act states that brattice or air pipes required for ventilation must be kept sufficiently advanced to supply adequate air to the working faces. A considerable amount of testimony indicated brattice and tubing were too far from the coal face. Many witnesses, from mine manager, through fire-bosses and pit-bosses, to timbermen and miners, all testified to a shortage of tubing and brattice, but the warehouse foreman testified that, except for short periods of time, he never was out of brattice. He also stated that from August 1941 to the time of the explosion on October 31, he had more brattice on hand than ever before. Commissioner Ewing said he had no reason to doubt any of the witnesses, and concluded that there was plenty of brattice in the warehouse and a shortage where it was needed, indicating that some undisclosed influence or authority must have intervened to prevent the brattice being at the point where it was needed.[10]

Questioning of numerous witnesses brought out the fact that, when shot-firing, the custom in the mine was not to test for gas between shots and, at times, not even before the first shot was fired unless there was suspicion of gassy conditions. The Mines Act required that, in any mine in which inflammable gas had been found within the preceding 12 months, the part of the mine to be worked, and the roadway to it, was to be inspected and a report made to the manager in charge. The report was to be recorded and signed in a book kept for that purpose. Testimony brought out the fact that no one ever reported the presence of gas in this book and the custom at the mine, without exception, was to indicate that everything appeared normal. Some of the fire-bosses pointed out that testing was time consuming, with one fire-boss stating that complying with all the provisions of the Mines Act would require 45 minutes to fire three shots. Another fire-boss stated that he did not always test for gas before firing if the ventilation tubing was fairly close to the face, because other miners were waiting to have shots fired.

Commissioner Ewing's conclusions were that the explosion would not have occurred if testing, as required by the Mines Act, had been done before firing each shot. He would not fix blame upon the pit-boss who had been killed when firing the shot since he was following the practice of all the fire-bosses/pit-bosses in this mine. Ewing stated there was a general disregard for safety on the part of all officials actively engaged in the operation of the underground workings of the Brazeau Collieries. He also stated that, although the miners may have been impatient to have their shots fired and may have condoned the breeches of the law in the mine, they did not have responsibility for the acts of their supervisors, and they had done all that reasonably could have been expected of them. Ewing declared that all officials must bear the responsibility, increasing in weight with the ascent in scale of authority.[11]

According to the Mines Act, the mine manager has the responsibility of the control and the daily supervision of the mine. The Company's agent, the general manager, on behalf of the owners, is responsible for the care and direction of the operation. However, the owner is not liable for contravening the provisions of the Mines Act if it is proven that the owner or agent is not in the habit of taking any part in the management of the mine, as long as all financial and other necessary provisions are provided to enable the manager to carry out his duty, and as long as the owner/agent has no knowledge of an offence against the Mines Act. Ewing stated that, since the general manager had been made aware of the situation in number 3 mine, it was his duty to follow up on the progress of the directives he had issued a month prior to the explosion.

Ewing also concurred with the fire-bosses' recommendation, which was followed shortly afterward by a petition, that all fire-bosses be appointed and paid by the provincial government, thus removing the fire-bosses from under the control and deployment of the mine owner and the mine manager. This recommendation was strongly supported by the miners. Ewing explained in his report that, if a fire-boss properly observes the law, he delays production and slows the whole tempo of the mine. The miners, naturally, are anxious to get on with their work of loading the cars, and management is desirous that there be no unnecessary delay. This places the fire-boss, or the pit-boss if it is he who is firing the shots, in a situation where he is under pressure to move quickly and, if he takes longer than other fire-bosses, it may make him feel he is not as efficient as the others.[12] One witness went so far as to say that, in lots of mines, a man cannot work for the Mines Branch and do his duty, and also hold a job; it is like trying to serve two masters.[13]

The investigation into the Brazeau Collieries' Number 3 Mine explosion resulted in Mine Manager Stewart and General Manager Shanks having their Mine Manager Certificates removed. Jimmy Stewart was moved to the surface operations, overseeing the tipple area. Shanks, as Brazeau Collieries' agent, continued as previously, looking after the business, finance, and general direction of the mining operations. In July, 1942, Dave Shanks, who had been managing Number 2 Mine, was assigned as mine manager of the considerably larger operation of the Number 3 Mine. Dave Shanks, brother of

Johnny Shanks, had come to Nordegg in 1915. Also in July, McMullen was asked if he would become manager of Number 2 Mine, while still continuing with his other responsibilities, which included running the briquetting operation. Two assistants, Tom Hodson and Bob Craig, would assist McMullen in surveying duties and in other aspects of the operation, as needed.[14]

The Brazeau Collieries Company was brought to trial in the Supreme Court of Alberta, in Red Deer, on a charge of criminal neglect in relation to certain specific carelessness; Chief Justice W. C. Ives presided. The indictment was a three page document. The Company already had been arraigned before Justice Tweedie, and had reserved plea and election. At the trial, the Company pleaded not guilty and elected to have a non-jury trial. The trial began on December 7, 1942, and was completed on January 16, 1943. Various charges were laid, including that Brazeau Collieries, between August 1, 1941, and October 31, 1941, did not see to it that adequate ventilation was constantly produced, that the current furnished by ventilation was circulated throughout, and that the current was in sufficient quantities to ensure that all working places were safe.

The verdict went against the Brazeau Collieries, stating that the Company had been found guilty of the criminal charges of not performing the "legal duty to take reasonable precautions against and use reasonable care" in the operation of the coal mine, "whereof in the absence of precaution or care might endanger human life." For this offence, the Company was fined the sum of $5000.[15] To place this sum in perspective for the time period: during 1930-1944, Brazeau Collieries had had six years of financial losses and nine years in which the Company made a profit. The overall net profit for these 15 years was $148 326, an average profit of $9888 per year.[16]

The fine was paid. An appeal by the Company was proposed, and allowed for, but a letter from the Clerk of the Court (Red Deer) to the Deputy Attorney General, dated June 18, 1943, indicates that the appeal had been abandoned.[17] In September 1943, the President of Brazeau Collieries, J. Boyd, sent a letter to Shanks notifying him that the Board of Directors had passed a unanimous resolution expressing their complete confidence in Shanks, and in his continued operation of the mining complex.[18]

The mines had remained closed for six weeks following the explosion. When the mines reopened, explosive shot-firing had been eliminated for loosening the coal. Thus, Brazeau Mines became the first Alberta coal mine to institute pneumatic picks throughout.[19] The use of compressor and air picks to mine coal increases the costs of mining, as opposed to shooting dynamite to loosen the coal.[20] The use of pneumatic picks made mining much safer but it also made digging the coal much harder. One characteristic of the coal was that ventilation seemed to increase its degree of hardness, making the coal more difficult to extract, and the air picks increased the ventilation in the mine. Some gas at the coal face seemed to make the coal softer, and easier to mine. While the majority of miners were pleased with the introduction of the pneumatic picks into the mine, an occasional old-timer complained that he preferred it the old way.[21]

By 1951, Brazeau was still the only Alberta bituminous producer not blasting coal with explosives, despite the 1942 report of Andrew Millar, Chief Inspector of Mines, which stated that the whole question of blasting loose the coal in Alberta bituminous mines needed to be considered because of the inherent danger of using explosives.

Occasionally it became necessary to use explosives when the coal seam became very narrow. Then it became essential to remove rock at the bottom so the track remained level, and horses could get through the passage way. Because Number 2 was the smaller mine, this was more likely to be the mine that needed to use explosives for removing rock. This was not a common occurrence and, when it was necessary to use explosives, they were used very cautiously. Dynamite to be used was carried in a sealed container, and caps were transported separately.[22]

By 1942, Brazeau once again was one of the top producing Collieries in Alberta. However, in 1943, the specific needs of the country at war, as dictated by the federal government, changed the flourishing eastward expansion of Brazeau's coal products. At that time the Coal Controller ordered Alberta coal to be shipped to British Columbia where there was a coal shortage, and eastern market customers were instructed to begin using United States coal. Brazeau officials knew it would be difficult to regain these markets when demands changed, but they were unable to control this situation. By the end of 1943, the West Coast demands for coal had vanished but no adjustments were made by the government to compensate for continuing to import United States coal into Manitoba and Ontario.[23] Sales of coal to the railway also had decreased by 1944, but the demand for coal still was high.

The prosperity of the early 1940s resulted in 60 new homes having been constructed. The extension of Martin Nordegg's original plan took place, with the grid pattern spoking out from the third circular street. These homes extended north, onto the flat valley floor, reaching almost to the location where the school (now the Nordegg Heritage Centre) later was built. Also, on Marcelle Avenue, the traditional home of senior management, the brush and trees which separated the largest two of the homes from the other three were removed, and three single-story homes were built in this space. Another home also was constructed just west of the general manager's home. Also at this time, the original tennis courts were removed and more homes were constructed to the east, along both sides of East Marcelle Avenue. These residences were built on lots originally designated for the management homes which had been constructed at the minesite instead. These newly constructed homes then were allocated according to who was on the list for homes. The result was a cosmopolitan mixture of labor and management living side by side along Marcelle Avenue, although an attempt was made to keep certain houses for specific job positions.

Some of the houses put up at this time were given the nickname Vancouver houses. These were smaller, three- and four-room prefabricated houses that were shipped in from Vancouver and assembled in Nordegg. Examples of this type of Nordegg housing have been relocated to the minesite, under the jurisdiction of the Nordegg Historical Society. The Royal Commission on Coal reported that by April 1945 there were 71 five-room homes with bath, water, and sewer, 168 four-room homes, 27 with three rooms, and 22 with two rooms.

By 1945, Johnny Shanks was 71 years old. He decided to ease into retirement by maintaining his position as general manager, but based out of his home in Calgary. He would run the operation as had been done in the early years, when Martin Nordegg had continued his role as general manager while based in his wartime refuge in the United States. Accordingly, Shanks arranged that the Chief Accountant, Archie Sturrock, would act as the on-site Company representative, looking after the Company's business, sales, correspondence, and financial affairs, under Shanks' direction, while Mining Engineer McMullen would look after all the technical operations of the Brazeau complex, also under Shanks' direction. Shanks intended to visit Nordegg on a semi-regular basis, and the rest of the time he would remain in touch by way of telephone, telegraph, and letter, as needed.[24] He instituted this policy in September 1945. Later that same year he was diagnosed as having cancer of the throat. He was in the Holy Cross Hospital, Calgary, on December 31, 1945, when he received a letter from the Minister of the Department of Lands and Mines, N. E. Tanner, returning his mine manager's certificate which had been taken from him after the explosion, and wishing him a speedy recovery. In a letter dated January 11, 1946, The Western Canada Bituminous Coal Operators' Association acknowledged Shanks' retirement:

> *We regret the necessity brought about by the condition of your health, of your now separating yourself from the Industry, and your retirement from the long service you have devoted to and enjoyed with the Brazeau Collieries.*[25]

Shanks died at home on February 28, 1946, at the age of 72.

The decision was made by Brazeau officials in Toronto to continue with the organizational set-up arranged by Shanks. Sturrock was appointed the Company's agent, assuming all business responsibilities, as well as the title of general manager. The day-to-day operation of the Brazeau Collieries would be directed and supervised by McMullen, as manager of all technical operations of the mining complex.

With the demand for coal remaining at a high level after the war, Brazeau began consideration of the direction to follow in order to remain an efficient and safe operation. In 1945, Gus Vissac was called upon to assess the operation, and to suggest the route for Brazeau to follow. By this time the original underground workings were widely spread, and timbers and areas of the mines' roofs were deteriorating in some tunnels. The mine tunnels also had extended a considerable distance underground, increasing hauling distance to the surface and the processing plant. These factors affected safety, efficiency and economy. Vissac, in his report, indicated the need to revamp much of the underground workings, abandoning all upper levels of present mines and developing new areas to be mined. He also suggested that Brazeau pay more attention to development of strip-mines at outcrop locations, as the coal return on these seams close to the surface could be as great as that from underground mines.[26]

Brazeau began work on this plan in 1946. Mannix Construction Company of Calgary was hired to do the strip mining. The mines were in the higher elevations of the mountains to the south. The coal to be strip-mined at Twelve Level and Stuart Valley were extensions of the coal in Number 3 seam where it had outcropped and then continued to run relatively close to the surface. In these locations the seam was quite flat, and suitable for open mining. Nelson Odlum was appointed the Stripping Engineer. Odlum had married Jo Sturrock, and they, with their young family, had moved to Nordegg after the war was over.

The strip mines were located in the higher elevations to the south. A. Belliveau collection.

By 1950, Brazeau Collieries had quit strip-mining because there was too much dirt and rock in the coal. A new underground mine was developed, with the mine entrance in the area of Number Twelve Level strip-mine. Another change made as a result of Vissac's 1945 report was the opening of a deeper level, fifth level, in the existing Number 3 mine. It was also at this time that Brazeau Collieries began looking at the possibility of opening one or more of the other coal lands belonging to the Company. The South Brazeau field, originally intended to be the first area developed, was given serious consideration. Major development of this area and, to a lesser extent, the Bighorn area, remained a distinct possibility throughout the late 1940s.[27] By 1947, development also was underway at the Brazeau Collieries' Kananaskis field on Mount Allan.

Turning Points

*I*n 1947, the Kananaskis Exploration and Development Company of Brazeau Collieries had begun a core drilling program on their Mount Allan Holdings and had opened a strip mine for a brief period, followed in 1948 by an underground mine. The village of Kovach, named for Joe Kovach, the district ranger from 1940 to 1953, came to life in 1948 as a result of the Brazeau Collieries development of the Kananaskis coal fields. The Olympic ski runs, which have been developed on Mount Allan, now pass directly over this underground coal seam, and follow along the area where mine employees once cut timber for the mine supports. This coal seam provided an excellent semi-anthracite coal with a very high heat content.[1] One purpose for developing this mine was the Ontario anthracite coal market, then being supplied from the United States. A second purpose was to make briquettes for fuel, an operation which had proven to be extremely successful for the parent company, Brazeau Collieries, located at Nordegg.

Following Marmot Road, the Kananaskis mine entrance was about two and one half miles (4 km) up the slope of Mount Allan, and approximately a mile (1.6 km) from the present ski runs. The underground mine was situated in such a way that, from the entrance, it was possible to see up the Ribbon Creek valley, and both north and south along the Kananaskis River valley. The underground mine entrance, located within the area which first had been strip-mined, is behind a shoulder or gradual bend in the mountain and cannot be seen from either the ski area or from the lower region, although it can be seen from the Alpine Village.

Prior to the Brazeau fire, up to 150 men were employed at the Kananaskis development, many of them from Drumheller Valley area. Brazeau Collieries had built bunkhouses for these men, most of whom were single. About 12 tar paper shacks were in evidence as well, not far from the boarding house, the power house, and the lamp cabin. These were used by couples and families, and many of them were built by the people who lived in them. However, the Ribbon Creek village of the late 1940s was considered to be only temporary. It was laid out along both sides of the road used by trucks to haul the coal, and close to the mining operational centre. Company plans were to build a permanent town at a later date, complete with all facilities, to be constructed on a flat area which, now, would be located between the road to Nakiska and the road to the Alpine Village.[2] Meanwhile, the temporary town had electricity supplied through transformers located along the Calgary Power (TransAlta Utilities) lines which passed close by, but there were no water or sewer systems. Water was taken from a spring behind the mine office, from Ribbon Creek, or from the boiler room at the plant. A small store was operated by Harold Falt, but most shopping items were purchased in Seebe. A number of grocery orders would be sent into Seebe where they would be compiled and then delivered to the doors of the people in Ribbon Creek village.

Horses were used for hauling the coal from underground when the mine first opened, and these horses were pastured between the town and the mine itself. However, the coal operation soon became fully mechanized and horses were no longer used in the mine. The mine tipple for the Kananaskis coal field was constructed along the Canadian Pacific Railway main line, near the station of Ozada on the Stoney Indian Reserve at Morley Flats. Some homes also were constructed there, as well as a dining room, and bunkhouses which could hold up to 50 men. This, however, was quite a distance to haul coal from the Ribbon Creek minesite to the Ozada tipple. During the winter the coal trucks frequently had to be winched up Barrier Hill, which had a much steeper grade before road reconstruction prior to the 1988 Winter Olympic Games.

By 1948, when the Kananaskis field was being expanded and an underground mine was in the development stage, the parent operation at Nordegg was producing 1250 tons (1 270 000 kg) of briquettes per day, and expected to reach an output of 1500 (1 524 000 kg) during the fall of that year.[3] The expansion was credited to the economics of the process. In the years prior to the fire which destroyed the surface installations of Brazeau Collieries, the future of the Company looked bright. Expansion was underway, total coal production had climbed to an annual production level ranging in the area of 300 000 tons (272 160 000 kg), and commercial orders were climbing.

During and after the fire at the tipple and briquette plant. G. Poscente collection.

Although Nordegg had seen a number of major fires erupt in the 1940s, the June 14, 1950, fire was the most extensive and the most far-reaching in effect. This fire demolished the tipple, coal preparation areas, and the briquetting plants, effectively halting all coal operations. Brazeau Collieries officials, at all levels, had known that much restructuring and rebuilding had been necessary, not only within the mines, as begun in 1946, but to the surface complex as well, if the Company was to remain a major player in the coal industry. This 1950 fire forced the issue into immediacy.

The Company had to make the decision whether to rebuild or to close down. This was not a decision to be made locally, but by the Board of Directors and the Administration of Brazeau Collieries, based in Toronto. This decision would necessitate intense consultation with representatives from the Canadian National Railway. One consideration was the discovery of oil at Leduc in 1947, creating a plentiful supply of a competitive fuel. Also, by the late 1940s, the federal government had made it clear that they were not going to act on Alberta's plea for a logical and permanent national fuel policy that could make Canada self-sufficient in relation to coal. The government considered it too expensive to develop an all-encompassing Canadian fuel supply.

The major and more immediate factor to be considered was the information given to the Brazeau Collieries by the Canadian National Railway of their intention to switch to diesel locomotives. However, Brazeau directors were under the impression that this was expected to be phased in over an extended period of time. The Brazeau directors informed local officials at Nordegg that the railway had guaranteed preferential treatment in buying Brazeau coal until sufficient diversified markets could be established and built up.[4] However, there is no mention of this on record, and John Boyd, President of the Brazeau Collieries, later admitted that there had been no commitment from the railway.[5] The Directors were convinced that, with a new, high-tech plant, more extensive domestic and commercial markets, unrelated to rail traffic, could be built up.[6] The Province of Alberta also gave substantial encouragement to the Brazeau Collieries in the form of a loan of sufficient funds needed to cover the balance of the costs not covered by insurance, in order to rebuild the surface installations that had burned.[7]

The decision was made to rebuild.

Although planning for reconstruction had begun within a relatively short time after the fire, the extensive amount of construction required, as well as other problems, kept the Nordegg operation from reopening until December 1951. The Brazeau Collieries still had orders to fill but their major producing plant had been destroyed. Brazeau attempted to hold onto their long-standing coal orders by rapidly increasing production in the Kananaskis coalfield until the new briquetting plant could be completed and operational at Nordegg. When the Collieries scrambled to save coal orders by increasing production at Kananaskis, some of the Nordegg miners were relocated to this field while other unemployed mine workers found jobs wherever they could, biding their time until the Brazeau Collieries' Nordegg operation would reopen. Renewed interest in the Shunda and Saskatchewan regions on the part of oil companies resulted in a flurry of activity, and some of the men who had spent their working years helping to extract coal from the ground now helped in the search for oil.

The Nordegg crew who journeyed to Kananaskis to organize the increased operations included an administrative team which was to organize the Kananaskis expansion process. This advance-party included Dave Shanks (Senior), John China, and mining engineer Zupido D'Amico. Dave Shanks, who was managing Nordegg's Number 3 mine prior to the fire, took over as Kananaskis mine manager, and Mr. McDonald, who had been the previous Kananaskis mine manager, then became the pit boss. Before long, up to 40 Nordegg miners had been relocated to work the Kananaskis seam in an effort to save existing Brazeau markets. Brazeau's Number 3 briquette press, previously

The present Kananaskis Alpine Village (left) and Kananaskis Lodge (right) were built in the blueberry field where Brazeau employees and families picked berries. Strip mined area is white patch behind flagpoles. A. Belliveau collection.

intended to be used for Nordegg's local market, was relocated to Ozada. Relatively tiny briquettes, which were characteristic of this press, added to the Kananaskis output.

During this 1950 expansion of Kananaskis operations, a few five-room prefabricated houses were erected; these were nice homes, put up on temporary foundations without basements. It was intended that these houses later be moved to the permanent townsite when it was created. A school also was built at this time, located in the general area of the present-day youth hostel. Prior to 1950, the children had had to travel 20 miles to Seebe school, but the population of Ribbon Creek village now was increasing dramatically; a new mining centre was being developed. Capitalizing on the mountain landscape of the area, recreational opportunities for the villagers centred around sporting activities and outdoor pursuits. Less than a mile from what used to be the settlement of Ribbon Creek, or Kovach, is the present Kananaskis Alpine Village which was constructed for the international ski events of the 1988 Winter Olympics. It is located in the blueberry field where many of the townspeople used to pick berries, and not far from where the townsite for this mining centre was expected to be built at a later date. Life was simple but happy in the little mining village located at the juncture of Ribbon Creek and the Kananaskis River.[8]

In December 1951, the new coal processing plant was opened at Nordegg. Dave Shanks returned there to resume his position as mine manager of Number 3 mine, while Zupi D'Amico, who had received his mining engineering degree in 1948, remained in the Kananaskis area, in charge of the mining operation. In February 1952, shortly after the new Brazeau Collieries installations commenced operation, the Kananaskis Exploration and Development Company ceased mining the coal in Mount Allan. The hauling distance from Ribbon Creek to Ozada was simply too far for it to be a profitable venture. Other reasons also contributed to the Brazeau Collieries' decision to close the Kananaskis mine. No cleaning plant had been constructed to prepare the coal, freight rates to Ontario had increased in April of 1951, and market outlets rapidly were declining. Brazeau Collieries bull-dozed over the mine openings on Mount Allan, sealing off the tunnels from the outside world. Coal development in the Kananaskis Valley was at an end. Most of the Ribbon Creek buildings had been demolished by 1969.[9] In 1976 a coal policy covering the Kananaskis Valley was issued by the Alberta government, stating that there would be no further exploration or development therein.

Nakiska on Mount Allan and the Alpine ski-area resorts which were host to the world during the 1988 Winter Olympics could not have existed in present form or location except for the decision made in a Brussels apartment in early 1910. This was when the decision had been made whereby one of the Brazeau Collieries' more northern coal holdings would be the first to be developed, rather than the Kananaskis field of the Rocky Mountain Collieries, as favored by both Martin Nordegg and William Mackenzie. If the Kananaskis coal-fields had become the major development, the topography of the area would have become quite different from what it is today. The minor development which took place at Ribbon Creek, as a subsidiary or satellite of the parent Brazeau Collieries, made very little lasting impact upon the landscape. Visitors to this area of Kananaskis Country now see only a lighter, cleared area along the lower south-east slopes of Mount Allan where the strip-mined section and the entrance to the underground tunnels once were located.

Between Nakiska and the Kananaskis Alpine Resort lies a road which runs west along the north shore of Ribbon Creek. At the end of this road is the starting-point of a hiking trail to the area where the mine once existed. There also, at the west end of the parking lot, are a few mine-cars and a historic marker. Little else remains to indicate that once this was an isolated but vibrant village, home to both man and industry during the earlier years of the 20th century. Across Ribbon Creek, south from Nakiska and not far from the Kananaskis River, lie the Kananaskis Resort buildings, offering a luxurious setting amidst the scenic grandeur that is Kananaskis Country. Both the Alpine Village and Nakiska appear to have been carved from a wilderness previously untouched by man. But appearances often are deceiving.

*T*he 1950 Brazeau Collieries fire, which had destroyed the entire tipple, preparation, and briquetting complex at Nordegg, and which had forced the rapid expansion of the Kananaskis operation, had served to highlight the extreme importance of briquetting to the continued survival of the Company. From the time the first briquetting plant had gone into operation in January 1937, Brazeau's focus had been upon the gradual development of a high quality product which would help the Company to diversify their markets for briquettes. This necessity now had become of paramount importance, especially in light of the fact that the major revenue source, the Canadian National Railway, had served notice that locomotives were in the process of phasing out coal as the fuel of choice. It was decided that Brazeau would concentrate on making briquettes since raw coal was no longer a profitable market.

The total funds estimated for the restructuring of both Brazeau and Kananaskis amounted to $1 695 000, of which the insurance covered approximately one half. Brazeau Collieries had requested that the Alberta government grant a loan to cover the other half. Funds also were required to maintain the reduced operation of the Collieries, now based out of Kananaskis, and this had been factored into the total requirements. An amount of $270 000 of the total insurance money was diverted to the Kananaskis operation. This was done in order to double the briquetting capacity of this field, and to expand and modernize its mining operation in order to continue to supply coal to Brazeau customers, since no coal was being produced at Nordegg.[10]

The Dominion Bridge Company of Calgary, and the Riverside Iron and Engineering Works, in which Dominion Bridge held the controlling interest, were selected to rebuild the surface works at Brazeau Collieries. Mining Engineer McMullen, who by this time was in charge of all Brazeau Collieries technical operations, was given a leave of absence from the Collieries in order to be hired by Riverside Iron Works as consulting engineer for the design and specifications for construction of the new Brazeau surface plant. Within two weeks the entire planning stage was completed; it was time to rebuild. The new plant incorporated all of the most sophisticated briquetting technology of the time, and very close contact was maintained between Riverside Ironworks, Dominion Bridge Company, and Brazeau's technical operations manager, in order to ensure that every step of the reconstruction process was done according to plan so that one of the best and most efficient briquetting operations on the North American continent would be the end result.[11]

The new plant incorporated the most modern technology of the time. A. Belliveau collection.

Creating briquettes out of the Nordegg coal land's abundance of fine coal always required a very precise and methodically organized procedure. Brazeau Collieries officials now had been made aware that rail transportation was in the process of eliminating coal as a fuel for locomotives, so production in the new plant was geared to making briquettes. It was felt that the Company could expand their commercial market outlets into areas other than the railway and, thus, survive the loss of revenue when locomotives were converted from coal. By the time the new plant went into operation in December 1951, a large number of changes had been made, in particular to the preparation of the coal for briquetting. The new preparation process became much more thorough and much more complex.

The objectives achieved in the design of the new Brazeau Collieries plant included a lower ash coal, a greater capacity for coal washing and for briquetting, a consistent quality of the end product, and the use of steel rather than wood for the plants. The general structural work was of steel girders, and the buildings were covered with aluminium sheeting with rock wool insulation, while large wall windows provided day lighting. Storage bins of laminated timber were connected to the production line, but isolated through the construction of steel fire doors. In all buildings, electrical switchgear of a no-fuse type was housed in separate rooms, while machine control was effected by means of push buttons at all operating points.[12]

Coal hauled to the surface was handed over to a ten-ton (10 160 kg) trolley locomotive for haulage to the tipple and, from there, was sent to be sized and cleaned. In the original briquetting plant operation, it had been sent to the Marcus shaker screen where the division was made at three-quarters of an inch (1.9 cm) in size. Coal larger than this was sent to the Vissac jig for wet washing and then to the Vissac thermal dryer. Coal that was one-quarter to three-quarters of an inch (.64 cm to 1.9 cm) went to steel air-cleaning jigs, and both sizes of coal then were delivered to a trough belt conveyor which conveyed this coal to waiting railway boxcars. The boxcars were loaded by using an Ottumwa gravity tipping cradle loader, which tipped the huge boxcars at an angle while the coal was loaded into them. After the coal had been separated by size on the Marcus shaker screen, the minus one-quarter inch coal (less than .64 cm), which was almost half of Brazeau's coal output, and which was used to make briquettes, was delivered to a belt conveyor over which was suspended a powerful magnet to remove tramp iron before the coal went to the storage bins.[13] One of the characteristics of Brazeau coal was the unusual cleanliness of the coal's smallest sizes, which allowed very fine coal to by-pass the washing process.[14]

As a result of Brazeau Collieries' decision to concentrate on briquetting in the new plant, mined coal that was larger than sizes used for briquetting purposes was broken and crushed into smaller

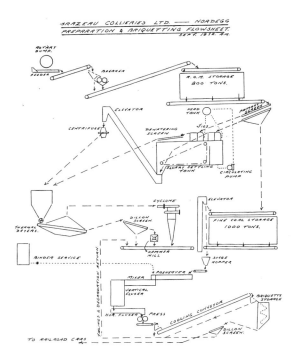

Flow chart of the full briquetting process. A. Belliveau collection.

pieces. In the new tipple, run-of-mine coal was conveyed to a stationary bar screen which by-passed the minus four inch coal, with larger sizes going to a double roll breaker. The broken and crushed coal then was reintroduced onto the conveyor belt, which carried it to a storage bin with a capacity of approximately 800 tons (812 800 kg). Fourteen control gates then controlled a varied feed of the coal into the cleaning plant.[15]

At this point, the more convenient and less expensive way to clean the coal would have been to wash all remaining sizes together. This would have been possible, to a limited extent, especially with the use of a jig. This also would have eliminated the need for an additional plant. However, careful attention had to be paid to the specific characteristics of Brazeau coal during the designing of this plant, especially in light of the fact that new markets had to be developed and the coal product had to be of a sufficiently high quality to draw these new markets. The extreme friability, as well as the actual cleanliness of the very smallest sizes, dictated the need for a pre-sizing operation. Sizing for washing purposes was done at three eighths of an inch (.95 cm) by a Robins Vibrex circle throw type screen, in which unbalanced and adjustable weights created a circular action. This screen was able to treat 130 tons (132 080 kg) of coal per hour, which then passed down chutes to coal cleaning equipment. Coal that was greater in size than three eighths of an inch was sent to a standard pulsator-type jig for cleaning, while the extremely fine coal, which did not require washing, passed directly to the 1000 ton (1 016 000 kg) fine coal storage bin, where the briquetting process actually began. A feldspar jig was used to clean coal which was less than three eighths of an inch.[16]

One of the adjustments that had been made in the restructured Brazeau Collieries washery was the introduction of the feldspar jig for cleaning the coal that was less than three eights of an inch (.95 cm) in size. McMullen was aware that feldspar filter-bed jigs were operated at mines in the part of Britain where he had trained, and that the feldspar had a cushioning effect upon the coal that was being cleaned. He contacted coal managers in northwestern England to obtain further information as to the efficiency and value of such jigs.[17] He then consulted with Gus Vissac regarding the possibility of incorporating feldspar into the design of a Vissac jig for Brazeau Collieries, as well as the possibility of such an addition being able to make a significant difference in handling the soft and weak coal which was characteristic of Brazeau mines. Vissac felt the idea had possibilities and might make a difference in addressing the problem of handling Brazeau coal, with its extreme friability. He proceeded with a design incorporating crushed feldspar about four inches (10 cm) thick, which was placed upon a grid with perforations larger than the the coal being washed but smaller than the feldspar lying on the grid. The feldspar allowed the refuse to pass through the filtering bed and the perforations of the grid to a conveyor below, while still cushioning the fine coal from the violence of the jig's pulsations. This feldspar jig was able to process forty tons (40 640 kg) of less than three eights inch (.95 cm) coal per hour. The unit, once operational, proved to be mechanically reliable and the results obtained were encouraging.[18] An outstanding feature of the Vissac jigs in the new washery was the consistency obtained in the final washed product. The jigs also combined the desirable characteristics of accessibility and simplicity of design.[19] The Vissac jigs located at the Brazeau Collieries Historic Site are thought to be the only complete units still in existence; they are part of the preserved and protected machinery situated there.

Water control valves for the Vissac jig. A. Belliveau collection.

From the jigs, the larger sizes of coal passed to an elliptical throw type dewatering screen upon which the unbalanced weights produced a compound centrifugal force. The smaller sizes of coal passed to a centrifuge. Within the centrifuge, the extraction of water from the coal/water mixture depended upon centrifugal force and impact, breaking the surface tension between solids, and solids and liquid. After this primary dewatering, the coal moved to Pulso Thermal Dryers for final dewatering. The angled screen had a reciprocating motion as the coal passed through the dryers. The heat source was maintained at a constant temperature by the addition of varying quantities of air, and the heating medium was directed by a forced draft fan to the underside of the screen deck. The coal was dried by a controlled pulsating flow of heat directed up through the bed of coal. The carefully controlled speed of the heated air distended the bed of coal so that all the coal particles were affected and, as the flow was cut off through the action of the pulsator, the coal bed settled onto the screen. The rise and fall of the coal, subjected to the heated air, was observable. This was a continual process, maintained until the dried coal reached the end of the screen. At no time did the material travel at high speed, so a minimum of coal dust was produced. Spent gases and evaporated moisture were passed through cyclones to remove the major portion of the coal dust before the waste was released into the atmosphere.

From the dryers, the coal was taken to a Dillon vibrating screen for further separation by size. Minus one quarter inch coal (.635 cm) was deposited on a conveyor belt, en route to the 1000 ton (1 016 000 kg) capacity storage bin in which the extremely fine coal, which didn't require washing, had been deposited previously. Coal larger than one quarter inch (.635 cm) was sent to a Jeffrey Swing Hammer Mill to be pulverized, after which it was deposited on the same belt conveyor, en route to the same storage bin. This storage bin was the starting point for the actual briquetting process.[20]

The briquetting procedure of the original plant, as compared to the new operation, was very similar in nature, but the addition of higher speed equipment, as well as new innovations in the procedure, helped to increase production capacity. From the storage bins, the coal was delivered to the briquetting line to undergo the procedure of binding the fine particles of coal with petroleum asphalt in order to create a solid, uniformly-sized, combustible fuel. This asphalt was brought into Nordegg in tank cars equipped with heating coils. High pressure steam then was used to heat the asphalt before transferring it to the Brazeau storage tanks. In both the old and the new plants, the Brazeau's three storage tanks allowed for storage of 40 000 gallons (103 592 litres) of asphalt. Each tank was equipped with steam coils and, while the old tanks were covered with asbestos insulation, the new tanks were wrapped in fibreglass, to maintain the asphalt at a temperature of 310 degrees Fahrenheit (154.5 degrees Celsius).

Briquette press rolls formed the hot mixture of coal and asphalt into briquettes. A. Belliveau collection.

To combine the fine coal with the hot petroleum asphalt binder, the fine coal was heated to 175 degrees Fahrenheit (79.5 degrees Celsius) and dumped into a revolving paddle mixer. The molten asphalt was sent to a special apparatus where it was foamed by steam at 100 pounds (45.4 kg) pressure, which increased the volume of the asphalt approximately 10 times and also thinned the mixture. This foamed binder then was mixed with the heated coal in the mixer, and the mass that was combining was subjected to high-pressure steam. The mixture of asphalt and coal then was passed into a vertical fluxer containing paddle arms which rotated, giving an action of slow kneading. Again, steam heat was applied to maintain the high temperature, and the action of heating and mixing gave the desired consistency, which was like a stiff plastic mass.

In the old plant, the material, which was in a hot doughy state, then travelled at a controlled rate on the tempering conveyor, which allowed the mass to cool to the proper temperature and degree of plasticity needed for it to be compressed into briquettes. In the new plant, this same hot doughy material was then passed from vertical to horizontal fluxers to continue the non-stop kneading of the briquette material. These horizontal fluxers of the new plant had both steam and water capabilities so that heat could be either added or subtracted, as needed, in order to reach the precise final temperature before entering the briquetting presses.

In the old plant, a conveyor delivered the briquetting material to a hopper fixed directly over the rolls of the briquette press, while in the new plant the horizontal fluxers delivered this material to the feed hoppers directly over the briquette presses. Two press rolls were used in each briquetting line and these were made of high-grade, abrasion-resisting steel, consisting of numerous half molds which, when revolving past each other, were almost touching. The presses of the new plant were made up of steel rims fitted on cast iron filler rings. These stainless steel rims were abrasion and corrosion resistant, with physical properties similar to high speed tool steel. The surface of the finished briquette reflected the hard, smooth surface of the molds in the new presses. These briquetting rolls, in both the old and the new plants, revolved horizontally in opposite directions, in a smooth and continuous action, creating briquettes at high speed as the plastic mixture of coal and asphalt passed between them. At the point of actual formation, the briquettes were subjected to a pressure of approximately 2500 pounds per square inch (175.8 kg per square cm) and a temperature of 165 degrees Fahrenheit (73.9 degrees Celsius).

As the two rolls revolved, the newly-formed briquettes fell out of the molds onto another belt conveyor which, in turn, delivered the finished briquettes to a cooling conveyor outside the building. As the briquettes passed from this conveyor en route to storage bins, they passed over a bar screen where the mold-formed joints of the briquettes were smoothed and imperfect briquettes were eliminated. Then they were delivered to spiral chutes, and a gentle lowering action into storage bins. Before final loading into boxcars situated on the Ottumwa loader, another belt conveyor transported the briquettes from storage to a vibrating screen where all degradation was removed prior to loading. In the new plant, a series of belt conveyors returned the excess briquetting material, now in the form of degradation and tailings within the briquette circuit, to the fine coal storage bins at the beginning of the briquette lines. In this way, good material which had been outside the form of the briquette and had been removed during the smoothing and handling processes was recycled.[21]

The well-planned layout of the new briquette plant occupied surprisingly little space, in relation to the large capacity of output. The original plant had an output of 65 tons (64 008 kg) per hour, while the new plant was planned to reach nearly twice the capacity, at 120 tons (121 920 kgs) per hour. However, with the generally poor climate for coal during the decade of the 1950s, Brazeau's new plant never was called upon to reach maximum output.

In the briquette plants, operators' platforms were placed so that binder service, metering, and mixing equipment all could be seen with a quick look. Each briquette line required two attendants, and an excellent signalling system was put in place between each line of operators in order to ensure correct mixtures of materials, as well as a continuous operation.[22] Great care had to be taken to ensure that every step of the procedure was carried out according to requirements, or the finished product would not be suitable for sale. The purchase cost of briquettes was approximately two dollars per ton higher than for coal, so it was necessary to provide value for money.[23] Tests were run on samples from each railroad car that was loaded, and a few briquettes from each car were subjected to both crushing and abrasion tests to see that they would do well during transporting and handling. This type of close quality-control went far in aiding Brazeau in maintaining an excellent reputation for creating a superior product.

Original expectations for Brazeau Collieries construction had been that the new plant would be completed and operational in 9 to 12 months. The plant needed to be operational in order to generate revenue, and this became an area of contention between the construction firm and the financial management officials of the Collieries. It had become increasingly more difficult, even impossible, for Brazeau to meet all their financial obligations. The Brazeau officials in charge of finances, both at Nordegg and in Toronto, considered the lost revenue, due to delays in having the plant ready for production, to be the responsibility of Riverside Ironworks, thus payments to Riverside Ironworks were slow in being sent. Considerable heated correspondence took place between General Manager Sturrock and officials of the construction company. Riverside Iron and Engineering works sent a proposal, accepted by Brazeau Collieries on January 9, 1951, to the Attorney General's Department, whereby title to the installations at Brazeau was to remain with the vendor (Riverside) until all costs were paid in full.[24]

When Brazeau operations resumed in December 1951, the Collieries was equipped to produce a superior product and to supply as much coal as demand dictated. However, the plant did not come into full operation until late January 1952. Brazeau had planned to increase their domestic markets with their improved briquettes but January 1952 saw a very poor domestic market. An extremely mild winter resulted in much less demand than usual for coal as a heating fuel. Brazeau had to depend upon sales to the railway to see the Company through until the buying season the following fall.[25] To compound Brazeau's problems, heavy oil was discovered at Coleville, Saskatchewan, which greatly accelerated the Canadian National Railways plan of converting all locomotives to oil burning machines.[26]

The 1950s saw considerable change in the demand for, and the supply of, fuel. Huge amounts of United States coal was being purchased for Canadian consumption and it was being shipped as far west as the eastern boundary of Saskatchewan. A running battle ensued between the Dominion Coal Board and the Canadian National Railway. The Canadian National Railway stated that Alberta bituminous mine coal was too friable, volatile content was too low, and ash content too high. The Canadian National Railway admitted that Brazeau briquettes were more efficient than mine run coal and were approximately equal to United States coal, but they considered Brazeau's product more expensive to purchase, as compared to United States coal.[27] United States coal could be shipped west in grain cars that were returning to the prairies, thus costing the Canadian National Railway relatively little to transport, while Alberta coal being shipped east was travelling in the same direction as grain shipments, thus creating an additional cost for transportation. Gus Vissac, who by 1952 was a member of the Dominion Coal Board, stated that the attitude of the Canadian National Railway was "roguish," and Brazeau had been caught in the battle between the Railway and the Dominion Coal Board over the use of Canadian coal.[28] Also, Luscar Mines, in the Coal

Branch area, now received considerably more orders for coal than did Brazeau, which had always been a privileged customer due to the original strong connection between Brazeau and the railway.[29]

The Brazeau plant needed to operate at 6500 tons (6 604 000 kg) per week in order to operate efficiently and to keep the work force in place. After much negotiation, the Canadian National Railway agreed to accept 5000 tons (5 080 000 kg) per week until May, 1952. However, further negotiations resulted in the railway continuing to purchase a good supply of Brazeau briquettes beyond this time limit.[30] Railway officials gave a number of reasons why they could not purchase greater amounts of Brazeau coal. However, the Canadian National Railway, at this time, was shipping large amounts of coal to Saskatchewan from the United States. While using less coal, in total, than in previous years, it still was increasing its importation of United States coal.[31]

The railway had restricted its use of Brazeau coal to briquettes because of the extreme friability of Brazeau's raw coal, but Canadian National officials began complaining about the higher price of purchasing briquettes. The Railway began to favor briquettes and screened coal from the Luscar Mines. Officials of the Canadian National Railway stated that this reduced the costs of hauling coal east, since Luscar was closer to the Canadian National's main line to eastern Canada.[32] Brazeaus objective of increasing and extending their commercial markets to the east was dealt another blow with the Canadian National Railway's announcement that the intention was to raise freight rates for shipments to the east. This would have made it practically impossible to develop further markets in Manitoba and Ontario, the areas targeted for expansion. Negotiations between railway officials and coal producers resulted in the projected freight rate increase being postponed for five years. Brazeau mounted an intensive campaign to increase sales in Ontario, but a succession of mild winters drastically reduced all fuel sales, and made it extremely difficult for Brazeau to increase its markets.[33]

Brazeau briquettes had expanded their markets as far east as Ontario, and they mounted an intensive campaign to increase those sales. Ad in Western Miner. Anne Belliveau collection.

By 1953, the only Alberta mines supplying the Canadian National Railway were Brazeau, Luscar, and Coal Valley, and by the spring of 1954, only 1200 tons (1 219 200 kg) per week for locomotive use were being purchased by the railway from Brazeau Collieries. Dieselization of the railway was proceeding rapidly. This, coupled with a succession of warm winters, and the high cost of shipping coal eastward, all combined to prevent the expected expansion of Brazeau's domestic and other markets, resulting in insufficient orders for the mines to work at an efficient capacity. Brazeau Collieries' financial difficulties had compounded, with considerable debt still remaining to be paid for the massive rebuilding of 1950/51. By this time it seemed obvious that the Collieries would not be able to continue producing coal, due to the many factors which influenced the collapse of the entire Alberta coal industry during the 1950s, and the Provincial Government now was concerned that the Provincial Treasurer might become responsible for the Brazeau Collieries debt, still not fully paid, to Riverside Iron and Engineering Works.[34]

Title to the installations at Brazeau still remained with Riverside Iron and Engineering Works, thus causing some concern for the Provincial Government, Attorney General's Department. Solicitor J. Hart of the Department of the Attorney General, in referring to the proposal of January 9, 1951, went on record as stating that, in his opinion, it had constituted a contract and, in case of default in payments provided for, the seller still retained the right to repossess the property. Hart went on to state that Riverside had priority over the Province in connection with the lien for machinery and fixtures supplied during reconstruction of the plant. The Deputy Provincial Treasurer, in a memorandum to the Department of the Attorney General, stated that it was doubtful that a loan of any kind would have been made to Brazeau Collieries if the debenture taken as security was not a first charge against the Collieries, as the total loans that had been made were considered to be sufficient to complete all construction and to pay the accounts of all suppliers.[35]

To compound Brazeau's ever-increasing problems, the climate for coal in all of Alberta had taken a severe down-turn and purchase orders for this fuel continued to drop dramatically at all mining centres. Despite the new, high-production, state-of-the-art briquetting plant, Brazeau Collieries coal orders continued to disappear. The previously optimistic outlook turned pessimistic once more. The final blow fell in January 1955. A general notice was posted, announcing that all areas of the Brazeau Collieries establishment, including the Bighorn Trading Company store, would be closed that coming summer.

By the time the June 1950 fire had occurred, a large number of Nordegg people had strong second and third generation roots in the town. Before the new plant opened in December 1951, 19 months had passed. Many families had been forced to relocate in order to survive but others had held on, scratching out a living as best they could. For those who remained, the fabric of Nordegg was woven together even more tightly. The idea of relocating to another area was not to be considered for many of the townspeople; Nordegg had become more than a place – it was part of what they were. Nordegg was an integral component of their identity.

Through the Years

*T*he collective identity which developed in Nordegg over the years was influenced by many of the same factors present in all mining towns. However, other strongly influential factors were unique to this specific mining centre. It was clear from the beginning "that coal miners would relate to their society largely on their own – and varying – terms."[1] In Nordegg, the common ground of schooling combined with the close contact of insular living, resulted in the development of a town personality which combined aspects of all the different ethnic groups, including those of the nearby Stoney Nation.

Horses were an integral part of the mountain community of Nordegg – an accepted fact of life. This does not mean that everyone in Nordegg had horses or even that everyone rode horses, but simply that horses were part of the locale. Corrals were constructed in locations that were convenient to the individual, but not immediately adjacent to residential buildings, while common pasture areas consisted of large tracts of land for grazing purposes, fenced in to prevent the horses from straying too far. The Forestry Department maintained a relatively large herd in their pasture, which stretched north of town toward the mountains. The David Thompson Highway, in the area of the access road to Nordegg town, now passes through what used to be Nordegg Forestry Station pasture land.

During late fall of each year, the majority of the townspeople's horses were turned loose so they could graze wherever they chose to spend the winter, and in early spring they would be rounded up. Some of the local horses and a couple of mules preferred to wander around town, foraging for food from the local inhabitants and in the garbage cans of the town's back alleys. It wasn't unusual to see a small herd of horses wending its way down the alley every few days, checking for what was edible. One of their favorite stopping spots was the back entrance to the Bighorn Trading Company general store. Produce, which had not been sold and was being replaced with fresh stock, was not thrown out but was kept for these wandering horses. When the weather was hot, this herd of horses often went down Main Street to the Lakeview Hotel. There, they congregated on the sloping hill of the hotel's lower level, in the shade underneath the hotel verandah and just outside the door into the hotel's beer parlor, known locally as The Submarine.

The use of horses was a common bond with the Native people who, as neighbors, were another of the unique factors which helped to shape the Nordegg collective personality. The townspeople had an easy relationship with the Wesley band who roamed the territory at will. In the spirit of cooperation, the Stoneys often maintained information on locations of local horses which, when not in constant use, were left to wander the area. Then, in time for spring round-up, the owners would be notified as to where their horses last had been seen. This cooperation also extended to the Stoneys and the Nordeggers helping each other build cabins and corrals, when needed.[2] Some aspects of Stoney philosophy and lifestyle were adopted by individual Nordeggers, and strong friendships flourished between Native and non-native individuals who had similar interests. As well as become a supply and mail centre for the Stoney band, Nordegg also became a place to meet and visit with friends. The Stoneys were an accepted part of life in Shunda Basin, and they also contributed to the development and maturation of the Nordegg common identity.

Like the Indians, mountain people such as those in Nordegg had a limited degree of self-sufficiency through their material culture.[3] The tangible benefits from this location were the availability of game, fish, berries, roots and greens, timber, wood, and fresh water. In more centrally-located areas the seasonal and market fluctuation of coal orders often resulted in miners finding part time work outside the coal fields. Since isolation and distance did not make this practical for Nordegg's permanent work force, hunting and gathering from the land was the chief method of supplementing income. This supplementation was used throughout Nordegg's history to protect from the harsh reality of insufficient funds, but it became even more important during depression times, strikes, and in times of low coal orders. A segment of Nordegg's population also added to their regular incomes by becoming licensed guides and outfitters for big game hunting parties. Other outfitting organizations from the Rocky Mountain House area also used Nordegg as a base for operations. Each fall, avid hunters would journey into Nordegg from as far away as Texas and Colorado. The outfitter whom they had hired then would guide their party into the back country in search of big game.

For the most part, the first generation officials, business people, nurses, and teachers had been of British origin. However, a comparison of attitudes of the first generation with those of the second indicates the extensive changes that took place. By the late 30s and early 40s the new generation of people, born and raised in Nordegg, were further blurring the lines of race, creed, and class consciousness. The number of inter-marriages between classes, ethnic groups, and different religions which occurred among second generation Nordeggers, as compared with the lack of such inter-marriage in the first generation, indicates the enormity of the attitude changes.[4]

Common experiences, common goals, shared lifestyles, and extreme isolation soon began to erase any feelings of heavily-drawn divisional lines. All Nordegg drank from the same water supply, shopped at the same few stores, walked the same trails, and swam and skated the same lakes. Nordegg's severe class structure of the early years had evolved into a less structured ethnic and religious base during the 20s and early 30s, although class structure based on job position never completely disappeared from Nordegg, any more than it has in today's world. However, it did change in nature over the years, going through various stages during the town's nearly 45-year existence. There was always awareness of socio-economic status among townspeople but there was little friction or division because of it.[5]

Church groups played a major role in Nordegg life and these groups helped create cohesiveness among church members, regardless of race or position. Such groups

Protestant church decorated for Harvest Festival (Thanksgiving). A. Belliveau collection.

opened the lines of communication between different ethnic groups which shared the same religion. Nordegg's Protestant Church was operational before Martin Nordegg was forced to leave the town.[6] The Protestant Minister's home was located on the upper-eastern edge of Elizabeth Avenue, on the south-west corner; traditionally this house was known as the Manse. In 1925, the Methodist, Presbyterian, and Congregational Churches had joined to form the United Church of Canada. Nordegg's Protestant Church, which early records (1918) indicate was Presbyterian, became a United Church and, over the years as ministers were rotated, the attempt was made to get different denominational ministers each time, in order to satisfy as many people as possible.[7] In 1918, Martha Fallow and her sister Mary Stewart both encouraged their Sunday School classes to begin collecting and saving pennies to buy a bell for the church. This was supported by all members of the congregation and soon it was possible to purchase a second-hand train bell, which then was installed in the Protestant Church belfry.[8]

Catholic services first were conducted in the Nordegg meeting hall/theatre and, later, in the school. In 1936, the Catholic Church was constructed just north of the railway station, at the crest of Main Street hill. Nordegg's first Midnight Mass was held in the new church on Christmas Eve, 1936.[9] A Catholic priest visited Nordegg once a month in the early days, then once every two weeks as the population increased, until eventually a full-time pastor was assigned. When the Catholic Church was built, an upstairs area was constructed at the rear to act as living quarters for the priest. With volunteer help Father Anthony Dittrich, who had become pastor in 1949, undertook construction of a separate residence on the west side of Main Street, directly across from the church.

Although Alberta mining towns did not have a high percentage of church-going members compared to total town population, some Alberta localities had sharp and, frequently, unfriendly lines in the context of religion. The British were usually management and also usually Protestant. European immigrant labor usually belonged to the Catholic church. With Nordegg's percentage distribution of ethnic groups, this resulted in a very even division of people between the Catholic and the Protestant Churches. Originally, all members of senior management, including Martin Nordegg, were Protestant, but this changed in 1928 when Arthur McMullen became a member of senior management. Unlike all other senior officials of that time, he was a practising Catholic. This helped to ensure a balance in treatment and funds for both United and Catholic congregations and to forestall the situation often found in mining towns whereby class or ethnic lines extended into religious lines. Nordegg functioned apart from mainstream Alberta life and the spirit of cooperation became more than a nice gesture – it often meant survival as a group. As a result, the two church congregations supported each other in bazaars, teas, and similar activities. In the same spirit, it was not looked on as unusual when, during the mid-years of the town's existence, the Protestant organist would ask the Catholic organist, who was an accomplished musician, to play the United Church piano for special services such as Harvest Festival, Christmas, and Easter. It was expected that people help each other when the need arose.[10]

In the early 1940s, when Father Neil MacKenzie of Rocky had been commuting to Nordegg to hold services, he had placed a request for a church bell with General Manager Johnny Shanks. This request was turned over to McMullen, who ordered a bell cast in the United States. This bell was about 3 feet tall and 30 inches across, and it had a deep, resonant tone. Later in the 40s, the old-country custom of ringing the church bell at six o'clock in the evening was begun by Father Dittrich and, from then until the town's closure, the Angelus bells could be heard each evening throughout the quiet valley, pealing the call for silent prayer. When the town closed, this bell was moved to the Catholic Church at Jasper, Alberta.

The United Church survived for 20 years after the town's closure, continuing to serve as a location for Protestant religious activities. In the late fall of 1975, it was completely destroyed by fire when the church's heating system was activated for the first time following the warm weather of summer. The loss of this early landmark left the Catholic Church, which now has become a non-denominational church, as the centre for any religious service conducted in the Nordegg area.

In the late 1930s, Harold Killick, of Killick Stores Ltd., Rocky Mountain House, began looking to expand his range of customers. He travelled to Nordegg twice a month, catching the Monday train west and returning to Rocky on Thursday. Competing with the Bighorn Trading Company for customers, he walked from house to house, taking orders, while at the same time making new friends and visiting with them. In recalling those days, he commented upon the great hospitality of the Nordegg people, stating that many times he "sat down with those grand people and enjoyed their food – sometimes Italian – then Ukrainian – Polish or English."[11] After arriving back in Rocky, he and his staff worked frantically to prepare the orders to go out on the Friday train to Nordegg. These orders then were delivered from the train to the purchasing customer.

Originally, the Brazeau Collieries provided a delivery service to the townspeople in the form of a flat-bed wagon drawn by two horses. This dray service delivered groceries from the Bighorn Trading Company to the home of the purchaser. It also met the thrice weekly train to pick up items shipped to Nordegg from outside centres. In 1947, a trucking service, Bighorn Transport, was instituted as a local haulage service, replacing the horse-drawn grocery wagon. This was established by Guido Blasetti, who also ran the bakery/coffee shop and the Bighorn Service Station. Bighorn Transport later expanded to haul mail as well. When mail was transported by the Canadian Northern Western Railway into the Brazeau station, the mail still had to be unloaded from the train and hauled to the Nordegg Post Office, just down the Main Street hill. Blasetti decided that it would make better sense to simplify the steps of getting the mail delivered so he arranged to become the mail carrier, hauling the mail into Nordegg from the outside world. Thus, Bighorn Transport became the first trucking service in Alberta to haul mail between centres.[12]

Big Horn Transport, founded in Nordegg, has become a successful Alberta business. Painting of Nordegg by Serena (D'Amico) Duncan. Big Horn Transport/Blasetti collection.

As well as the grocery delivery wagon, Brazeau Collieries also provided another form of horse-drawn delivery – the local milk wagon – which provided house to house delivery of dairy items. The Bighorn Transport haulage service to Nordegg was expanded to include not only mail, but grocery orders from both Rocky Mountain House and Red Deer. Later, further expansion resulted in Blasetti purchasing an old Greyhound bus, which he used to carry miners to and from the Brazeau Collieries plant. As well as save the miners from inclement weather on their way to and from work, this convenience also saved time. Some Brazeau employees took advantage of the time saved, prior to their evening meal, to drop into the local beer parlor to "wash the coal dust out of their throats." After Nordegg closed, Bighorn Transport first was relocated to Red Deer, and later to Calgary, where it underwent further expansion. Owned and operated by Guido Blasetti and family, Bighorn Transport now has become a successful and well-known Alberta company which covers territory extending from the Northwest Territories, to south as far as Texas.[13]

Other Brazeau Collieries' horse-drawn door to door services were the garbage removal, done during the day, and also the "honey wagon" which, at night, visited homes with outdoor privies, removing and hauling away the refuse.

*B*y the 1940s and early 1950s, Italian entrepreneurs had taken over a large percentage of the business district, operating the bakery/coffee shop, one of the two service stations, two boarding houses, the town's only hotel, the beer parlor, a shoe repair shop, and Bighorn Transport service. These entrepreneurs also opened a second cafe, located within one of the boarding houses.[14] Second generation Brazeau Collieries officials included Zupi D'Amico in senior management, as well as both Italian and Central European men who were appointed middle and junior management in various areas.

The enforced isolation of life in Nordegg, especially during the early years, had made it necessary for people to depend upon each other for companionship and for help, as needed. As time passed, relationships began to depend more and more upon the individuals involved. "There was no question about it, the town became a melting pot."[15] Many retained some forms of earlier biases, but the lines were no longer formal forms of segregation and prejudice, but that of individual choice. These arguments could sometimes cause arguments leading to fist fights. It was extremely rare, although not completely unknown, for a grudge to escalate into violence causing death.[16]

Nordegg also was known for the usual small town problems of gossip and bickering, and a common complaint was that everyone knew everyone else's business. In some ways, it resembled life in a goldfish bowl, open for everyone to see. But, along with petty differences, there remained a strong feeling of solidarity and belonging. People were expected to look out for each other. According to retired Royal Canadian Mounted Police Constable George Krause, the typical resident of Nordegg was peace-loving and law-abiding. Krause, who was stationed in Nordegg for five years, stated that it was the best place in the world to be stationed.[17] He commented that he had less juvenile trouble in Nordegg than in any of the nine other stations at which he had served.

Any class-structure lines, and the ethnic divisional lines of the following years, had gone through many forms and changes. By the 40s and early 50s the community lines were tightly woven. Both class and ethnic lines had become sufficiently indistinct to be relatively unimportant. Strangers or newcomers to the town during this time were looked upon with some degree of suspicion, an attitude of "we've got a good thing going here; don't rock the boat." A new face in town was very noticeable, since everyone knew everybody else by sight, even if not always by name. However, once the initial hesitancy and curiosity had worn off, newcomers were absorbed into mainstream Nordegg life.[18]

What had evolved over the years of Nordegg's existence was very close to a singular identity for the townspeople: whatever else they might be, they were Nordeggers first.[19] Ideas of differences, whatever type they might be, were individual things, and became whatever a person wanted to make out of them. Personal feelings or grudges were exactly that – personal; they did not reflect upon the community. "All those living there enjoyed a good relationship with all others."[20] There was individual pride in one's ethnic group, work position, and religion but, even more important, there was respect for, and tolerance of, each other's differences.

A look at the 1953 housing arrangement of Marcelle Avenue, traditionally known as Snob Hill, indicates a mixture of ethnic groupings and job classifications. Once considered the exclusive domain of management, this now had become simply another street within the town. Although the original five large homes continued to be assigned to people in senior management positions, other houses on Marcelle Avenue were assigned according to an accommodation waiting list. As houses became vacant, they were filled by those whose turn it was to be assigned a location. The same policy applied to the homes situated above the minesite. While an attempt was made to retain some management personnel in these homes, the policy of need and availability took precedence.[21] Unlike the more traditional coal towns, labor and management now lived side by side.

The concept of "village" as the centre of the world had become the general attitude of all Nordeggers toward their town, an attitude developed and nurtured partly through isolation. Telephones were relatively non-existent, except for a few maintained for business purposes. A central switchboard and a private telephone booth were situated in the Drug Store. When this store closed at the end of normal business hours, the switchboard closed as well, although a 24-hour direct-contact line was maintained through Rocky Mountain House to the Brazeau Collieries mining complex.

The method of message transmission to all townspeople was through a series of signals blasted out by the mine whistle. These included whistles which signalled specific times of day and by which clocks were set. There was a signal to signify fire and signals to indicate when a particular work shift had been cancelled due to lack of coal orders or boxcars. But the sound that struck terror into the hearts of all townspeople, uniting them as one, was the whistle signal cancelling a work shift already in progress, indicating a death had taken place at the mine. The ensuing wait to see whose life had been irrevocably changed was an agonizing one. Fortunately, this was an infrequent event in Nordegg, but the sound of this whistle, and the accompanying terror, is a memory not easily forgotten.

Although language often had been a barrier for the first generation European immigrant, all children spoke English in school regardless of the language spoken at home. They learned the same lessons from the same teachers, and they made friends according to whom they liked, not according to ethnic group, father's job, or church attended. Any ideas of individuals being different from each other was straightened out very quickly when children first went to school.[22] Town activities, whether social, recreational, or spiritual, became cross-cultural, open to all. A number of local people took teacher training and came back to Nordegg to work. Teaching staff included second generation Nordeggers with names such as Blasetti, Pasechnik, Stagg, Vecchio, and Minue, indicating the wide range of ethnic backgrounds being brought to Nordegg's school by the 1940s. Education was held in high priority among all ethnic groups and what appears to be a disproportionately high number of individuals educated in Nordegg continued into professional careers.[23]

By 1915, there were four teachers and 132 school-aged children in Nordegg. As the town's population increased, over-crowding of the original school building resulted and, in the early 1940s, a separate primary school building was constructed across the

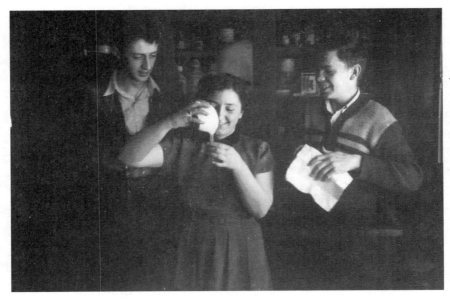

All students learned the same lessons from the same teachers. A. Belliveau collection.

square from the main school. Primary classes continued at that location even after fire destroyed the main building on January 9th, 1945, and until the new school building was opened in the fall of that year.[24] A number of residential buildings now occupy the area where these schools once stood.

The fire, which completely destroyed the original school, forced students into makeshift classrooms until the new school could be built. High school classes were located in both the bank building and also across the street, on the stage of the Empress Theatre, better known as The Show Hall.[25] Elementary classes were also located in The Show Hall, with brattice-cloth partitions dividing the three separate areas. Out of necessity, Nordegg experimented with "open area classrooms" long before it became educationally fashionable. Other elementary classes took up residence in the United Church, and junior high classes went underground – into the recently completed gymnasium/teen activity centre, located in the basement underneath the Miner's Club. It is a tribute to both the teachers and the students of the time that education continued under adverse conditions, with minimum interruption.

Construction of the new school was begun almost immediately by Morin Brothers of Edmonton who, at that time, also contracted to construct more residences for the rapidly increasing population of Nordegg. Classes moved from their temporary locations into the new school building in the fall of 1945. Nordegg's new school also had a new location. It was built on the Flats, at the northern end of the town and on the west side of Stuart Road. This building still is standing, and now is the summer branch-office location of the Nordegg Historical Society, as well as the District Tourist Office. This location gave students access to the Sports Field, including a baseball diamond, and plenty of open play area, something which the location of the other school had not provided.

This new school was in the shape of a large box, with four classrooms on the main floor and four more upstairs. The old school had had outdoor privies, but the new school had the bathrooms located in the basement, a much warmer arrangement. The front entrance had two sets of doors and, in keeping with the customs of that time period, both the doors and the stairs were designated as "the boys side" (west) and "the girls side" (east). Since the two sets of stairs went only half way to the top floor before rounding a corner and becoming just one large set of stairs for the final climb, this boys/girls division was used as a guide for traffic purposes rather than as a rule.

Classes moved into the new school in fall, 1945. A. Belliveau collection.

The Option courses offered at the Nordegg school were totally dependent upon the talents of the teaching staff and whatever class trades they might make, but at least one, and usually two, Fine Arts courses were offered each year. There was neither a Home Economics lab nor an Industrial Arts shop built into the new school, but this was partially solved by one of the houses on Lily Street being converted into a wood-working area. Once a week, all the students in a particular grade would walk up Stuart Road to the Shop and spend the day learning the finer points of construction. This resulted in a generation of Nordegg girls who may or may not have learned to cook, but who certainly could build and paint a set of shelves.

Not too long after the new school was operational, construction began on a sports complex for the people of Nordegg. It, too, was located at the edge of the Flats, just across Stuart Road from the school. Condominium type housing now is located where this sports complex had been built. This close proximity provided the opportunity to incorporate both skating and curling into the school program, much to the delight of the students. Class sizes were large, as compared to present acceptable standards, with the usual number being approximately 40 students per teacher, but major discipline problems were minimal. Serious problems were swiftly dealt with by both teachers and parents. Education was important to the people of Nordegg, most of them immigrants who wanted the best for their children and who were willing to work hard to see that it came about. The younger generations had the benefit of this example of hard work, so they, in turn, learned that if you wanted something badly enough and were willing and able to work hard enough to get it, anything was possible.

The final 15 years of Nordegg's existence involved a number of crises which affected the total community. By far the most catastrophic was the 1941 underground explosion which killed 29 men. Most of the remaining crises were fires which involved major structures. By this time, the majority of Nordegg's wooden structures were more than 30 years old and they were becoming somewhat run down, although the report of the 1944 Royal Commission on Coal stated that the houses in Nordegg were kept in good repair. Also, Alberta's dry climate had taken a heavy toll; the wooden buildings were becoming dry and brittle. The Company attempted to paint homes and mercantile buildings, but demands of the Collieries superseded other requirements, so a set schedule was not maintained.[26]

As well as the fire which destroyed the school in 1945, an earlier fire had occurred when the Bighorn Trading Company store and the bakery/coffee-shop burned to the ground. This fire broke out at approximately 11:00 p.m., Saturday, March 25, 1944.[27] The first indication that this was a fire of major proportions came when both the bell and the whistle of a recently-arrived train began emitting solid streams of sound, joined almost immediately by the Brazeau Collieries' whistle signal which indicated fire. The Collieries' whistle continued raising the alarm well beyond the usual length of time and, while the train whistle stopped blowing, the bell continued to ring for nearly 20 minutes. The train, which had arrived less than two hours previously, was berthed for the night at the south end of Main Street, up the hill from the commercial section. One of the train crew, after spotting the fire and sounding the alarm, hung the metal poker used to stoke boilers onto the cord which rang the bell. He then went down the street to watch the fire.

The fire, which had begun in the Bighorn store, spread to the bakery/coffee shop and it took considerable effort on the part of those fighting the fire to prevent it from spreading one more step up the street, to the Drug Store. The Post Office, north of the

The Bighorn and Bakery/Cafe both were destroyed by fire in 1944. Maggie Morris collection.

Bighorn, was watched carefully as well, but the wind was pushing the flames south, up Main Street hill. Eventually the flames subsided, but not before totally destroying two of Nordegg's main commercial buildings. The Bighorn carried a plentiful supply of canned and bottled goods, including a basement area stocked with additional supplies to replenish shelves. For a considerable time following the fire it was considered safest to pass the area by walking on the opposite side of the street. For days the over-heated cans and bottles continued to explode, sending contents and pieces rocketing skyward. A temporary store was set up in the Miner's Club while both buildings were being reconstructed. The new Bighorn store was of brick construction with a heavy metal firewall separating it from the bakery next door.

In March 1949 one of the five large homes originally built for Senior Management was completely destroyed by fire. Until 1939, this had been Stuart Kidd's home and, after he left Nordegg, it continued to be the residence for subsequent Managers of the Bighorn Trading Company. When this house was rebuilt it became the residence of Mining Engineer Zupido D'Amico, his wife, Maitha, and their young family. Another major community building destroyed was the Lower Boarding House, which caught fire approximately 8:00 a.m., June 13, 1949. The local Legion, which was next door, also caught fire, but that building was only scorched.[28] When the boarding house was replaced, a coffee shop was made part of this structure, now providing the town with two centrally-located lunch and meeting spots.

Boarding House fire, 1949. John Janigo collection.

Later that same year, the coal bins of Number 5 briquette plant were destroyed by fire. But the most extensive and expensive of Nordegg's major fires was the June 1950 fire which destroyed much of the surface structure at the minesite. There was a collective sigh of relief from the townspeople when the decision was made that Brazeau would rebuild its surface works. However, it was 19 months before the new construction was completed and the Collieries resumed operations; the climate for coal had changed drastically in that time.

Four years after reopening the Collieries with all-new, high-technology briquetting equipment, the decision was made to close operations permanently. During 42 years of production, over 10 million tons of coal had been produced by Brazeau Collieries. Now this was at an end. Quiet desperation swept through the population. This town was their life – the only one that many of the people had ever known; leaving it seemed unthinkable. When the announcement of final closure was posted, a feeling of desolation and anguish gripped the townspeople. Their world had been taken from them.

Bright Spaces, Special Places

The changes to this area have been relentless since Nordegg closed in 1955. Little of the town is still in existence, and the whole Upper North Saskatchewan River Corridor is very different from what it used to be. Once the Brazeau Collieries had ceased operations and the townspeople had relocated elsewhere, the abandoned houses became available to buy for $700. But the cost of dismantling and relocating them resulted in only a few sales. The curling rink was taken to Rocky Mountain House and the ice arena to Rimbey. A few hardy individuals continued to live in the Nordegg area but the nearest post office and supply centre now was Rocky Mountain House. During this time a caretaker was appointed to keep an eye on the Brazeau's property, but limited public access still was available into both the town and minesite. A number of newspaper articles, which speculated on what was to become of the buildings and the mining infrastructure, kept the idea of Nordegg in high profile. A large number of people visited the region to wander through this example of a new generation of ghost towns, created through termination of many of the province's coal mines. Many of these visitors returned home with souvenirs – items which had been abandoned when the mine closed. For years, the town lay in silence, deteriorating, and gradually being stripped by visitors to the location. Brazeau Collieries records lay where they had been left.

The town of Nordegg, as a factor of both identity and unity for the townspeople, had become so firmly entrenched by the time Brazeau Collieries ceased operations, that efforts were begun almost immediately to facilitate individuals keeping in touch with each other. By 1956, a year after the town had closed, the Nordegg Recreation Association was created in order to "maintain contact with friends and former neighbours." This group hoped to maintain the ties of Nordegg people who now had scattered in many directions. The Association began to organize activities and reunions so that people could "maintain that link with each other which was forged by parents and grandparents in the early years of Alberta's history."[1]

In 1956, Canada Cement considered the possibility of a cement plant at Nordegg. This did not materialize although, in 1984, Canada Cement (Lafarge) obtained the surface lease, and this company remained involved in the Brazeau site until historic reclamation was begun. Also, in the years after Nordegg closed, the timber and pulpwood industry expanded in the area. By 1961, the Canadian National Railway which, under the name Canadian Northern Western Railway, once hauled coal and briquettes from Nordegg, now had a scheduled weekly run for hauling out pulpwood.

In 1958, the Farmers' Union of Alberta began development of the Goldeye Centre just west of Nordegg, with the initial emphasis directed toward education and youth. The first programs were presented in 1963. In 1979 the Centre became a charitable organization and, since 1985, the Centre has promoted adult use as well. It now operates all year as a site for retreats, family gatherings, seminars, business conferences, and school field trips.

In 1959, a Youth for Christ wilderness camp for troubled youth was begun in the area along the northeast edge of Fish Lake. The following year, this camp adopted the name Frontier Lodge. During the 1970s, a social services program was run for delinquent boys. In the mid-1980s, this camp became a non-denominational Christian wilderness camp for boys and girls. This camp, with the wilderness experience as their specific focus, now runs programs for all young people of Junior High School age and older, including adults. They have both group and individual bookings for various wilderness activities and, since 1992, this has included an annual Mountain Bike Festival.

A number of major changes took place in the 1960s. The First Nations' camping area, which had become known to Nordeggers as Grouch Camp and which had been a Brazeau Collieries timber camp, now became the site of the Nordegg Youth Hostel. The Shunda Flats prehistoric campsite, near the southern end of the First Nations' Big Fish Trail, became the Upper Shunda Recreation area and, in 1970, this became a public campground.

In the early 1960s, plans were put forth to reopen the Nordegg post office. During the years 1962-1963, the Attorney General's department of the provincial government began consideration of a minimum security prison facility in the town of Nordegg. This began as a tentative experiment, but it soon became a permanent institution, lasting until October, 1994, although the final group of prison personnel did not leave until 1995. The Nordegg facility originally was launched as a satellite of the Bowden Institute, to deal with first-time, and young, offenders. The Lower Boarding House became a barracks. One of the first jobs undertaken by the prisoners was a clean up of three of Nordegg's cemeteries. These cemeteries included the special cemetery created for the men killed in the 1941 mine explosion and the two original town cemeteries. The presence of the minimum security facility required enforced restricted access to the town and mine, thus aiding in preserving what still remained of the original residential and industrial complexes.

When the minimum security camp first was opened, the Nordegg Ranger Station and the residences for Forestry personnel, previously located on an up-slope at the northwest end of the lower Flats, were relocated to the junction of the David Thompson Highway (Highway 11) and the Forestry Trunk Road (Highway 734). In 1981, the Forestry Ranger Station office again was relocated to its present site a short distance east of Nordegg, along Highway 11.[2]

In mid-June 1964 the Alberta Coal Company of Calgary, a subsidiary of Mannix Company Limited, in reaction to the demand for certain types of coal, began testing coal samples from the Bighorn area. Testing was done in the same general area that first had been tested over half a century before, and traces of the activities of previous years were found in beginning tunnels and shafts along the coal seams.[3] No commercial activity came about as a result of this testing.

Shunda Quarry was once the place where prehistoric tribes gathered chert to make their arrowheads. In early years it had become the Railway's Rock Crusher, supplying ballast for the railway. Now it is the scene of present day quarry activity, supplying limestone for the Rocky Mountain House plant of Fish Creek Excavating of Calgary.

Calgary Power, now TransAlta Utilities, in answer to ever-increasing demands for power to supply a rapidly expanding provincial population, began planning a massive water storage structure to harness the Saskatchewan River west of Nordegg. By August, 1972, construction was completed and the dam had begun to fill. Once information became available about a new lake to be formed in the west country, developers began speculating about the region. In 1969, an organization calling itself Cline River Development Corporation proposed a $50 000 000 Odyssey Resort Project to be built near the eastern end of the new lake. This 336 acre (136 hectare) site was planned to incorporate a 300-room, all-seasons luxury resort, with an indoor swimming pool and an 18-hole golf course. The Alberta Social Credit government approved this project in 1971.[4] Six environmental groups joined forces to create the Alberta League for Environmentally Responsible Tourism (ALERT) and, spear-headed by Rocky Mountain House's Dr. Martha Kostuck, this coalition fought the project over a 15-year period. In 1984, three appeal court judges ruled that the project must be taken back to the Development Appeal Board.[5] Two years later the government cancelled the development lease of Cline River Development Company.

In 1968, the David Thompson Highway was opened, although paving was not completed until 1974 and the official opening did not take place until August 3, 1975. This road continues to grow in popularity as an alternate route through the mountains. In July 1996 an unofficial proposal was made to create another highway through the Rocky Mountains, extending the present David Thompson Highway beyond Saskatchewan Crossing through Howse Pass, thus opening another route westward to British Columbia. Industrialists were quick to jump on the bandwagon, while environmentalists were horrified at the idea of further invasion into the wilderness areas of the Rocky Mountains.

By 1972, the David Thompson Resort Lodge had been constructed on the west side of Lake Abraham. Presently, this establishment is run by descendants of Harold Killick of Rocky Mountain House.

In 1991, new developers unveiled proposals for recreation resorts for the same general area that previously had interested Cline River Development Corporation. Development is looked upon favorably by the David Thompson Local Integrated Resource Plan for the Highway 11 Corridor, which has identified a large development node in the area of Whitegoat Lakes, as well as a node for Bighorn Canyon area. Environmentalists keep a watchful eye on such proposals, especially anything relating to the Kootenay Plains area. The ecologically sensitive Kootenay Plains, a semi-arid mountain zone, is an important wintering ground for wildlife and also is the site of Stoney Indian burial grounds. Spokespersons have suggested that developers look instead at more ecologically compatible areas which can be found closer to the Nordegg region. Accordingly, the Shunda/Goldeye development node has been identified in the Goldeye and Fish Lakes areas, west of Nordegg, and a fourth node is in the Saunders/Alexo region.

The north branch of the Forestry Trunk Road is now a connector road which joins Nordegg to Coal Branch country. This road, which passes through the region that originally was the focus of Martin Nordegg's prospecting ventures and coal claims, now is the main north/south route through the Forestry Reserves, areas that not all that long ago were accessible only on horseback. Approximately 6 miles (9.66 km) northwest of Nordegg, the Blackstone Road branches west from this north Forestry Trunk Road. After this "improved earth" branch road crosses the Blackstone River near Beaver Flats it becomes "unimproved," but relatively passable for vehicles suitable for back roads. This road/trail follows the Blackstone River until it is quite close to Blackstone Gap in the Bighorn Range of mountains. At this point the route becomes a hiking trail. The Gap is narrow, and walking through this region requires both following and fording the river. The scenery is spectacular, and high cliffs tower above the river on both sides. Approximately 4 miles (6.44 km) west of this Gap, along the Blackstone river, is the area first selected to be the headquarters and major centre for the Brazeau Collieries mining empire. Some of the original stakes laid out for the South Brazeau townsite can still be seen.[6]

The south leg of the Trunk Road, the Bighorn Highway, runs south from Nordegg and then works its way in a south-easterly direction. The road, constructed in the early 1960s, has opened up many more areas of this west country. It has given access to the spectacular and now well-known Ram River Falls and to Corkscrew Mountain, on its route southward. Other roads now connect this Trunk Road with Caroline, on the Highway 22 connector, and with Sundre, in Red Deer River country. Following this road south from Nordegg, it passes west of the Brazeau Collieries' Nordegg minesite, crossing over what once was the walking trail to Fish Lake. Approximately 1 mile (1.9 km) from the junction with Highway 11, the old Indian/Fur Brigade Trail is visible to the east/northeast, coming from the Nordegg region. For the next 2 miles (2.8 km) the main Indian Trail and the Trunk Road are one and the same. At this point, approximately 3 miles (4.7 km) from Highway 11, is the location of The Forks. At this ancient and long established Forks, the west arm of the Native trail still remains clearly visible; it has not been touched by the passage of time, other than to become heavily covered with moss. This trail is the remnant of the historic First Nations/Fur Brigade land route westward, still clearly defined as it passes through the trees, wending its way along the Saskatchewan route toward the Bighorn.

From the Forks where the two arms diverge, the east arm of the trail continues to be part of the Bighorn Highway. It approximates the First Nations route southward toward the North Saskatchewan River, although the east arm of the original trail rejoins the river considerably upstream from the vehicle bridge which now spans the North Saskatchewan River.

A number of guide and outfitter companies are active in the Upper North Saskatchewan River corridor, with each company working out of a predetermined region. Some of these companies have strong family ties to the Nordegg area. North of the David Thompson Highway, and across the road from the David Thompson Resort, is the base camp of McKenzie's Trails West. Ed McKenzie, who first began working with guiding and outfitting in 1948, instituted this company in 1966 in partnership with his wife, Millie. Ed was the grandson of Nordegg's first sawyer, Gilbert McKenzie; the son of

Nordegg's first "pony express" mail and supply rider, Tom McKenzie; and a nephew of both Alan McKenzie, of Baird and McKenzie, who constructed Nordegg's business district and first houses, and of Vic McKenzie, who was one of Nordegg's first school teachers. Since Ed's death in December 1994, Millie and eldest son Ron have continued the operation of this family business.

Another outfit was developed by ex-Nordegger Jim Colosimo. Diamond Jim's Guide and Outfitting Company was based out of Rocky Mountain House. Jim and his son, Jim Jr., ran trail rides into areas northwest of Nordegg. Since Jim Sr.'s death in March 1996, young Jim has attempted to maintain the family business. Diamond Jim's base camp is located at Beaver Flats, southwest of the bridge across Blackstone River on the old Chungo road. Both McKenzie's Trails West and Diamond Jim's Company ride into territory where most of the Brazeau coal lands once were, and where the original town of Brazeau was to have been located.

A long time guide and outfitter, who is new on the scene of trail riding for tourists in the Upper North Saskatchewan River Corridor area, is Charlie Abraham. For a number of years, Charlie has worked with the forestry, supplying horses and wrangling for their patrols. Charlie is a descendent of Ta Otha, or Peter Wesley, who led the Wesley Stoneys back to the Kootenay Plains in the late 19th century. He also is the grandson of the well-respected Stoney, Silas Abraham, for whom Lake Abraham was named.

Another long time guide and outfitter, based out of the Wapiabi region, is Clayton Grosso, whose grandfather and uncle both worked in Nordegg mines. Born and raised in Big West Country, Clayton rode in Nordegg's final Sports Day bucking bronc event. During spring and summer, Clayton now guides trail rides through Nordegg, and to Eastbush Falls.

*I*n 1971, Consolidated Coal acquired the Nordegg coal leases and 132 acres (53.42 hectares) of surface lease. In 1973, a "heritage resource impact assessment" was prepared for the Consol Nordegg Coal Lease area to determine the effect on the region of an active mine development, then being considered. Various recommendations were made with regard to the heritage resources of the area. One recommendation included preservation of a section of the historic First Nations/Fur Brigade Trail, with an interpretive road-side exhibit to be erected. The authors of the assessment also made a number of recommendations for preservation of the history and artifacts of Nordegg, the Brazeau Collieries, and the Shunda region. They stated specifically that the value of the Brazeau Collieries historic site was of national significance in relation to Alberta's first coal mining era, as this plant was the least impaired of any in existence. The final recommendation was for Consol, in order to present a positive image of corporate responsibility in preservation of heritage, to consider development of a Heritage Interpretation Program, along with completion of the other recommendations.[7] No development of either a coal mining operation or of heritage resources took place through the Consolidated Coal Lease. In 1984, Consolidated Coal assigned their right of surface lease renewal to Canada Cement Lafarge Limited, who wanted to make use of the remaining piles of slack coal which were piled near Number 2 mine.

Due to various circumstances, over the years since Brazeau Collieries closed the Nordegg operation, the records and files of this company were widely scattered. The individuals who were involved in preparing the Consolidated Coal Lease assessment in 1973 found Brazeau Collieries records in the mine office, 18 years after closure of the mine. These records were sorted and boxed, and the recommendation made for their immediate removal. However, there are gaps in the continuity and completeness of these files. Although most of the records were sent to the Public Archives of Alberta, in Edmonton, a number are in the Glenbow Archives in Calgary, some have been destroyed, some are privately controlled, and some have been traced as far as Colorado before the trail was lost.

Little was heard of the Brazeau Collieries after the mines closed, but the company remained in existence. It later was purchased by Vern VanSant, of Whitehall Mining, although no development resulted from this.[8] In 1991, dissolution notices were posted by the legal firm of Macleod Dixon of Calgary, but unspecified difficulties prevented the final dissolution from taking place at that time. These difficulties now have been resolved. Brazeau Collieries, as of June 25, 1996, was federally dissolved and registration was cancelled in Alberta.

For over 15 years after Nordegg closed, there was a relatively high degree of preservation of the town. Although the houses were abandoned and untended, most of them were still standing and in relatively good condition. However, except for the buildings and the area utilized by the Attorney General's department of the provincial government, the community, planned with such loving care by Martin Nordegg in the early years of the 20th century, gradually began to disappear. It was noted in the 1973 Consol Coal Lease study that, of the 270 homes standing when the town was abandoned, 175 of them, as well as some of the commercial structures, had been razed. Alterations had been made to other structures for use by the prison establishment.[9] Without the presence of townspeople and of the wandering horses, the grass and bushes grew high; the Forestry Department became concerned about the danger of fire. Under Forestry direction, the Solicitor General's Department removed the remaining homes, bull-dozing, burying, and burning what remained.

According to the terms of Lafarge Canada's lease of the Brazeau Collieries minesite, Lafarge was required to remove the structures still standing at the mine. Plans were made for dismantling the buildings and clearing the site. During the early 1980s, both Lafarge and the Solicitor General's Department had begun hauling out bricks and metal. Donna Dahms, who had lived in Nordegg from 1970 to 1976, had been witness to the increased deterioration and destruction of this historic area. In the fall of 1982, she called the first meeting of a group of individuals interested in preserving the fast disappearing heritage of the Nordegg area. This group began meeting on a regular basis in 1983, planning and organizing ways to protect these remnants of Alberta history. In November, 1984, this group became the Nordegg Historic Heritage Interest Group. The mandate of this group was to promote, protect, and preserve the Brazeau Collieries minesite and what remained of the town.

Lafarge's plan of reclamation was presented to the Province of Alberta in 1985. The efforts of the Nordegg Group managed to have the demolition of the mine buildings postponed; Canada Cement Lafarge agreed to postpone reclamation. If the site did not receive designation as a historic resource, or if there was insufficient private sector response for preservation, Lafarge would reclaim the site by October 1, 1992, totally dismantling all buildings, leaving only the concrete bases.[10]

A feasibility study, commissioned by Alberta Culture and Multiculturalism and by the Nordegg Historic Heritage Interest Group was completed by Great Plains Research Consultants and Associates in September 1987. The study indicated that the interpretive value of the minesite was rated high because of historical significance and because of the well-preserved presence of the last coal-mining industrial plant which represented Alberta's coal boom of mid-20th century. The study also recommended redevelopment of the townsite be considered, with the stipulation that "all residential and commercial development be in strict conformity with appropriate heritage design controls."[11]

Dennis Morley (right), a mainstay of the guided tours for many years, now has a plaque and an interpretive walk at the minesite, a gesture of appreciation from the Nordegg Historical Society Board (1997). A. Belliveau collection.

By 1990, three town buildings had been leased to the Nordegg Historic Heritage Interest Group, Alberta Culture had designated 6 mine buildings for restoration, and the Group had taken over the old Nordegg school building. The entire lease, all buildings and assets, were placed under the control of the Nordegg Group. A major project undertaken by this group was the compilation and organization of a photo archives, under the supervision of John Galloway. Guided tours of the town and minesite were instituted, with tours conducted by ex-Nordeggers. A mainstay of this portion of the historic presentation to the public has been Dennis Morley, who once worked for Brazeau Collieries. In April 1997, one of the interpretive walks at the Brazeau minesite was named "The Morley Trail" in his honor, and a commemorative plaque was mounted at the entrance to this walkway.

After the Brazeau mines had ceased operating, the mine entrances had been sealed off by being bulldozed shut. In 1990, the decision was made to reopen the entrance to Number 2 mine, with the possibility of eventually restoring the tunnel for a short distance underground so that it would be suitable to include in the tours of the minesite. However, it would take considerable time to ready it for visits by the public. But this

Tourists are able to see into the mine and to feel the temperature change. A. Belliveau collection.

decision to reopen the entryway has made it possible, once again, to see into the old Number 2 mine from the (barred) entrance, and to feel the difference in temperature of the air coming from the underground mine. A building stabilization and land reclamation program of the industrial complex of the old minesite also was implemented. But this massive venture by a relatively small group ran into financial difficulties. In the spring of 1992, the Nordegg Historic Heritage Interest Group was brought under the umbrella of the Municipal District of Clearwater, which controls the development of the whole Upper North Saskatchewan River Corridor. Joe Baker, of Rocky Mountain House, was made Nordegg Site Manager. The Board of Directors was then made up of representatives of various municipal organizations and the Group's somewhat unwieldy name was shortened to the Nordegg Historical Society.

On August 25, 1993, the entire minesite lease – over 75 acres (30.35 hectares) and all standing buildings – was designated a Provincial Historic Resource, thus preserving for future generations this record of Alberta's pioneer years. A plaque was erected at the crest of the hill which overlooks the historic buildings of the briquetting operation.

*T*he Canadian National Railway removed the rail tracks and wooden trestles constructed between Rocky Mountain House and Nordegg, dismantling the last one during the winter of 1993. However, two of the trestles just east of Nordegg, the rail line into the town and the mine, and the wooden trestle spanning the small ravine between Hospital and Mine hills all came under the jurisdiction of Public Lands, so these were not removed during the dismantling process. Although trees and underbrush continually attempt to reclaim the terrace where the Canadian Northern Western Railway once thundered into Brazeau station, the tracks remain in place, staking their claim. In 1998, the C.N.R. donated a railway boxcar to the Historical Society. It now has been transferred to the Brazeau Collieries minesite and it sits on the Ottumwa Loader, located at the completion end of the briquetting lines, much of which is still in place in these historic buildings.

In 1998, the CNR donated a boxcar, which now sits on the loader at the completion end of the coal processing plant. A. Belliveau collection.

Redevelopment of Nordegg, as a town, is becoming more of a reality all the time. By 1993, water studies had been done and surveying had begun. By 1998 a new water supply system had been designed and intalled for the old townsite. This consists of two wells hooked into the system, with a third well in reserve. The new water holding tower (reservoir) has been constructed beside the old tower. On December 15, 1998, the new water system was turned on. At present, there are no plans to dismantle the old townsite dam east of Nordegg. After more than 80 years' existence, major leaks had developed in this structure. As it drains, it well be assessed to see if repairs are feasible, with the idea of it being used to form a storm-water catch basin and a nice pond stocked with fish. There is also the possibility of this becoming a park area.

Nordegg townsite, and the surrounding area, were transferred to the Municipal District of Clearwater on March 18, 1996. The M.D. began developing a subdivision on the lower slope of Coliseum Mountain north of the David Thompson Highway, with acreage lots for sale. The M.D. visualizes the possibility of a large part of Shunda Basin – 1600 acres (647.5 hectares) – as residential land. Ideas for a new town go well beyond the area of the old Nordegg site, extending north across the lower valley and to the up-slope of the Brazeau Range outlier mountains of Baldy and Coliseum. Tentative, long-range plans for the concept of Nordegg would maintain certain segments of the old town as historical in nature. Suggestions for historical restoration include a commercial area on Main Street, and homes on parts of east and west Elizabeth Avenue intersecting with Main, as well as homes along Marcelle Avenue. The duplexes which were constructed where the Sports Complex had been now have all been sold to the private sector. There has been extensive planning for 1999 in relation to all aspects of the old town. Proposals include carrying out geotechnical work, architectural designs and historical controls, street planning, historical streetscaping, and trail and pathway planning. It also has been proposed that a waste water system be developed, as well as a storm water drainage plan. Also proposed is a 19-lot subdivision on Elizatbeth West and presently, negotiations are ongoing with Pipestone Developments of Calgary to reconstruct some of the main commercial buildings, as well as a condominium aand commercial development of approximately 15 acres. Development and expansion within the Upper North Saskatchewan River Corridor seems inevitable, and Nordegg appears to be part of the long range plans.

Carefully planned and controlled development of this historic Corridor would allow an unparalleled opportunity to maintain the integrity and the historical value of this region which figured so prominently in the early history of Native people, of European movement throughout Canada, and of the settlement of the western prairies. This is a region that, for over 200 years, was a focus for numerous plans for exploration, for early settlement, and for expansion. Paradoxically, it is a region still relatively unsettled.

When the town closed, Nordeggers were at the height of solidarity; the town was functioning as a huge family. It was a second and third generation, multi-cultural, tightly-knit microcosm of Canadian society. Whether this cohesiveness could have been maintained during following years is open to speculation, but it is extremely doubtful, given the changes which have taken place in familial and social structure, and the advances in technology which have opened up the areas of communication and travel. However, Nordeggers, who were dispersed in many directions at the height of the dream, have managed to capture that cohesiveness in a time capsule through their regularly scheduled reunions. The Nordegg Recreation and Heritage Association, established in 1956, and formed of ex-Nordeggers and their descendants, has continued to organize activities and meetings for its membership wherever and whenever possible. Now, each year on the August long weekend, a Nordegg reunion and Sports Day is held. These Sports Days incorporate many of the same activities which once were part of the regular Nordegg Sports Days. A fall reunion, in the form of a dinner and dance, also is held each year in a central location, usually Red Deer.

In 1985, the Association was successful in obtaining a 21 year lease from the government for a parcel of land north of Nordegg, at the foot of the mountains which face the town. The Nordegg Association's present lease will expire, or be renewed, in 2006. In this Nordegg campground area, locally known as The Airstrip, small street signs of "Lily Street," "Marthe Street," etc., have been put in place, as well as a bobolinko court and horseshoe pits. During mid-summer, life in Nordegg is re-created here. In many cases, the people who attend these reunions and campouts are too young to have their own memories or even to have been a part of this town, but they are a part of this land because it is the heritage of their extended family. Even now, decades after the final closing of the Nordegg mining complex, its people and their descendants still meet each year, some coming thousands of miles to renew old friendships and to keep in touch with each other. They are bound by a common bond and a common heritage which neither time nor distance has altered. Whether this will be maintained during subsequent generations by those whose ties are through ancestry rather than through the reality of habitation, also is open to speculation. This can be answered only through the passage of time.

In recent years, more and more ex-Nordeggers have begun to spend their summer months living in recreation vehicles adjacent to the Nordegg school and among the hills and valleys of the Shunda Basin, and beyond. In varying ways, those who knew this land as it once was have come to terms with the changes that have taken place. Once again they are able to walk these hills and find peace. They are at home in the present as well as in the past.

Despite all the changes, the mountains are still the same. They are the constant – the unchanging, yet ever-changing face of this country. They are still the sheltering arms which signify 'home'. The road from the east, into Nordegg, has changed and so has the road out, to the west. The old Five-Mile Bridge train trestle at Shunda Gap, east of Nordegg, first was cut, then later dismantled, making way for the newer, straighter road westward. But a stop just west of where the David Thompson Highway now cuts through the Cadomin Conglomerate at the eastern edge of Shunda Gap where this wooden trestle once stood, and a walk down the old road which once passed beneath this wooden arch, is a journey into the past. Here the memories crowd closer, closing in. The present disappears.

At Nordegg, the David Thompson Highway runs through what once was the Forestry pasture, behind the hill where the log buildings of the Forestry Station were located. The swooping wings of the roadways, built over what earlier had been First Nations trails before becoming the east-bound and the west-bound roads which met just north of Nordegg, are still discernible but they are roads no longer. A connector road from the highway now comes directly through their centre onto the flats below the old town. The eastern wing of the old road still can be seen from the highway into Nordegg; the western wing of the old road, into which had been incorporated the short connector trail for the numerous Native pathways converging in this area, is still a roadway, passing north of the present golf course and ball diamond. But the extension which followed around the northern end of Nordegg's two lakes at the foot of the town is no longer in use.

To the southeast of the old townsite, the Burnt Patch of south mountain has renewed its growth and the scar of the 1919 fire that threatened the town has all but disappeared. The beautiful meadow now is filled with new growth. This meadow, near Eastbush Falls, was one of two locations for Nordegg's earliest bush camps which supplied timber for the mines.

On the southern edge of Nordegg, the Service Station, part of which was once Reed's Garage, is still in operation. Here also, north of the Garage, is the Nordegg Resort Lodge. Portions of this establishment are located on the western edge of what used to be the community horse pasture. When Don Reed, as a teenager, took up flying, this was where he landed his single engine plane after first buzzing the field to herd the horses out of his way. Seismic crew helicopters now occasionally use this area. Although there are more of them now, planes have been part of this pasture before. Oil exploration activities are still at a high pitch, but the crews no longer work out of Nordegg's Lower Boarding House, as they did during the early 1950s. The search continues, as it has since the early years of this century, for the elusive big field believed to exist somewhere in this territory of the Upper North Saskatchewan.

The lower Flats, painstakingly created into a sports field by the Nordegg inhabitants of earlier years, is now a hodgepodge of various structures. The smooth lines and open spaces of by-gone days are noticeably absent. But the old golf course has been reopened and golfers still play through parts of the original course on the Lower Flats. The ball diamond is now at the north end of the Flats, rather than the south end where it once was.

The exterior of Nordegg's last school seems not to have changed over the years, but the inside now houses the tourist office for the area, as well as a display mounted by the Nordegg Historical Society. This building also contains both a gift shop and a coffee shop. Local tours of the mine and town begin and end at this building. Close by the school is the special cemetery set aside for the 29 miners who died in the explosion of October 31, 1941. It remains a silent tribute to the horrific price too often paid by the pioneers of this province. A little further south along Stuart Road are the community cemeteries, which have been given a new entryway and sign.

Nordegg's old school is now the Heritage Centre, and the Nordegg Historical Society staff the Centre each summer. A. Belliveau collection.

Going even further south into the area of the old town, the visitor must look through the eyes of the past to see what was once a vibrant and close-knit community. The neat rows of houses all are gone now. The forests have begun to move closer, ready to obliterate signs of those small moments in time when the Shunda Basin was teeming with the sounds of industry and community life. The terrace upon which the railway tracks were built soon became overgrown with underbrush and new trees. It became impossible to walk there until clearing took place as part of historic restoration. But, between the tracks and Marcelle Avenue, and slanting toward the southwest, the old trail that was once part of the Native network is still in place, although mossy overgrowth now covers what once was hard packed earth.

The two lakes lying in the valley north of Nordegg were part of the charm and beauty of the town's location, despite one having been turned into the sewage receptacle. When the sun settled to the edge of the Bighorn Range of mountains lying to the west, the lakes took on the color of molten gold. By the time the sun sank behind the horizon, the gold shifted subtly until the lakes became shining silver, reflecting the ever-darkening sky above. Now the shores of these lakes have closed in. They have become badly overgrown with weeds and, from the old town, they have become less discernible as lakes.

A few of the Main Street buildings still remain, and the remnants of Elizabeth and Cherie Avenues still sweep in a grand S-curve past Main Street and on to the train trestle at the small ravine between Hospital and Mine Hills. Both the high and low roads to the mine still are evident, although entrance is restricted, and people must be accompanied to the old minesite area by a tour guide from the Nordegg Historical Society. The miners' path, south of the high road, is still reasonably navigable, but brush and undergrowth are much thicker than in earlier years. The buildings at the mine are as big and as impressive as ever, but the constant hum of machinery now is stilled. The only sound to break the silence comes when the wind blows, rattling through the sheets of metal that are part of the briquette plant. It is then you can feel the ghosts of the past all around you, whispering stories of by-gone days.

A few of the Main Street buildings still remain. A. Belliveau collection.

The beautiful Saskatchewan River country south of Nordegg, where Brewster's Flats is located, now is fully accessible through the Bighorn Highway of the Forestry Trunk Road. The adventurous men of the fur-trade era completed the short overland route through the Shunda Basin and around the mighty gorges of the Saskatchewan prior to returning to this river along the same pathway. And for centuries before, countless generations of First Nations people walked this land, as the numerous prehistoric campsites and burial grounds confirm. From Saskatchewan River Crossing on the Bighorn Highway, can today's fisherman, gazing upward into the nearby hills, sense the ghost of long-gone campfire smoke winding lazily toward the sky?

The Saskatchewan Gap, where that mighty river once thundered through the rocky gorge, thwarting efforts of David Thompson and of other explorers in their attempts to reach the mountains, is still a river barrier of sorts. However, the fury of the river at The Gap now depends not so much on spring run-off as upon flow control from the upstream Bighorn Dam.

To the west, Fish Lake, once the summer place of Nordegg people, is as beautiful as ever. The lake-side camping area is in the same place but now there are designated camping pads and fire pits. A wooden bridge has been constructed across the creek which flows into the lake just beyond the camp area, and a respectable path has replaced the old trail to the upper end of the lake where Frontier Lodge now is located. Near the lower end of the lake, part of the gently sloping hill that once was used to hold wiener roasts has become a parking lot. The old pier, with its high and low diving boards, has disappeared from the lower end of the lake and has been replaced by a bridge across the outlet creek. Paths and park benches follow around the lake beyond this outlet. A new, but much smaller, pier has been located opposite the entrance road but it is utilized only by fishermen and canoeists. Swimming does not seem to be the popular pastime it once was. Could the water be colder now than it was in earlier years?

West and north of Fish Lake is the little jewel, Goldeye Lake. High on a hill over-looking this lake is the Goldeye Centre. Carved out of the wilderness, but part of it still, this Centre maintains the spirit of the west country.

Bighorn Falls, near the Bighorn Reserve of the Stoney Indians, was renamed Crescent Falls in deference to the other Bighorn Falls located near the Yaha Tinda forestry ranch, west of Sundre in Red Deer River country. Bighorn (now Crescent) Falls is part of the history of the Upper North Saskatchewan River Corridor. This is the immovable starting point, selected by D. B. Dowling and Martin Nordegg, to be used for staking when they first began coal prospecting in this part of the west in 1907. Along the river above the falls, the large rocks that jut into the flowing current still catch and hold the sun's warmth. The falls now have a guard rail along the northern edge, and further up the river's rocky shores are picnicking and camping areas. But, so far, the changes here are minimal; it still is very much a part of the past. A short distance downstream from Bighorn Falls is Bighorn Canyon, an awe-inspiring slash in the earth which bears testimony to the power of this river, and to the length of time it has been cutting itself into the ground.

Bighorn (Crescent) Falls now has a guard rail. A. Belliveau collection.

Before and After: The original cliffs of Windy Point were topped with a few small spruce trees, permanently bent against the unceasing wind through this mountain gap. The navigable road, which in early years ceased high above the North Saskatchewan, is now on a level with Lake Abraham. A. Belliveau collection.

Southwest of Bighorn, the road to Windy Point has been lifted well above the valley and now follows along what once was the top of the cliffs above the river. That wall of rock once known as Windy Point jutted into the valley of the Saskatchewan. The navigable road ceased there, suspended between earth and sky, with a rocky cliff towering above, and the mighty Saskatchewan River far below. The original cliffs of Windy Point were topped with a few small spruce trees, permanently bent against the unceasing wind howling eastward through this gap in the mountains. That wall, once so high, has been blasted through to make way for the David Thompson Highway as it passes southwest, out of the Bighorn Valley, along the top of the cliff. The termination point of the old road to Windy Point is now nearly submerged under the deep waters of Lake Abraham. But a small road leads around the rocks south of the highway and a very vague resemblance to the upper reaches of old Windy Point still might be sensed.

Across the Saskatchewan from Windy Point is the distinctive mountain topped with a crooked talon. This mountain, easily seen while following the Saskatchewan River route westward, was the early guide and sentinel for the pass through which the river flowed. It, too, was known as Windy Point. On August 26, 1979, this peak was named Mount Michener in honor of Roland Michener of Lacombe and Red Deer, who was Canada's Governor General from 1967 to 1974.

Despite the desecration of this portion of the Kootenay Plains through flooding when the Bighorn Dam was opened in 1972, there is something hauntingly beautiful about the resultant Lake Abraham. There is a remoteness and a haughty grandeur to these waters which hint at the danger they can present to an unwary visitor. The extensive Kootenay Plains in which Lake Abraham lies is a wide valley which acts as a funnel for the fierce and unpredictable winds which race down the eastern slopes of the Rockies and roar eastward.

Beyond the south-western end of Lake Abraham, the Kootenay Plains are comparatively similar to what they used to be. Two O'Clock Creek flows toward its confluence with the Saskatchewan River, passing under the David Thompson Highway not far from the Two O'Clock Creek public campground. An improved earth road to the east follows near this creek, and the south arm of this road leads to the one remaining cabin of Tom Wilson's horse ranch. Two of these ranch cabins were moved from the confluence of White Rabbit Creek and the Saskatchewan to this higher ground at Two O'Clock Creek when Lake Abraham first came into being, but one of the cabins has since burned.

This same Two O'Clock Creek location was once the home of the Barnes' Kadonna Ranch in the early 20th century, and remnants of the ranch house chimney still are evident near the south end of these Flats. Between the ruins of the chimney of the Kadonna Ranch and the one remaining building of Tom Wilson's horse ranch and trading post is the Stoney Indian grave site created when First Nations graves were destroyed in the creation of Lake Abraham, which began forming behind the Bighorn Dam in August, 1972.

On the David Thompson Highway, a short distance south of Two O'Clock Creek public campground and on the west side of the roadway, is the Cavalcade Campground. This was created in commemoration of the David Thompson Cavalcade adventurers of the mid years of the 20th century. And further south, Whirlpool Point, once a major challenge to the early travellers of the David Thompson Cavalcade, now is only a side trip and a scenic view along the western end of the David Thompson Highway shortly before it joins the Icefields Parkway.

The Upper North Saskatchewan River Corridor of today is no longer the same isolated territory where the mountain people, both Indian and immigrant, once wandered freely, recognizing every turn in the roads and trails. But now the world has changed also. Civilization and technology have taken over peoples' lives, compressing space. The concepts of access and distance have changed. The world no longer stretches with silent prairie and mountain regions, inhabited by scattered settlements whose people look to larger centres for relief from the vast space and loneliness of the Canadian West. Now the tide is reversed, and people attempt to seek out the silence that would allow them to hear their inner selves. The majesty and harmony that is part of the Upper North Saskatchewan River Corridor acts like a magnet. Each year thousands of people have begun to find their way into this lost wilderness.

The intrusion of Europeans into the Shunda Basin in the early 20th century was a very recent development, in light of the total history of this area. This land has known many different groups of people over an extended period of time. The numerous well-defined trails and deeply embedded pathways throughout the region bear testimony to the many feet which trod this same ground during countless years prior to the European presence in this West Country.

When you are in this land of Nordegg, the Shunda Basin, and the Upper North Saskatchewan River Corridor, treat it with the care and respect it deserves. This land is your link with history – a history which goes back through the mists of time – beyond that of the mighty Egyptian pyramids and the glories of ancient Greece and Rome. Here, in the Upper Saskatchewan and the Shunda, you are in tune with the past.

Here, you can touch eternity.

The younger generations belong to this land because it is their heritage. A. Belliveau collection.

Notes

The Land Before Time

1. Coues, Elliott. *New Light on the Early History of the Greater Northwest: The Manuscript Journals of Alexander Henry and of David Thompson.* New York: Francis P. Harper, 1897, p. 701.
2. These rapids are adjacent to the present day Rocky Mountain House National Historic Park, and are part of the Park's Long Walk of the Interpretive Trail System. The Brierley family once owned the land upon which the two chimneys, remnants of Rocky's last fort, were located. In 1929 the land was donated by the Brierley family and, in 1931, the Historic Sites and Monuments Board of Canada erected a cairn and plaque.
3. Spry, Irene, ed. *The Palliser Papers 1857-60.*Toronto: The Champlain Society, 1968, p. 208.
4. Hower, Charles.*Report on the Properties of the Rocky Mountain Collieries Limited, Brazeau Collieries Limited, Sixth Meridian Coal Lands.* Berlin: Buexenstein, 1910, p. 6.
5. Strachan, Dick, and Caufield. "The Coal Mining Industry of Western Canada." Edmonton: Empire Mining and Metallurgical Congress, Sept. 20th, 1927, pp. 101, 103, 125, 147.
6. Today, coal strata can be seen along the David Thompson Highway in the Bighorn region, especially in areas near the Bighorn River.
7. Larner, J.W. "The Kootenay Plains (Alberta) Land Question and Canadian Indian Policy, 1799-1949: A Synopsis." *The Western Canadian Journal of Anthropology, 612* (1976), p. 87.
8. Campbell, M.W. *The Saskatchewan.* Toronto: Clarke, Irwin and Company Limited, 1950, pp. 235-237.
9. Dolph, J. (Geologist, Gulf Canada Resources, Calgary). Interview.
10. Whyte, Jon. *Indians in the Rockies.* Banff: Altitude Publishing, 1985, p. 68.
11. Wilfred Jacob, elder, Ktunaxa First Nation: *Rocky Mountaineer*, March 17, 1998. Many First Nations now have reverted to their original tribal names; previously, the Ktunaxa Nation has been known in Canada as Kootenay, and in the United States as Kutenai.
12. Leo Letourneau - Brazeau fire lookout on Coliseum Mountain, 1951. Built in 1927, this was the first mountain lookout in Alberta. The present lookout station is on Baldy Mountain, which is 150 feet higher than Coliseum. Potter, Mike. *Fire Lookout Hikes.* Banff, Alberta: Luminous Compositions Ltd., 1998.
13. Reeves, Brian K.O., Getty, Ian A., Calder, James M. *Heritage Impact Assessment Consol Coal Lease, Nordegg, Alberta.* Calgary: Lifeways of Canada Ltd., 1973, p. 4.
14. *Rocky Mountain House Echo*, Sept.17, 1912.
15. Coues, pp. 554, 676, 679.
16. Mele, Tony. Interview.
17. Coues, p. 681.
18. Reeves, et al., *Heritage Impact Assessment . . .*, pp. 3, 6-7.

19. Thompson, David. *David Thompson's Narrative of his Explorations in Western America, 1784-1812.* ed. J.B. Tyrell, Toronto: The Champlain Society, XII, 1916, p. lxxxvi.
20. Reeves, et al., *Heritage Impact Assessment . . .*, p. 10.

As Long as the Sun Shines

1. Coues, p. 550.
2. Laurie, J.W. *The Stoney Indians of Alberta, Volumes I and II.* Calgary: Glenbow Foundation, 1957-1959. Glenbow Archives, p. 131.
3. Ossenberg, N.S. "Origin and Relationships of Woodland Peoples: The Evidence of Cranial Morphology," *Aspects of Upper Great Lakes Anthropology: Papers in Honour of Lloyd A. Wilford.* Elden Johnson, ed. St. Paul: Minnesota Historical Society, 1974. p. 34.
4. *Stoney History Notes*, compiled by Peter Jonker, copyright Chiniki Bank, Stoney Tribe, Morley, Alberta, 1983, p. 4.
5. Ibid.
6. Laurie, J.W. *The Stoney Indians of Alberta, V.2*, p. 106.
7. Butler, Sir William Francis. *The Great Lone Land.* Toronto: Macmillan Company of Canada, p. 278, 280.
8. Butler, p. 280.
9. Marty, Sid. *A Grand and Fabulous Notion.* Toronto: New Canada Press, 1984, p. 23.
10. Dempsey, Hugh. *Indian Tribes of Alberta.* Calgary: Glenbow Museum, 1979, p. 43.
11. Whyte, pp. 44, 49.
12. Butler, p. 279.
13. Whyte, p. 46.
14. Laurie, J.W. *The Stoney Indians of Alberta, V.1*, pp. 109, 162; *V.2*, p. 2.
15. Ibid., *V.1*, p. 43; *V.2*, p. 144
16. At Rocky Mountain House, the Walking Eagle Motor Inn displays copies of some of Paul Kane's paintings.
17. Snow, Chief John. *These Mountains are Our Sacred Places: Story of the Stoney Indians.* Toronto: Samuel Stevens, 1977, p. 18.
18. PAC, RG 10, File 339151; John Abraham to the Secretary, Dept. of Indian Affairs, May 31, 1909.
19. Snow, pp. 35, 37.
20. Butler, p. 364.
21. *Stories of the West Country.* Banff: Archives of the Canadian Rockies, 1971.
22. Chief Peter Wesley, who died in the Bighorn area in 1936, had a namesake who was 11 years old when the move was made to Kootenay Plains. This second Peter Wesley, who rests in the Indian burial grounds on Kootenay Plains, was born May 10, 1883, and died June 8, 1989, at the age of 106.
23. Getty, W.E.A. "Perception as an Agent of Socio-Cultural Change for the Stoney Indians of Alberta," M.A. Thesis: University of Calgary, 1974, p. 93.

Native and Immigrant

1. Belliveau, Anne. "Horse Ranching in the Rockies," *Canada Rides*, 2, 1973, p. 19.

2. Snow, p. 79.
3. Wilson III, T.E. Scrapbook No. 4; Scrapbooks of Father, Grandfather, and Nordegg Information. Personal collection.
4. Although Tom Wilson did not live in the town of Nordegg, three of his six children, John, Ed (T.E. Wilson II), and Rene all became long time residents there.
5. PAC, RG 10, File 339151, to Director of Forestry, Ottawa, July 12, 1911.
6. PAC, RG 10, File 339151, sub-files 37-45.
7. PAC, RG10, File 339151, October 3, 1910. Assistant Deputy Superintendent General of Indian Affairs to P.G.Keyes.
8. PAC, RG10, File 368174, Nov. 10, 1909.
9. When Lake Abraham began forming behind TransAlta Utilities' Bighorn Dam, flooding the north-eastern regions of Kootenay Plains, two of the buildings which remained from the original horse ranch/trading post of Tom Wilson were moved to higher ground on the west side of the river. One of these buildings now has burned down but the other is still standing. It is located close to the Native burial ground on a plateau near the Saskatchewan River, in the area of Two O'Clock Creek. Ironically, this is the area once occupied by the Barnes' Kadonna Ranch, and on the north-east end of these Flats the remnants of this ranch house chimney still can be seen. This, also, is where the disturbed Native graves were relocated when flooding of the eastern portion of Kadonnha Tinda was to take place. The majority of the relocated graves were from the family plot of Silas Abraham, after whom the new lake was named.
10. PAC, RG 10, File 339151, McDougall to Dept. of Indian Affairs.
11. Snow, pp. 62-63, 81-85.
12. Memo: Nordegg to Kidd, April 28, 1913. Kidd Collection: Personal correspondence to and from Stuart Kidd. Custodian: Virginia Kidd, Edmonton.
13. Nordeggers, including the youngsters, also used this system to trade furs. These furs were required to be fully prepared – dried, scraped, and stretched (Tony Mele, interview).
14. Wilson III, T.E. Scrapbooks, p. 32.
15. Kidd, Fred. Interview.
16. Kidd, Fred A. "The Stuart Kidd Story." *Chaps and Chinooks: A History West of Calgary*, 1976, p. 404.
17. "Alberta, a Cold Hard Winter," *Time Magazine*, Nov. 21, 1960; p. 28
18. Marasco, Mario. Interview.
19. Larner, J.W. "The Kootenay Plains Land Question..." p. 89.
20. "Clearwater Forest," Rocky Mountain Forest Reserve, Department of Lands and Forests, 1965. Locations of Stoney hunting and trapping territory added separately. Nakoda Institute Archives, Morley, Alberta: Maps, Kootenay Plains (Clearwater) File.
21. Marasco, Mario. Interview.
22. Calgary Power, informational pamphlet on the Bighorn Dam, 1972, p. 5.
23. Getty, W.E.A. "A Case History and Analysis of Stoney Indian-Government Interaction with Regard to the Bighorn Dam: The Effects of Citizen Participation – A Lesson in Government Perfidy and Indian Frustration." MSW Project, University of Calgary, 1975, p. 185-86.

West Country Legend

1. Warkentin, J. *The Western Interior of Canada: A Record of Geographical Discovery*. Toronto: McClelland and Stewart Ltd., 1964, p. 49.
2. Eccles, W.J. *The Canadian Frontier*. Toronto: Holt, Rinehart and Winston, 1969, pp. 8, 88-89, 186.
3. Eccles, W.J. "La Mer de l'Ouest: Outpost of Empire," *Rendezvous: Selected Papers of the Fourth North American Fur Trade Conference, 1981*, Thomas C. Buckley, ed. St. Paul, Minnesota, 1984, p. 11.
4. Ibid., pp. 4, 8.
5. Ibid., p. 9.
6. Eccles, W.J. *The Canadian Frontier*, p. 94.
7. Eccles, W.J. "La Mer...", p. 7.
8. The 1928 report by the Geographic Board of Canada lists the Baptiste River as appearing by that name on Palliser's map of 1865, but no further explanation is given for this name. (Geographic Board of Canada. *Place Names of Alberta*. Ottawa: King's Printer, 1928, p. 6.) It is also referred to in David Thompson's journals, but without explanation of origin.
9. Geographic Board of Canada, p. 6.
10. Warkentin, J., p. 49.
11. Eccles, W.J. "La Mer...", p. 9.
12. Noble, W.C. "The Excavation and Historical Identification of Rocky Mountain House," *Canadian Historic Sites: Occasional Papers in Archaeology and History, #6*, Ottawa: National Historic Sites Service, 1973, p. 135.
13. Ibid., pp. 111, 115, 135, 161.
14. Ibid., pp. 84-85, 87.
15. Ewers, John C. *The Blackfeet: Raiders of the Northwest Plains*. Norman: University of Oklahoma Press, 1958, p. 24.
16. Ewers, John C. *Blackfeet Indians: Ethnological Report Commission Findings*. New York: Garland Publishing Inc., 1974, p. 28.
17. Men of the fur trade were known to wear brightly colored wool sashes called the Assomption Sash, a name derived from an area northeast of Montreal from which the NorthWest Company recruited many of their *voyageurs*. The majority of these sashes were hand woven for the NorthWest Company, but the high demand for these sashes by Native tribes resulted in the Hudson's Bay Company having them made mechanically in England and shipped to Rupert's Land. An original Assomption sash is located in the Rocky Mountain House National Historic Park Interpretive Centre. (T. Poworoznik, Historical Interpreter, Rocky Mountain House National Historic Park. July 31, 1991.)
18. Grinnell, George Bird. "The Coming of the White Man." *The Story of the Indian*. New York: D. Appleton and Company, 1911, p. 224-232.

Through the Shining Mountains

1. Coues, p. 701.

2. Rocky Mountain House National Historic Park, File EE, Paper 6; Smyth, David. "The Fur Trade Posts at Rocky Mountain House." Manuscript Report #197, National Historic Parks. Ottawa: Parks Canada, 1976.
3. "Extracts from Fur Trade Journals, Stoney Indians 1826-68," Hudson's Bay Company Files. Calgary: Glenbow Archives.
4. Thompson, David. *David Thompson's Narrative...*, ed. Tyrrell, p. lxxx.
5. Thompson, David. *David Thompson's Narrative 1784-1812*. Richard Glover, ed., Toronto: the Champlain Society, 1962, pp. lxxxvii-lxxxviii.
6. Thompson, David. *Travels in Western North America, 1784-1812*. Victor J. Hopwood, ed., Toronto: Macmillan of Canada, 1971, pp. 228, 233-235.
7. Dempsey, Hugh. "A History of Rocky Mountain House," *Canadian Historic Sites: Occasional Papers in Archaeology and History #6*, Ottawa: National Historic Sites Service, 1973, p. 11.
8. Bond, Rowland. *David Thompson and the Native Tribes of North America*. Nine Mile Falls, Washington: Spokane House Enterprises, 1972, p. 188.
9. Nisbet, Jack. *Sources of the River: Tracking David Thompson Across Western North America*. Maps and Illustrations by Jack McMaster. Seattle: Sasquatch Books, 1994, p. 89.
10. Thompson, David. *David Thompson's Narrative 1784-1812*. Richard Glover, ed. XII, p. 431.
11. Ibid., pp. xlvii-xlviii.
12. By the time David Thompson arrived in Montreal in 1812, it had been 27 years since he last had been in a city. (Nisbet, p. 243).
13. Thompson, David. *David Thompson's Narrative 1784-1812*. Richard Glover, ed. p. liii.
14. Coues, pp. 651-652.
15. Brewster's Flats is a short distance west of this widening of the Saskatchewan.
16. Thick forestation, combined with dense undergrowth, often complicated by fallen timber, appears to be a characteristic of a majority of the wetland portion of the Upper North Saskatchewan River Corridor. Between the time that Henry recorded his comment and the town of Nordegg was constructed, fires cleared large areas of this growth. However, there has not been an extensive major fire in this area during the 20th century, and once again there is evidence of dense growth, or "strong woods."
17. Coues, p. 684.
18. Nisbet, p. 211.
19. However, the NorthWest Company opened a number of trading posts within the Columbia district and competed with the Pacific Fur Company. When the 1812 war broke out between Canada and the United States, the Pacific Fur Company management, knowing that they were outnumbered by Nor'westers, sold their fur company to these Nor'westers, who then took over complete control of the trade in the Columbia River region.
20. Nisbet, pp. 254-255, 684.

Explorers, Prospectors, and Other Visitors

1. Dempsey, Hugh. "A History of Rocky Mountain House...," p. 9.
2. Spry, Irene. *The Palliser Papers 1857-60*, pp. 211-212, 214-215.
3. Ibid., pp. 330-331.
4. Ibid., pp. 331-335.
5. Southesk, Earl of. *Saskatchewan and the Rocky Mountains*. Edinburgh: Edmonston and Douglas, 1875, pp. 223-224, 228-230.

6. Ibid., pp. 230, 234.
7. Ibid., p. 234.
8. Ibid., pp. 235-236.
9. Butler, pp. 197, 278-279, 354, 356, 358, 376-377, 386.
10. Ibid., pp. 363-364, 378-379.
11. Rogers Pass booklet, p. 8.
12. Fraser, Esther. *Canadian Rockies: Early Travels and Explorations.* Edmonton: Hurtig Publishers, 1969, p. 231.
13. Berton, Pierre. *The National Dream/The Last Spike* (abridged by author), Toronto: McClelland and Stewart, 1974, pp. 106, 133, 137, 228, 247-250, 351.
14. Washburn, Stanley. *Trails, Trappers and Tenderfeet in Western Canada.* London: Andrew Melrose, 1912, pp. 204-205.
15. Ibid., pp. 5, 34-37.
16. It is entirely possible that this mining engineer to whom Washburn spoke was James McEvoy, who had been hired in 1908 by Martin Cohn on behalf of the German Development Company to do coal prospecting in that general area.
17. Washburn, pp. 126-129, 132-138.
18. Palmer, H. *Patterns of Prejudice.* Toronto: McClelland and Stewart, 1982, introduction pp. ix-xi, 2-4, 9.

Nordegg and the Changing Face of the West

1. Koch, John. *Martin Nordegg: The Uncommon Immigrant.* Edmonton: Brightest Pebble Publishing Co. Inc., 1997, pp. 37-38, 40-41.
2. The term Anglo-Saxon indicates the non-Celtic, Germanic-speaking people who settled in England over 1500 years ago.
3. PAC: MG30, A 19, Vol. I & II, M. Nordegg ms, pp. 3-7.
4. Cohn "admired this statesman enormously" and occasionally was invited to Laurier's home to visit. (PAC: MG30, A 19, Vol. I & II, M. Nordegg ms, p. 37.)
5. PAC: MG30, A 19, Vol. I & II, M. Nordegg ms, pp. 15-16.
6. See the numerous references to "Andy" whenever Martin Nordegg came upon troubled times (Nordegg, Martin. *The Possibilities of Canada Are Truly Great: Memoirs 1906-1924.* T.D. Regehr, ed. Toronto: Macmillan Company, 1971). Haydon became a Canadian Senator in 1924.
7. Although concrete supporting evidence has not come to light, it is reasonable to suppose that Andrew Haydon was financially involved in the German Development Company through his law partner, H.B. McGiverin. The Bighorn coal area, first of the coal lands to be staked by the German Development Company, shows ten sub-divisions; each of the sub-divisions was given a name, as follows: S.W. Haydon, E.J. Haydon, H.B. McGiverin, Hurdman, A. Haydon, E. Haydon, L. Barber, W. Haydon, J. Haydon, and L. Haydon. (Hower, C. p. 26) The memoirs of Martin Nordegg describing his discussions with Andy Haydon when the Toronto syndicate staked the same territory as the German Development Company in 1907, suggest joint ownership in the statement: "The end of my recital to Andy was that we must move Heaven and Earth to become the legitimate owners of our staked coalfields." (PAC: MG30, A 19, Vol. I & II, M. Nordegg Ms., p. 132.)
8. After resigning as geologist for the German Development Company, Barlow relocated to Montreal where he became a Consulting Geologist. By 1912, he was lecturing at McGill

University and also was Vice President of the Canadian Mining Institute. In 1914, he was drowned when aboard one of two ships which collided in the St. Lawrence River. (PAC: MG30, A 19, Vol. I & II, M. Nordegg Ms., pp. 218-19.)
9. PAC: MG30, A 19, Vol. I & II, M. Nordegg Ms, p. 59-60.
10. Silesia, once part of the kingdom of Bohemia in the empire of the Hapsburgs, is a rich mining country with numerous valuable industries.
11. Arthur "Mac" McMullen, interview.
12. No coal mining legislation was in place for western Canada when Martin Cohn began staking his claims. He was permitted to stake claims under the regulations for quartz mining and to purchase these claims from the federal government. Hemphill, C.R., Jennings, E.W. Eighth Annual Field Conference, Nordegg, 1958. Edmonton: Alberta Society of Petroleum Geologists and the Edmonton Geological Society, p. 5.
13. PAC: MG30, A 19, Vol. I & II, M. Nordegg ms, p. 65
14. Fred Kidd Jr., p. 404.
15. Fred Kidd and Donaldson Bogart Dowling had become friends during Dowling's previous trips to the west. Mount Kidd, which lies in Kananaskis Country, south of Ribbon Creek, was named by Dowling for Fred Kidd. North of Ribbon Creek lies Mount Bogart, which Dowling named for himself. (Fred Kidd, son of Stuart Kidd; unpublished papers).
16. Hower, C. p. 27.
17. PAC: MG30, A 19, Vol. I & II, M. Nordegg ms, pp. 105-106.
18. Ibid., p. 112-114
19. Kananaskis Country Environmental Education. *History, Kananaskis Country*. Edmonton: Government of Alberta publication (Heritage Fund), p. 45.
20. PAC: MG30, A 19, Vol. I & II, M. Nordegg ms, pp. 130-131
21. Hower, C. p. 7.
22. PAC: MG30, A 19, Vol. I & II, M. Nordegg ms, p. 133.
23. Hower, C. pp. 7, 27.
24. Regehr, T.D. *The Canadian Northern Railway: Pioneer Road of the Northern Prairies 1895-1918*. Toronto: MacMillan Company, 1976, pp. 25-26, 201n.
25. Nordegg, Martin. *The Possibilities of Canada...* p. 127n.

An Unusual Alliance

1. Regehr, T.D. *The Canadian Northern Railway*. pp. 20-21, 27-28.
2. Nordegg, Martin. *The Possibilities of Canada...*, p. 131n.
3. Hower, C. pp. 6-7, 73.
4. PAC: MG30, A 19, Vol. I & II, M. Nordegg ms, pp. 208, 276.
5. PAC, RG 46, V.1444, blueprint; Regehr, T.D. *The Canadian Northern Railway*. pp. 248, 288-289.
6. The present-day coal centre of Grand Cache is located in Townships 56 and 57, Range 8, West of the 6th meridian. The Brazeau Collieries' five separate coal claims, called the Sixth Meridian coal holdings (with different claim names), were scattered in Townships 53 and 54, Ranges 3, 5, and 6. In 1910, another application was being considered for areas of outcrops along the Smoky River, in Township 58, Ranges 8 and 9, West of the sixth meridian. (Hower, C. p. 82.)

7. The Nordegg coal holdings, which were not part of the Brazeau Collieries at this time, were 5120 acres (2072 hectares), or 8 square miles (20.72 sq. km) in size, which would bring the total Brazeau Collieries holdings to 38 080 acres (15 411 hectares), or 59.5 square miles (154.1 sq. km).
8. Regehr, T.D. *The Canadian Northern Railway*. p. 202.
9. PAC: MG30, A 19, Vol. I & II, M. Nordegg ms, p. 216.
10. In Martin Nordegg's memoirs, *The Possibilities of Canada Are Truly Great*, he relates that he and Mackenzie attended the Grunau regatta on the day following final negotiations. (PAC: MG30, A 19, Vol. I & II, M. Nordegg ms, p. 214.) According to information from the German periodical "Wassersport," as supplied by Staatsbibliothek Preussischer Kulturbesitz, Berlin, the 1909 Grunau rowing regatta was held from Saturday, June 12th, to Monday June 14th. (personal correspondence).
11. Koch, John. *Martin Nordegg*, pp. 111-113.
12. PAC: MG30, A 19, Vol. I & II, M. Nordegg ms, pp. 220-221.
13. Regehr, T.D. *The Canadian Northern Railway*, pp. 216, 305.
14. PAC; RG 46; Vol.1444, blueprint.
15. Hower, C. p. 9.
16. PAC; RG 30; Canadian Northern Railway Stocks and Bonds.
17. PAC; RG 43; Records of the Department of Railways and Canals – Place and Work.
18. PAC; RG 30; Canadian Northern Railway on the Prairies. III C, 19-20.
19. PAC; RG 30; file 15321 #149213; letter from Alberta Central Railway Company legal department to Hon. Charles Murphy, Secretary of State, Ottawa, April 17, 1911.
20. PAC; RG 30; Canadian Northern Railway Stocks and Bonds.
21. It is thought to have been on a height of land north of Innisfail that the Blackfoot pointed out the route westward into the mountains to Hudson's Bay explorer, Anthony Henday. For many years packtrips into the west began at Innisfail, crossing the North Saskatchewan River where Rocky Mountain House was located, and then travelling the First Nations' trails through the Upper Saskatchewan River Corridor. This route from Innisfail also became one of the routes used occasionally by Martin Nordegg. (Hower, C. p. 10.)
22. Gheur, Ernest. Report on Nordegg Coal Claims. Brazeau Collieries Limited, 1912, p. 19.
23. PAC; RG 30; file 15321, #149213; letter from Alberta Central to Secretary of State.
24. PAA:67.258, Alberta Central Railway Company, Rowbotham.
25. PAC; RG 30; file 15321 #149213; letter from Alberta Central to Secretary of State.
26. Regehr, T.D. *The Canadian Northern Railway*, pp. 200, 285.
27. Dolph, J. geologist; interview.
28. PAC; RG 46; V.1444, blueprint – Feb. 15th, 1911. In 1912, a new location was decided upon for the settlement then known as Prairie Grange. The village of Rocky Mountain House came into existence in 1913. Use of this name for events occurring prior to this time is in reference to the general area, rather than to the specific location of the town.
29. PAC; RG 30; Records of CN Railways, Schedule – Canadian Northern – Stettler to Nordegg.

Unfolding the Dream

1. PAC: MG30, A 19, Vol. I & II, M. Nordegg ms, p. 229.

2. Hower, C. pp. 10, 46.
3. Stuart Kidd, as told to Mac McMullen, and to Stuart's son, Fred Kidd.
4. Martin Nordegg would then be following a portion of the Big Fish Trail. The mountain which looks like an extinct volcano is Shunda Mountain, always known locally as "Baldy." In Martin Nordegg's write-up for his daughter, Marcelle, based upon their 1912 trip through the Upper Saskatchewan, he refers to this mountain as Mount Nordegg: "From the top of the hill we had a gorgeous view of the two mountains to the north: Mount Nordegg lying to the west, Mount Coliseum in the east" (Translated from the German by Maria Koch)
5. PAC: MG30, A 19, Vol. I & II, M. Nordegg ms, pp. 237-238.
6. According to the *Rocky Mountaineer* newspaper of September 28, 1938, George Pearkes (who was visiting Rocky at that time) had been employed in 1910 hauling freight into Brazeau fields. Pearkes once homesteaded near Rocky. He later became a war hero, eventually going on to become Minister of Defence in the Conservative government of J.G. Diefenbaker.
7. In 1907 Nordegg and Dowling had given George Creek its name after Georg Buexenstein, a director of the German Development Company, and President of the Deutsches Kanada Syndikat. (PAC: MG30, A 19, Vol. I & II, M. Nordegg ms, p. 101.)
8. Hower, C. p. 44-63.
9. The trail south, now known as Bighorn Trail, which passes along the Wapiabi, was the general route followed from the South Brazeau to the Bighorn coal holdings (Hower, C. facing p. 44.)
10. On the 1934 Geological Survey map of the Nordegg area there was a Crescent Falls located on the Bighorn River, but this falls was located a distance upstream from Brazeau Collieries' Bighorn Falls, which now has been renamed Crescent Falls.
11. The present picnic area at Crescent Falls is in the location where the town of Bighorn was to be located, while the camping areas further upstream are where the mine complex was to be built.
12. Hower, C. p. 24.
13. Alberta Map – Department of the Interior, 1913. (Comments written on map) Glenbow Library.
14. Hower, C. p. 94.
15. Ibid., p. 90.
16. Kidd Collection; Personal correspondence to and from Stuart Kidd. Custodian, Virginia Kidd, Edmonton. – March 7, 1911, from Hower.
17. Dowling previously had recognized the geological Kootenay strata in this area and noted that coal likely would be in this region. (R. Green, "Eighth Annual Petroleum Geologists," p. 6).
18. At 5120 acres, or 8 square miles, the only other Brazeau coal holding that was larger than the Nordegg field was the Kananaskis field at 5440 acres.
19. Arthur "Mac" McMullen, interview.
20. PAC: MG30, A 19, Vol. I & II, M. Nordegg, ms, p. 266.
21. PAC: MG30, A 19, Vol. I & II, M. Nordegg, ms, p. 271.
22. Fallow-McMullen, Martha. Interviews.
23. Brewster, F.O. "Pat". *They Came West*. Banff: Altitude Publishing, 1979, p. 40.
24. Tom was the father of Ed McKenzie who, with his wife Millie, established McKenzie's Trails West Guide and Outfitting in 1966, which, under Tom's grandson Ron, operates in the Whitegoat region and north.

25. PAC: MG30, A 19, Vol. I & II, M. Nordegg, ms, pp. 258, 274, 281.

Nordegg: A Town is Born

1. Regehr, T.D. *The Canadian Northern Railway.* p. 322. A plan of diagonal streets converging into a star-shaped centre intersection can be traced back to the 19th century's Second Empire of France, under Napoleon the Third and Empress Eugenie, when Paris was reconstructed "into a city of broad boulevards and grand open spaces." (Burns, Edward McNall, et al., *Western Civilizations: Their History and Culture.* 9th ed., New York: W.W. Norton and Company, 1980, p. 694.) Montreal's Mount Royal, sometimes referred to as the "Garden city," may have been influenced by Ebenezer Howard's Garden-city concept. (Marsan, Jean-Claude. *Montreal in Evolution.* McGill-Queen's University Press, 1981, p. 326.) The model city design is similar to that of Washington, D.C., with diagonal streets and the rail terminal at the centre. (Norman Lowe, retired Historic Resources Officer, Canadian National Railway, interview.)
2. The similarities between the Nordegg town plan and the western portion of the plan for Mount Royal (The Mount Royal Tunnel, Montreal, Quebec, Canada, Being Built by Mackenzie, Mann and Company Limited. Printed Privately, December 1913. Copy at CNRHQ, blueprint.) are easily recognizable. Many times Arthur (Mac) McMullen, Mining Engineer and Surveyor at Nordegg, spoke of Nordegg's town plan being "lifted" from the C.N.R. townsite in Montreal. He stated that Martin Nordegg related the story to Johnny Shanks, who had been hired as Mine Manager in 1914, and Shanks, in turn, had told him.
3. Arthur "Mac" McMullen, interview. Blueprints or sketches showing only the lots without the constructed buildings could be confusing to anyone not realizing that all the lots shown were not necessarily developed but were available for construction, as needed, following Martin Nordegg's original plan. Construction that was carried out in the later years of the town's existence was faithful to the wishes of Martin Nordegg's plan for his town.
4. PAC: MG30, A 19, Vol. I & II, M. Nordegg ms. p. 281. This booklet, referred to by Martin Nordegg, possibly is the Brazeau Collieries' September 1913 publication, *Specifications for the Mining Plant at Nordegg, Alberta.* This booklet contains detailed plans for various surface buildings at the minesite, as well as for the commissary (Bighorn Trading Company) and the two-story boarding house. (Copy in possession of the author.)
5. Rocky Mountain House established two nursing homes during the third decade of the 20th century, but these did not include surgical facilities. Rocky's first hospital was opened in July, 1938. (*Rocky Mountaineer*, 75th Anniversary supplement, July 29, 1987, p. 19.)
6. PAC: MG30, A 19, Vol. I & II, M. Nordegg ms., pp. 281, 285.
7. Until a gravel road was constructed into Nordegg in the 1950s, this corduroy road technique also was used, as necessary, to permit car and truck travel over the improved-earth road which was built in the 1930s.
8. Gheur, pp. 5, 7, 9-12, 37. As the mine extended underground, the Number 2 coal seam was actually closer to five and one half feet (1.7 meters) on average, while Number 3 seam averaged 15 feet (4.57 meters).
9. The 1916 Prairie Provinces census indicated that Nordegg's population was 738, of whom 538 were men. However, in early peak years the number of workers actually was over 800.

10. Fallow-McMullen, Martha. Interviews. Gilbert McKenzie was the father of Tom McKenzie, who operated the pony express from Rocky to Nordegg prior to rail construction, as well as father of construction contractor Alan McKenzie. Alan was a partner in the construction firm of Baird and McKenzie, the contractors who built the houses and business district at Nordegg, and who also did construction in Banff and Medicine Hat, and portions of the Hudson Bay Company building in Calgary.
11. Arthur "Mac" McMullen, interview.
12. Told to Martha Fallow-McMullen by Alan McKenzie, construction contractor.
13. Fallow-McMullen, Martha. oral interviews.
14. The location of Martin Nordegg's Swiss chalet is shown on the original Nordegg blueprint, now in the Nordegg Heritage Centre. Plans for this six-room chalet remained at the Brazeau Collieries mine office until the mine closed. (McMullen and D'Amico, interviews.) These blueprints are among the numerous Brazeau Collieries items which have disappeared over the years since the operation ceased.
15. Arthur "Mac" McMullen, interviews.
16. Fallow-McMullen, Martha. Interviews.
17. In 1923, the Alberta Provincial Police representative, Constable Norman McDonald, commented to Martha Fallow-McMullen that the majority of his work, for both that year and the previous one, had consisted of flushing out moonshine stills from the brush country north of Nordegg. Prohibition came into effect following a 1915 binding referendum, and it was repealed by another referendum in November 1923.
18. Fallow-McMullen, Martha. Interviews; Fallow-McMullen correspondence of Jan 20, 1923, in possession of author.
19. March 3, 1914, *Red Deer Advocate*, p. 3.
20. PAC, RG3, D.3, Nordegg postal history card
21. Arthur "Mac" McMullen, Interview.
22. *Rocky Mountain House Guide*, August 11, 1914.
23. Guido Blasetti, interview.
24. Over a span of years, other buildings and institutions were developed, giving the townspeople access to various religious, sporting, cultural, and business establishments.
25. Seager, C.A. *A Proletariat in Wild Rose Country: The Alberta Coal Miners, 1905-1945*. PhD dissertation. Toronto: York University, 1981, pp. 168-169, 176-177.
26. PAC: MG30, A 19, Vol. I & II, M. Nordegg ms, p. 291.
27. Gheur, p. 23; Brazeau Collieries 1913 Specifications, pp. 7-8, 13-14.
28. *Rocky Mountaineer*, p. A-2, Feb. 26/92.
29. *Days Before Yesterday: History of Rocky Mountain District*. Rocky Mountain Reunion Historical Society, eds. Winnipeg: Friesen Printers, 1977, p. 95.
30. Arthur "Mac" McMullen, interview; Zupido D'Amico, interviews; TransAlta Utilities pamphlet – history: Public Affairs Dept., TransAlta Utilities Corp., May 9, 1990.
31. Calgary Henderson Directory, 1914, Henderson Directories Alberta Ltd., p. 126.
32. PAC: MG30, A 19, Vol. I & II, M. Nordegg ms, pp. 281, 313.
33. Seager, C.A. *A Proletariat in Wild Rose Country*. p. 170.
34. Arthur "Mac" McMullen, interview.

Dreams and Reality

1. Guido Blasetti, interview.
2. Weatherbee appears to have specialized in working with mining companies while they were instituting initial operations; then he would move on to another location.
3. Kidd Collection; Memo to Stuart Kidd from Martin Nordegg; April 28, 1913.
4. PAA: 171/1-2. Brazeau Files, Letter from Stirling to F. Aspinall, Oct. 17, 1916.
5. PAA: 76.507. Ira Gray, notes. Records of the Official Receiver of Brazeau Collieries, Brazeau Collieries Files.
6. PAA: 171/1-2. Inspector's Report, J.A. Richards, Feb. 16, 1915.
7. Zupido D'Amico, interview.
8. PAC: MG30, A 19, Vol. I & II, M. Nordegg ms. p. 309.
9. Ibid., pp. 326-327, 333-335.
10. J. Koch Collection: Letter to M. Nordegg from S. Hughes, Aug. 18, 1914.
11. According to Johnny Shanks, Martin Nordegg blamed Shanks for these incidents, and for using his (Shanks') strong influence among the Italians to create unrest among the townspeople (Shanks to McMullen, oral) Although Martin Nordegg kept his feelings and his personal life very private, his dislike of Shanks was made evident in personal correspondence (Kidd collection). He also relates, in his memoirs, *The Possibilities of Canada Are Truly Great* how, in 1922, after riding horseback into Nordegg along the river from Harlech, he confronted the General Manager (Shanks) in the Brazeau Collieries mine office and asked why Shanks had "antagonize(d) [him] during the war." Shanks "maintained that he had not." PAC: MG30, A 19, Vol. I & II, M. Nordegg ms, pp. 406-407)
12. Koch, John. *Martin Nordegg: The Uncommon Immigrant*, pp. 107-212.
13. The Canadian Bank of Commerce and the Imperial Bank of Canada merged on February 3, 1961, forming the Canadian Imperial Bank of Commerce.
14. Letter of R.P. Ormsby to J. Shanks, April 13, 1917, Glenbow Archives: M1124-2.
15. PAC; RG30, Canadian Northern Railway on the Prairies, IIIC, 19-20.
16. Ironically, in later years, D.B. Hanna, a nephew of Canadian National Railway's President D.B. Hanna, became the conductor on the mixed passenger/freight train which travelled into Nordegg/Brazeau 3 times a week.
17. PAC: RG 30 United Mine Workers of America, District 18 – Morgan to Thornton, 1923
18. Kidd Collection; Letter of Nordegg to Kidd, June 22, 1921.
19. Kidd Collection; Letter of Nordegg to Kidd, Feb. 13, 1922.
20. PAC: MG30, A 19, Vol. I & II, M. Nordegg ms., pp. 409-410.
21. Arthur "Mac" McMullen, interview.
22. Millie (Mrs. Sam) Morley, interview. As a young bride, Millie Morley and her husband, Sam, farmed during the summers and spent their winters at Nordegg, where Sam worked for Brazeau Collieries. In 1922 they lived in a tent behind the Bank of Commerce on Main Street and, in 1923, with a small baby, they were part of the tent town which sprang up near Martin Creek. In 1926, after new construction had eased the housing situation, they made a permanent move to Nordegg and became long-time residents.
23. Koch, John. *Martin Nordegg: The Uncommon Immigrant*. p. 214.
24. Ibid., pp. 288-290.
25. Kidd Collection; Letter of Nordegg to Kidd, Sept. 20, 1945.
26. Wilson Scrapbook #4; Letters of Nordegg to T.E. Wilson, May 29, 1947, and July 19, 1948.

Nordegg: Its People

1. Seager, *A Proletariat in Wild Rose Country*, p. 164.
2. *Report of the Alberta Coal Commission 1925*. Commissioners Evens, Drinnan, Wheatlye. Edmonton: King's Printers, 1926, p. 180.
3. Guido Blasetti, interview.
4. Marasco, Mario. Interview.
5. Gibbon, John Murray. *Canadian Mosaic: The Making of a Northern Nation*. Toronto: McClelland and Stewart, 1938, pp. 313, 315.
6. Marasco, Mario. Interview.
7. Dibus, Rudolph. Interview.
8. M.Fallow-McMullen, interviews. A cast photo of the musical play, "Nautical Knot," is in the Nordegg Heritage Centre, and in Glenbow Archives, Calgary.
9. The small mining centres of Alexo, established in 1920, and West Saunders, established in 1918 and closed in 1927, were located approximately 18 miles (30 km) east of Nordegg. In 1948, Alexo had a hotel, cookhouse, bunkhouse, store and 30 houses. During normal production the payroll showed 70 men, of whom 30 were miners. These people depended upon Nordegg for medical care, entertainment, and many of their supplies. (Pullen, P.F. and Tennant, R., "Alexo Has Quality Products," *Western Miner*, Aug. 1948, pp. 88-9.) During the mid-years of the 20th century, there was an independent timber camp, run by Pete LeClerc, which was located at Harlech, approximately 9 miles (14.5 km) east of Nordegg. Timber from this camp was shipped east. The small number of people based in Harlech also depended upon Nordegg as a support system.
10. Fallow-McMullen, Martha. Interviews.
11. The Nordegg Recreation and Heritage Association Campground, located near the foot of Coliseum Mountain north of Nordegg, includes a bobolinko court.
12. Mele, Tony, interview. The soccer change rooms under the grandstand later were converted to concession stands from which food and refreshments were available for purchase during Sports Days and ball tournaments. This was accomplished by cutting holes in the back wall of the change rooms and attaching hinges to the loose wood, thus creating lift-up doors which could be secured from the inside.
13. Brian Shaw became coach of the Edmonton Oil Kings in 1971. In the fall of 1972 the Alberta Oilers, of the now defunct Western/World Hockey Association, came to Edmonton. The following year they were renamed the Edmonton Oilers, and Brian Shaw was appointed their coach, which he remained for close to two years. Brian left Edmonton when, in 1976, the Oil Kings hockey franchise became available for purchase; Brian was one of the purchasing group, as was Dale Fisher, another ex-Nordegg resident. This team moved to Portland, Oregon, and was renamed the Portland Winter Hawks. (B. Shaw, interview.) Many of the young hockey players that Brian worked with after he left Nordegg went on to play in the National Hockey League. On July 27, 1993, Brian Shaw died in hospital in Portland, Oregon, at the age of 62; his ashes rest in the family plot in the Nordegg cemetery.
14. Bareback horse wrestling consisted of 2 individuals, bare to the waist, mounted on horseback without benefit of a saddle. The contestants had to manoeuvre their horses into position and then attempt to wrestle the opponent until he was dislodged from his horse.
15. This connector road is still evident, and is used for light traffic north of the present ball diamond and golf course, but it now is a "no exit" roadway.
16. *Rocky Mountaineer*, July 18, 1934.

17. The bridge across the North Saskatchewan River was opened officially in 1946 by A.J. Hooke, Alberta's Social Credit Minister of Economic Affairs.
18. *Red Deer AdViser*, July 30, 1975. There still is a Cavalcade campground site on the Kootenay Plains. This now is available for pre-reserved group camping.
19. The 1945 Christmas concert, sponsored by the Nordegg Young People's Association, included songs and dances by the C.G.I.T. girls, two musical numbers by the High School Music Class, a pantomime by the Brazeau Cadets, piano solos by Johnny Blasetti and Anne McMullen, a skit by the High School Students' Union, a play directed by Nick Kozmenuik, and another play put on by the Young People's Association. (Concert program, in possession of the author.)
20. Kidd, Fred. Interview.

The Brazeau Collieries Mining Operation

1. Arthur "Mac" McMullen, interview.
2. Brazeau Collieries, *Specifications for the Mining Plant*, September, 1913.
3. McMullen, A. "Canada's Largest Briquetting Operation: Brazeau Mines Fine Product," *Western Miner*, August, 1948, pp. 62-63.
4. Dennis Morley, interview.
5. Mario Marasco, interview; Ibid.
6. PAA: 171/1-2, Brazeau Collieries Files; Letter from District Inspector to Chief Inspector Stirling, Aug. 1913
7. Peele, Robert. *Mining Engineers' Handbook, Volume II.* London: John Wiley and Sons, Inc., 1918. pp. 23/04-23/10.
8. Arthur "Mac" McMullen, interview. One such mine outcropping occurred close by the David Thompson Highway. The mine tunnels had passed underneath the highway, reaching the surface on the north side of the road, between Nordegg and the Fish Lake turn-off, a short distance west of the intersection of Highways 11 and 734. Numerous mine tunnels, from both Number 2 and Number 3 Mines, pass underneath both of these highways. (Brazeau Collieries tunnels blueprint. Nordegg Historical Society Heritage Centre)
9. Peele, Robert. *Mining Engineers' Handbook*, pp. 23/11-12.
10. Janigo, John. oral interview.
11. Brazeau Collieries Limited. *Specifications for the Mining Plant*.
12. Seager, C.A. *A Protelariat in Wild Rose Country*, pp. 110-112.
13. Zupido D'Amico, interview.
14. Seager, C.A. *A Protelariat in Wild Rose Country*, p. 179.
15. Annual Reports of the Mines Division of the Department of Mines and Minerals of the Province of Alberta. Edmonton: King's Printer. 1919.
16. McMullen, A. "Cleaning Fine Coal in a Feldspar Jig at Brazeau." *Canadian Mining and Metallurgical Bulletin*, February, 1954, pg. 1.
17. Analysis of Alberta Coal, Scientific and Industrial Research Council, 1925.
18. PAC, RG81, Dominion Coal Board. Volume 42, File 14-2-1. "Memo: Brazeau Collieries," Feb 9, 1954.
19. PAC, RG81, Dominion Coal Board. Volume 207, Files 71-71, Study of Coal from Brazeau Mines #2 and #3, 1940.
20. Arthur "Mac" McMullen, interview.

21. Ibid.
22. During the late 1930s, in one year of jig sales, Vissac made a profit of $40 000. (Vissac to "Mac" McMullen, interview.)
23. PAC RG81, Dominion Coal Board. Memo to P.F. Hannal from C.L. O'Brien, June 7, 1937.

Challenge and Change

1. McMullen, A. "Canada's Largest Briquetting Operation." pp. 62-63.
2. PAC RG81, Dominion Coal Board. Volume 41, Memo: The Use of Canadian Coal in Western Canada by the CNR, 1948.
3. PAC RG 33/63. Royal Commision on Coal, 1944, Volume 57, Files 13-2-2. Brazeau Collieries Questionnaire: 3-2-2, Annual Report, 1942.
4. PAA: 76.507. Records of the Official Receiver of Brazeau Collieries, Box 11, Item 495. G. Vissac: "Report on the Brazeau Coal Field of Alberta, 1945;" "Brazeau Collieries Mining Operation."
5. Ewing, A.F. Commission Report, Public Inquiry. Nordegg Mine Disaster, October 31, 1941, to the Lieutenant Governor in Council, Edmonton, 1942.
6. Ibid., p. 4.
7. Ibid., pp. 9, 20.
8. Ibid., pp. 14, 20, 26.
9. *Calgary Albertan*; 12/1/43.
10. Ewing, pp. 15-17.
11. Ibid., pp. 7-10, 21-22.
12. Ibid., pp. 29-33.
13. Heeley, William Grafton. Evidence 1942, Volume II. *In the matter of the Public Inquiries Act and in the matter of a commission...to conduct the inquiry to ascertain...the cause of the disaster...at Brazeau (Nordegg), Alberta, on the 31st day of October, A.D. 1941. Evidence and proceedings commencing January 6, 1942.* Glenbow Archives, M502 A H453. pp. 597-598.
14. Arthur "Mac" McMullen, interview.
15. PAA; 87.246; Supreme Court of Alberta, Judicial District of Red Deer. Between His Majesty the King and Brazeau Collieries Limited. Box 93, Feb. 10, 1943.
16. PAC RG33/36, Royal Commission on Coal, 1944, Volume 44, "Submission to the Royal Commission on Coal re. Living Conditions in a so-called Closed Town – the Town of Nordegg." April 11, 1945.
17. PAA; 87.246; Letter from Clerk of the Court, Supreme Court of Alberta, Judicial District of Red Deer, to Deputy Attorney General. Box 93, June 18, 1943.
18. Shanks, John (Nordegg General Manager, 1914-1945). Unpublished papers, Glenbow Archives, A/S528A M1124.
19. Ewing, p. 27.
20. PAC RG33/36, Royal Commission on Coal, 1944.
21. Marasco, Mario. Interview.
22. Arthur "Mac" McMullen, interview; Dennis Morley, interview.
23. PAC RG 33/63. Royal Commission on Coal, 1944.
24. Arthur "Mac" McMullen, interview.
25. Shanks, John. Unpublished papers, Glenbow Archives.
26. PAA: 76.507. Box 11, Item 495. pp. 16-20, 43-45.

27. Arthur "Mac" McMullen, interview.

Turning Points

1. Zupido D'Amico, interview.
2. Ibid.
3. McMullen, A. "Canada's Largest Briquetting Operation."
4. PAC, RG 81, Dominion Coal Board. Volume 41, File 14-2-1 (Part 2). Letter: Vice-President of Brazeau Collieries, Brigadier Kindersley, to President of CNR, Donald Gordon, March 4, 1952.
5. PAC, RG 81. Dominion Coal Board. Volume 41. Letter: President of Brazeau Collieries, John Boyd, to Dominion Coal Board, March 31, 1952.
6. Dieselization was expected to take up to five years to accomplish, with a gradual phasing-in period. However, it proceeded at a much more rapid pace than expected and, by 1956, both the Canadian National Railway and the Canadian Pacific Railway had ceased to burn coal. This resulted in the disappearance of a 13 million ton per year coal market. (den Otter, A.A. "Railways and Alberta's Coal Problem, 1880-1960," *Western Canada Past and Present*. A.W. Rasporich, ed. Calgary: McClelland and Stewart West, 1975. pp. 96-97.)
7. PAC RG 81; Memo re. Brazeau Collieries, February 9, 1954.
8. Zupido D'Amico, interview.
9. Oltmann, Ruth. *The Valley of Rumours...The Kananaskis*. Exshaw: Ribbon Creek Publishing Company, 1985, p. 117.
10. PAA: 76-507; Memorandum – J. Boyd, President of Brazeau Collieries, to Deputy Provincial Treasurer, K.J. Hawkins, August 14, 1950.
11. Arthur "Mac" McMullen, interview. These buildings still are standing at the abandoned minesite; they have been declared a Provincial Historic Resource and are protected. The Nordegg Historical Society is a separate body, working under the umbrella of the Municipal District of Clearwater (based out of Rocky Mountain House), restoring these buildings with assistance from the Provincial Government.
12. McMullen, A. "The Brazeau Story," *Western Canada Coal Review*. October 1952; p. 7, 35.
13. McMullen, A. "Canada's Largest Briquetting Plant," p. 63.
14. McMullen, A. "The Brazeau Story," p. 8.
15. Ibid.
16. McMullen, A. "Cleaning Fine Coal in a Feldspar Jig at Brazeau," p. 1.
17. Ibid., pp. 1-2.
18. Ibid., pp. 3-4.
19. McMullen, A. "The Brazeau Story," p. 8.
20. Ibid., p. 8, 34.
21. McMullen, A. "Canada's Largest Briquetting Plant," pp. 63-64; McMullen, A. "The Brazeau Story," pp. 34-35.
22. McMullen, A. "The Brazeau Story," p. 7.
23. PAC, RG 81; Dominion Coal Board, "Memo: Brazeau Collieries," Feb. 9/54.
24. PAA; 76.507; 399. Records of the Official Receiver of Brazeau Collieries. Total reconstruction costs overran original expectations, with final costs exceeding two million dollars.
25. PAC, RG 81, Dominion Coal Board, Volume 41, File 14-2-1, (part 2) Memorandum: Canadian National Railway and Brazeau Briquettes, March 17, 1952.

26. PAC, RG 81, Dominion Coal Board, Volume 42, File 14-2-1 (part 3), Letter: J.J. Frawley, Executive Council of Alberta, to C.L. O'Brien, Dominion Coal Board, March 19, 1954.
27. PAC RG 81 Dominion Coal Board, Volume 42. Letter: CNR (purchasing and stores) to W.E. Uren, Dominion Coal Board, February 6, 1950.
28. PAC, RG 81, Dominion Coal Board, Letter: G.A. Vissac to W.E. Uren, April 10, 1952, Volume 42, File 14-2-1.
29. PAC RG 81, Dominion Coal Board, Volume 41, File 14-2-1 (Part 2), Mar 4/52 and March 26/52.
30. PAC, RG 81, Dominion Coal Board, Volume 42, File 14-2-1, (part 3). Letter: Dominion Coal Board to Mr. Gordon (President of the CNR), June 13, 1952.
31. PAC, RG 81, Dominion Coal Board, Volume 41, File 14-2-1 (part 2), Memorandum.
32. PAC, RG 81, Dominion Coal Board, Volume 42, File 14-2-1 (part 3), Letter: J.J. Frawley to C.L. O'Brien.
33. PAC, RG 81, Dominion Coal Board, Volume 42, File 14-2-1, Memo, February 9, 1954.
34. PAA; 76.507; 399.
35. PAA; 76.507; 399. Hart to Hawkins, August 24, 1954, and Hawkins to Hart, August 26, 1954. In 1955, when the Brazeau Collieries officially closed and went into receivership, the Alberta Industrial Corporation became the registered receiver. (Great Plains Research Consultants, *The Nordegg Site: A Feasibility Study – Final Report*, Part II, pg. 43, September 15, 1987.)

Through the Years

1. Seager, C.A. *A Protelariat in Wild Rose Country*. p. v, introduction.
2. Marasco, Mario. Interview.
3. Seager, C.A. *A Proletariat in Wild Rose Country*. pp. 172-173.
4. Guido Blasetti, interview.
5. Art McMullen Jr., interview; Rudolph (Red) Jahelka, interview.
6. PAC: MG30, A 19, Volumes I and II, M. Nordegg Ms, p. 329.
7. Willda (Stagg) Greenwood, interview. According to Mrs. Greenwood, who has done extensive research on the history of the Protestant Church in Nordegg, the first records which indicate the denomination of this church are dated 1918, when it was indicated that this was a Presbyterian Church.
8. Martha Fallow-McMullen, interview.
9. Arthur "Mac" McMullen Sr., interview.
10. Ibid.
11. *Rocky Mountaineer*, May 7, 1986.
12. Raymond Blasetti, interview.
13. Guy Blasetti, interview.
14. The Italian individuals and families involved in these various business ventures were Joe Blasetti, Mele/Marasco, Guido Blasetti/Poscente and D'Amico. Also involved in the business venture of the D'Amico family members were spouses Duncan, Morris, and Neilsen.
15. Rudolph Dibus, interview.

16. The *Rocky Mountaineer* reported in January, 1935, that there had been an axe murder of a long-time resident. Railway and road routes were watched closely, and trains were checked. A suspect was arrested in February.
17. Liddell, Ken. "Part Four: The Northwest Corner." *Alberta Revisited,* Toronto: Ryerson Press, 1960; *Calgary Herald,* Oct. 6, 1965.
18. Rudolph Dibus, interview; Rudolph (Red) Jahelka, interview.
19. A statement made in later years by an individual who was not himself a Nordegger sums up this feeling: "You can't mistake anyone from Nordegg because they're always talking about it." (Mario Marasco, quoting minister's comment at Jimmy Kidd's funeral).
20. T.E. Wilson scrapbook, commenting on having lived in Nordegg from 1914 to 1950.
21. Arthur "Mac" McMullen, interview.
22. Kidd, Fred. Interview.
23. Nordegg High School reunion, Nov. 10, 1990.
24. Mafalda Marasco, interviews, with reference to personal journal.
25. This building, throughout Nordegg's existence, was well used; it was the community centre, theatre, bazaar and tea centre, dance hall, badminton courts, concert hall, meeting hall, and anything else deemed necessary.
26. Albert Ciccato, interview. The Company would supply paint to those individuals wishing to paint their own dwellings.
27. Mafalda Marasco, interview.
28. Serena Duncan, interview.

Bright Spaces, Special Places

1. Zupido D'Amico – Nordegg Historic Heritage Interest Group correspondence.
2. Nordegg Ranger District History, Nordegg Ranger Station files, Nordegg, AB.
3. Nordegg files-Glenbow Library, Calgary, Museum Library Clipping File.
4. *Calgary Herald,* March 12, 1986.
5. *Calgary Herald,* March 15, 1984.
6. Galloway, John. Interview.
7. Reeves, Brian K.O. et al., pp. 23-24.
8. Vern VanSant was the father of well known Hollywood film director, Gus VanSant, who was nominated for a 1998 Oscar as Best Director for his 1997 film, *Good Will Hunting*.
9. Reeves, Brian K.O. et al., pp. 18-19.
10. Canada Cement Lafarge Limited, *Nordegg Mine, Alberta: Remedial Action by Canada Cement Lafarge, Ltd.,* September 25, 1985.
11. Great Plains Research Consultants, pp. v-ix.

Additional References

Alberta's Coal Industry, 1919. D.J. Bercuson, ed. and introduction. Calgary: Historical Society of Alberta, 1978.

Alberta. Department of Public Works. Annual Reports. 1914-1917.

Alberta. Mines Branch. Annual Reports, 1918-1956.

Alberta Resource Management Zones for the Eastern Slopes, Central Map Sheet, August, 1977. Nakoda Institute: Maps, Kootenay Plains (Clearwater) File.

Allan, J.A. and Rutherford, R.L. "Saunders Creek and Nordegg Coal Basins, Alberta, Canada," *Fourth Annual Report on the Mineral Resources of Alberta, 1922, Part 1.* Edmonton: King's Printer, 1923.

Analysis of Alberta Coal. Scientific and Industrial Research Council, 1925.

Anderson, F.W. *Canada's Worst Mine Disaster: Hillcrest 1914.* Frontier Book No. 18, 1969.

Anderson, Raoul R. "Alberta Stoney (Assiniboine) Origins and Adaptations: A Case for Reappraisal", *Ethnohistory,* Vol. 17, 1970. pp. 49-60.

Annual Reports of the Mines Division of the Department of Mines and Minerals of the Province of Alberta. Edmonton, King's Printer. For the years 1918, 1920, 1921, 1922, 1923, 1942, 1950, 1951.

Annual Reports of the Department of Public Works; Mines Branch. Edmonton: King's Printer, 1914-1917.

"A Storehouse of Fuels: Most Favoured Province Depends on Export," Prepared by Department of Economic Affairs, Government of Alberta. *Western Miner.* August, 1948. pp. 82-83.

Belliveau, Anne. "Nordegg Memories: Brazeau Collieries and Kananaskis Country," *Rocky Mountaineer.* Feb. 11, 1987.

Belliveau, Anne. "Nordegg Memories: Dreams and Reality", *Rocky Mountaineer.* Sept. 24, 1986.

Bercuson, David J. *Fools and Wise Men.* Toronto: McGraw-Hill Ryerson Ltd., 1978.

Bercuson, David Jay. "Labour Radicalism and the Western Industrial Frontier, 1887-1919", *Twentieth Century Canada.* D. Bercuson, et al. eds. Toronto: McGraw-Hill, 1986. pp. 136-160.

Bercuson, David J. *Opening the Canadian West.* Toronto: Grolier Limited, 1980.

"Bighorn Project Revs Up," *Red Deer Advocate,* Sept 6, 1969.

Blueprint – undated. Road, Glaciers, Rivers, and Tributaries, and all Cabin Construction From Western Side (B.C.) of Rocky Mountains to Horburg – West of Rocky Mountain House, South to Mount Hector, and North to Brazeau River. A. Belliveau collection.

Blueprint – undated. Plan of Nordegg Townsite; Buildings Erected, Available Sites for Four Roomed Cottages, Available Sites for Five Roomed Cottages, Hydrants and Stand Pipes Installed. A. Belliveau collection.

Brazeau Collieries Employee Records, 1920s. Glenbow Archives, Calgary.

"Brazeau Name Etched on West," *The Edmonton Journal*, Wednesday, April 29, 1964.

Brebner, J.B. *The Explorers of North America 1492-1806*. London: Adam and Charles Black, 1933.

Brewster, F.O. "Pat." *Weathered Wood*. Banff: Crag and Canyon, 1977.

Bryce, George. *The Remarkable History of the Hudson's Bay Company*. Toronto: William Briggs, 1900.

Burnet, Jean. "The Social and Historical Context of Ethnic Relations," *A Canadian Social Psychology of Ethnic Relations*. R.C. Gardner and R. Kalin, eds. Toronto: Methuen, 1981. pp. 17-35.

Burns, Robert J. *Inverarden: Retirement Home of Fur Trader John McDonald of Garth*. Ottawa: Parks Canada, 1979.

Burpee, Lawrence J. *Discovery of Canada*. Plainview, New York: Books for Libraries Press, 1976.

Burpee, Lawrence J. *Pathfinders of the Great Plains: A Chronicle of La Verendrye and his Sons*. Toronto: University of Toronto Press, 1964.

Burpee, Lawrence J. *Search for the Western Sea*. Toronto: Thomas Nelson and Sons, 1937.

Busfield, J.L. "The Mount Royal Tunnel," *The Journal of the Engineering Institute of Canada*. Montreal: Engineering Institute of Canada, vol ii, no. 4, April 1919. pp. 267-298.

Campbell, M.W. *McGillivray: Lord of the Northwest*. Toronto: Clarke, Irwin and Company, 1962.

Campbell, M.W. *Northwest to the Sea: a Biography of William McGillivray*. Toronto: Clarke, Irwin and Company, 1975.

Canadian Northern Timetable.

Canadian Pacific Air Lines, Aerial Surveys Division, Photographs for Gulf Oil. September 10, 1944. 9:21 a.m., height 14 4000 feet above sea level. Maps Department, University of Calgary. Call #83C 19 1944; Roll #D17, photos #67, #68, #69.

"Canadians Sight Hairy Creatures", reprinted from the *New York Times*. *Tales Tall and True*. Theresa M. Ford, managing editor. Edmonton: Alberta Education-Alberta Heritage Savings Trust Fund, 1979. pp. 179-180.

City Directories – Toronto, Ottawa, 1906-1936.

City of Calgary. Calgary: Clear-View Street Maps Limited, 1984-85. (map)

"Clearwater Forest", Rocky Mountain Forest Reserve, Department of Lands and Forests, 1973.

Dawe, Wellington. History of Red Deer. M.Ed. Thesis, published by Kiwanis Club of Red Deer.

Den Otter, A.A. "A Social History of the Alberta Coal Branch." M.A. Dissertation, University of Alberta, 1974.

Den Otter, A.A. "Social Life of a Mining Community: the Coal Branch." *Alberta Historical Review*. (Autumn, 1969) pp. 1-11.

Documents Relating to the NorthWest Company. W. Stewart Wallace, ed. Toronto: the Champlain Society, 1934.

Dugas, Abbe G. (translated from the French). *The Canadian West: Its Discovery; Its Development*. Montreal: Librairie Beauchemin, 1905.

Francis, Daniel. *Battle for the West: Fur Traders and the Birth of Western Canada*. Edmonton: Hurtig Publishers, 1982.

Francis, Daniel. "Traders and Indians," *The Prairie West*, R.Douglas Francis and Howard Palmer, eds. Edmonton: Pica Pica Press, 1985. pp. 58-70.

Friesen, John W. "John McDougall: The Spirit of a Pioneer", *Alberta Historical Review*. (Spring, 1974) pp. 9-17.

Fryer, Harold. *Alberta: The Pioneer Years*. Langley: Stagecoach Publishing Co, Ltd., 1977.

Gallatin, Hon. Albert. *A Synopsis of the Indian Tribes Within the United States East of the Rocky Mountains, and in the British and Russian Possessions in North America.* New York: AMS Press, 1836.

"Game Laws Apply to Treaty Indians," *Calgary Herald.* June 30, 1973.

Geological History of Western Canada. R.G. McCrossan and R.P. Glaister, eds. Calgary: Alberta Society of Petroleum Geologists, 1970.

Gerow, C. *The Story of Canada's Coal.* Ottawa: Mortimer Ltd., 1948.

Gilpin, John F. *Nordegg, Alberta: 1907-1955.* Alberta Culture, Historic Sites Service, September 1985.

Haig, Bruce. *James Hector: Explorer.* Calgary: Detselig Enterprises Ltd. 1983. pp. 51.

Haig, Bruce. *Paul Kane: Artist.* Calgary: Detselig Enterprises Ltd., 1984.

Hamilton, Jacques. *Mountainmen: Our Alberta Heritage Series 2.* Calgary: Calgary Power Ltd., 1975.

Harmon, D.W. *A Journal of Voyages and Travels in the Interior of North America.* Toronto: The Courier Press, 1911.

Harney, Robert F. "Men Without Women: Italian Immigrants in Canada, 1885-1930." *Twentieth Century Canada.* D. Bercuson, et al. eds. Toronto: McGraw-Hill, 1986. pp. 231-253.

Henry Alexander and Thompson, David. *The Manuscript Journals of Alexander Henry and of David Thompson 1799-1814.* vol ii Elliott Coues, ed. Minneapolis: Ross and Haines, Inc., 1965.

Heritage Resources: Nordegg, Alberta, prepared by Dr. B.K.O. Reeves for Lifeways of Canada, 1973.

Howard, Ebenezer. *Garden Cities of Tomorrow.* 1902. pp. 50-57, 142-143.

Hudson's Bay Company 1670-1763. Volumes I & II. E.E. Rich, general editor. London: Hudson's Bay Record Society, 1959.

Kennedy, Chief Dan (Ochankugahe). *Recollections of an Assiniboine Chief.* Toronto: New Press, 1972.

Kucera, Richard E. *Exploring the Columbia Icefields.* Canmore, Alberta: High Country Publishing, 1981.

Lake, David Wayne. "The Historical Geography of the Coal Branch." M.A. Dissertation, University of Alberta, 1967.

Lafitau, Father Joseph Francois. *Customs of the American Indians Compared With the Customs of Primitive Times, Vol. 1,* 2 vols. Trans. and ed. William N. Fenton and Elizabeth L. Moore. Toronto: The Champlain Society, 1974.

Larner, J.W. "The Kootenay Plains (Alberta) Land Question and Canadian Indian Policy, 1799-1947," Ph.D. Dissertation. West Virginia University: Morgantown, West Virginia, 1972.

Laurie, J.W. "Home on the Kootenay Plains," *Canadian Cattlemen.* August 1950. pp. 22-23.

Laurie, J.W. Personal Papers. Glenbow-Alberta Institute, Calgary, Alberta.

Les Bourgeois de la compagnie du Nord-Ouest - Original Journals, Narratives, Letters, etc. Relating to the Northwest Company. Vol.II. New York: Antiquarian Press Ltd., 1889-90.

Long, James Larpenteur. *The Assiniboines. From the Accounts of the Old Ones Told to First Boy (James Larpenteur Long).* Norman: University of Oklahoma Press, 1961.

Long, James Larpenteur. *Land of Nakoda: The Story of the Assiniboine Indians.* Helene, 1942.

Lowie, Robert H. *Indians of the Plains.* Lincoln: University of Nebraska Press, 1954.

Malloch, G.S. "Bighorn Coal Basin, Alberta", Canada Department of Mines: Geological Survey Branch. Ottawa: Government Printing Bureau, 1911. pp. 14-19.

Maps Alberta. Grand Cache location and information. (Telephone information)

Matheson, C.W. *A History of Rocky Mountain House*. Memorial Collection.

McGillivray, Duncan. *The Journal of Duncan M'Gillivray of the North West Company at Fort George on the Saskatchewan, 1794-95*. Toronto: Macmillan, 1929.

Metal Prices in the United States Through 1991. United States Bureau of Mines, 1993.

Montreal 1914. National Map Collection, Public Archives of Canada.

Morton, Arthur S. *History of the Canadian West to 1870-1871*. Toronto: Thomas Nelson and Sons Ltd., 1939.

Morton, A.S. *Under Western Skies*. Toronto: Thomas Nelson and Sons Limited, 1937.

Nakiska, Alberta's Olympic Legacy. Edmonton: Alberta Olympic Secretariat.

Nelson, Samuel J. *The Face of Time: A Geological History of Western Canada*. Calgary: Alberta Society of Petroleum Geologists, 1970.

Nix, J.E. *Mission Among the Buffalo: Labours of the Reverends George M. and John C. McDougall in the Canadian Northwest, 1860-1876*. Toronto: The Ryerson Press, 1960.

Nordegg – April 1914. 3 documents. Blueprint of original plan Nordegg – 1914; Blueprint of Nordegg – undated, but post-1944; Drawing of 1944 street plan showing first phase of construction. (1914 Blueprint and drawing on file with the Nordegg Historic Heritage Interest Group, Rocky Mountain House Museum, post-1944 Blueprint – A. Belliveau collection).

Nordegg, Martin. *The Fuel Problem of Canada*. Toronto: Macmillan, 1930.

Ondrack, Jack W. *The Sasquatch Phenomenon in Alberta*. Edmonton: University of Alberta. pp. 51-56.

Ossenberg, Dr. Nancy; Associate Professor of Anatomy, Queen's University, Kingston, Ontario. Personal Correspondence (October 6, 1986.)

PAA: Brazeau Collieries Limited. Department of Consumer and Corporate Affairs, Companies Branch, File 2100 1472.

PAA: Board of Managers' Minutes and Minutes of Congregational Meetings Nordegg. United Church Records Accession 746/3.

PAA: Department of Energy and Natural Resources, Mine Inspector's Reports. PA 171/1-2.

PAA: Report to the Lieutenant Governor in Council, Edmonton, Alberta; Pursuant to the Public Inquiries Act, Chapter 26, Revised Statutes of Alberta; Inquiry into the cause of a disaster at Brazeau Collieries Number 3 Mine, October 31, 1941. Commissioner: A.F. Ewing. 1942. Accession 86.3/1.

PAC: RG30, V.1156, Minutes of Canadian Northern Railway Shareholders Meeting, Feb. 10, 1911.

PAC: RG30, Canadian Northern Railway Branch Lines.

PAC: RG30, file 15321, #122307, #127520, #129551, correspondence between Secretary-Treasurer, Stettler, and Board of Railway Commissioners.

PAC: RG30, Records of Canadian National Railways.

PAC: RG46, file 15321, #122307, #127520, #129551, correspondence between Secretary Treasurer of Stettler and Board of Railway Commissioners, Ottawa.

PAC: RG46, Synopsis of correspondence between Secretary Treasurer of Stettler and Board of Railway Commissioners, Ottawa. Aug.6, 1910, to October 17, 1910.

PAC: RG81, Dominion Coal Board. Volume 41. Letter: CNR Fuel Department to Urem, Dominion Coal Board, Oct.27, 1949.

PAC: RG81, Dominion Coal Board. Volume 42. Letter: CNR Purchasing Agent to Dominion Coal Board, April 2, 1952.

PAC: C-870, 148810-148811; PAC: C-879, 158631-2; PAC: C880, 159626-159629, Laurier Papers.

PAC: C-2269, 90054-90058; PAC: C-3674, 168176-7, letters from Martin Nordegg to Mackenzie King.

PAC: C-3683, 172593-172595, letter from Martin Nordegg to Mackenzie King.

PAC: MG27III C4, V.2, 1938. letters to Mrs. Macphail from Martin Nordegg.

PAC: MG30, A 19, 20cm. Martin Nordegg correspondence and clippings.

Pyszczyk, Dr. Heinz. "Little Fort on 'Des Prairie', Fort la Jonquiere: Fact or Fiction?", Unpublished paper, 1995.

Regehr, T.D. "William Mackenzie, Donald Mann, and the Larger Canada," *Western Canada Past and Present*. A.W. Rasporich, ed. Calgary: McClelland and Stewart West, 1975. pp. 69-83.

Regehr, T.D. "Western Canada and the Burden of National Transportation Policies", *The Prairie West*. D. Francis and H. Palmer, eds. Edmonton: Pica Pica Press, 1985. pp. 257-276.

Regehr, T.D. *Canadian Northern Railway: Agent of National Growth, 1896-1911*. Ph.D. Dissertation, University of Alberta, 1967.

Regehr, T.D. "The Canadian Northern Railway: The West's Own Product," *Canadian Historical Review*. LI June 1970.

Reeves, B.K.O. "Prehistoric Archaeological Research on the Eastern Slopes of the Canadian Rocky Mountains 1967-1971," Reprinted from: *Canadian Archaeological Association Bulletin 6*. 1974.

Reeves, Brian O.K. *Archaeological Resource Inventory, Department of Highways and Transportation, Proposed Construction Projects*. Contract Report (University of Calgary) for the National Museum of Man, Archaeological Survey of Canada.

Reeves, Brian K.O. "The Rocky Mountain Eastern Slopes: Problems and Considerations," *Alberta Archaeology: Prospect and Retrospect*. T.A. Moore, ed. Lethbridge: Archaeological Society of Alberta, 1981. pp. 31-38.

Report of the Royal Commission on the Coal Mining Industry in the Province of Alberta – 1907. Edmonton: Government Printer, 1908.

Report of the Royal Commission on Coal – 1946. Chairman: Mr. Justice W.F. Carroll. Ottawa: King's Printer, 1947.

Rocky Mountain House National Historic Park Library. File EE Paper 2, File EE Paper 3, File EE Paper 6, File EE Paper 9.

Ross, Toni. *Oh! The Coal Branch*. Calgary: Friesen Printers, 1974.

Rutter, N.W. "Late Pleistocene Ice Limits in Western Canada," *Alberta Archaeology: Prospect and Retrospect*. T.A. Moore, ed. Lethbridge: The Archaeological Society of Alberta, 1981. pp. 21-30.

Saint Pierre, Jacques Repentigny Legardeur de. *Memoir or Summary Journal of the Expedition of Jacques Repentigny Legardeur de Saint Pierre, Knight of the Royal and Military Order of Saint Louis, Captain of a Company of the Troops detached from the Marine in Canada, Charged with the Discovery of the Western Sea*. Archives, Series B, Vol. 26, pp. 1, clix-clxxi.

Seager, C.A. "Socialists and Workers: The Western Canadian Coal Miners, 1900-1921," *Labour/Le Travail*, 16 (Fall 1985). pp. 23-59.

Shaffer, Marvin and Associates. *Socio-Economic Impacts of the Western Canadian Coal Industry*. Calgary: Canada West Foundation, 1980.

Smith, G. Hubert. *The Explorations of the La Verendryes in the Northern Plains 1738-43*. W.R. Wood, ed. Lincoln: University of Nebraska Press, 1980.

Spry, Irene. *The Palliser Expedition*. Toronto: The Macmillan Company of Canada, 1963.

Stansfield, E. and Genge, C.A. "Alberta Coals and Automatic Domestic Stokers," Research Council of Alberta; Report Number 46. Edmonton: King's Printer, 1945.

Stansfield, E., Hollies, R.T., and Campbell, W.P. "Analysis of Alberta Coal," Scientific and Industrial Research Council; Report # 14. Edmonton: King's Printer, 1925.

Stansfield, E. and Lang, W.A. "Coals of Alberta; Their Occurrence, Analysis, and Utilization," Report Number 35: Research Council of Alberta. Edmonton: King's Printer, 1944.

Stelter, G.A. and Artibise, Alan F.J. "Canadian Resource Towns in Historical Perspective," *Plan Canada*. (March 1978) pp. 46-59.

Stenson, Fred. *Rocky Mountain House National Historic Park*. Toronto: New Canada Publications, 1985.

Stoney Country Stoney Cultural Education Program. Morley, Alberta. August, September, December issues, 1973.

Street Map of Montreal and Vicinity. Whitby, Ontario: Peter Heiler. (map)

Tales From the Canadian Rockies. Brian Patton, ed. Edmonton: Hurtig Publishers, 1984.

This is Kananaskis Country. Government of Alberta: Heritage Fund.

Trace, H.D. *An Examination of Some Factors Associated With the Decline of the Coal Industry in Alberta*. University of Alberta, 1958, unpublished.

Uhlenbeck, C.C. and Van Gulik, R.H. *An English-Blackfoot Vocabulary*. New York: AMS Press, 1979.

VanKirk Sylvia. "Fur Trade Social History: Some Recent Trends," *The Prairie West* eds. R.Douglas Francis and Howard Palmer. Edmonton: Pica Pica Press, 1985. pp. 71-82.

V. VanSant estate, Calgary. Brazeau Collieries files and photographs of Nordegg and Kananaskis fields, and Nordegg town.

Vissac, Gustave A. Copies of Patented Drawings for Coal Cleaning and Preparation Machinery. Dates of Certification of Drawings: March 14, 1934; April 7, 1934; April 9, 1937.

Wilson, Dick, Information Representative, Calgary Power, February 2, 1972. Personal Correspondence.

Wilson, Thomas E. (as told to W.E. Round.) *Trail Blazer of the Canadian Rockies*. Historical Paper No.3. Hugh Dempsey, ed. Calgary: Glenbow-Alberta Institute, 1972.

Wood, Kerry. *The Map Maker: The Story of David Thompson*. Toronto: Macmillan 1957.

Workmen's Compensation Board of the Province of Alberta For the Year Ending 31st December, 1927. Tenth Annual Report. Edmonton: King's Printer, 1928.

And all photos, information packages, files, and materials in the collection of: Nordegg Historical Society (formerly the Nordegg Historic Heritage Interest Group; Museum and Archives.

Additional Interviews

Abraham, Charlie; Margaret (Shanks) Armour; Baker, Joe; Beaver, Pete; Bechtold, Suzanne; Blasetti, Julia; Colosimo, Jim, Sr.; Colosimo, Jim, Jr.; Duncan, Robert; Foltinek, Bryan; Galloway, John; Grosso, Clayton; Hawkins, Matt; Humphries, J.T.; Janigo, Olga; Janigo, Nita; Johnson, Steve; Kupfer, Walter; Letcher, Bob, and Letcher, Nellie; Loblaw, Ted; Lucarelli, Arturo; Mazza, Brian; McKenzie, Ed; McKenzie, Millie; Morley, Mrs. Sam (Millie); Morris, Maggie and Alfred; Murphy, Peter; Park, J.; Slaymaker, Martha.

Audio Tapes

Banff National Park: Tape I. Comprehensive Communications Incorporated. Scarsdale, N.Y.: Audio Tape Tours Division, 1969.

Jasper National Park: Tape II. Comprehensive Communications Incorporated. Scarsdale, N.Y.: Audio Tape Tours Division, 1969.

Glenbow Archives: M1124-6. Sturrock, Bernie. (son of Nordegg's last General Manager) Oral Interview: Audio Tape.

PAA: 75.417. Basso, Pietro, with Basso, Barbara. (Ex-Nordegg residents). "Coal Mining at Nordegg, 1927-1947." Taped interview; interviewer: S. Ingram.

Index

Selected People, Companies and Towns

Abraham, Charlie: 195
Abraham, John: 32
Abraham, Silas: 35-36, 195, 211
Acton House: 53
Alberta Central Railway Company: 85-86
Alberta Coal Company: 192
Alexo (town): 49, 130, 193, 221
Alix (town): 87
Astor, John Jacob: 59-60, 62
Baird and Mackenzie: vii, 105, 195, 219
Baker, Joe: 198
Banff (town): 16, 35, 72, 84, 137
Barlow, Alfred E.: 72, 214
Barnes, E.C.: 35-36, 40-41, 43, 57, 206, 211
Beament, George E.: 126
Bearspaw band: 28
Beaver, Chief Morley: 38, 42
Beveridge, Josephine: 138
Bighorn Dam: 15, 21, 27, 41-43, 49, 203, 206, 211
Bighorn Reserve: 40, 43, 204
Bighorn Trading Company: vii, 37, 39, 107, 109, 114, 178-179, 182-183, 188-189
Bighorn Transport: 183-184
Blackfalds (town): 87
Blackfoot: 28-29, 50, 55, 58, 216
Blasetti, Guido: viii, x, 183, 225
Blood (Indians): 28
Blue Diamond Coal Company: 110
Boomer, Dr. E.H.: 158
Boyd, John: 161, 167
Brazeau, Joseph Edward: 63, 67
Brazeau Collieries: v, vii-viii, x-xi, 20, 24, 37-38, 56, 80-87, 89-90, 92-95, 97, 99, 101-105, 107-108, 110-111, 113-123, 125, 131, 137, 141, 143-156, 160-172, 174-178, 183-185, 188-189, 191-192, 194-196, 198, 215-216, 219-220, 225
Brewster and Moore: 84, 95, 97

Brewster, George: 24, 40, 95, 97
Brule (town): 77, 110, 150
Buck, Tim: 149
Buexenstein, Georg: 71-72, 75, 82, 94, 113, 217
Bury, Sir George: 86
Butler, Sir William Francis: 33, 67-68
Calf Child (Hector Crawler): 30
Calgary: 74, 84-86, 102, 110, 114, 137, 162-163, 170, 183, 192, 196, 199
Canada Cement (Lafarge): 191, 195-197
Canadian Bank of Commerce: 81, 115, 119, 150, 220
Canadian National Railways Corp.: 120, 123, 151-152, 154, 167, 169, 176-177, 191, 198-220, 224
Canadian Northern Railway: 77, 79, 83, 86, 89, 100, 108, 117, 119-120, 141
Canadian Northern Western Railway: vii, 81, 84-87, 120, 183, 191, 198
Canadian Pacific Railway: 31, 35, 69, 76-77, 79, 81, 85-86, 93, 123, 166, 224
Canmore (town): 16
Caroline (town): 85, 194
China, John: 167
Chiniki band: 28
Cline River Development Corp.: 193
Coal Branch: 16, 65, 75, 81, 84, 91, 94, 115, 129, 149, 176, 194
Cohn, Martin (see Nordegg, Martin)
Colosimo, Jim: 195
Communist Party: 110, 149-150
Consolidated Coal: 195-196
Constable, Jack: 108, 114
Cree: 28, 40, 42, 47, 54-55
Crowsnest Pass: 16-17, 72, 76, 113, 115, 129, 151
D'Amico, Zupido: x, 167-168, 184, 189
Dahms, Donna: 196
David Thompson Cavalcade: 137, 206

David Thompson Highway: 17, 22-23, 25, 41, 57, 105, 135, 137, 179, 192-194, 199, 201, 206-207, 209, 222
Dawson, G.M.: 82
Deutsches Kanada Syndikat: 72, 75, 82, 119, 217
Dittrich, Father Tony: x, 19, 181-182
Dominion Bridge Company: 170
Dowling, Donaldson Bogart: 36, 72-76, 93, 204, 215, 217
Drumheller (town): 16, 86, 110, 165
Duncan, Helen: 109
East Bush Camp: 130, 141-142
Eckville (town): 87
Edmonton: 16-17, 53, 57, 64-65, 76-77, 79, 82, 84-86, 102, 110, 115, 149, 186
Edson (town): 65, 84
Ewing, A.F.: 156, 158-160
Falt, Harold: 166
Farmer's Union of Alberta: 191
Fidler, Peter: 28
Fish Creek Excavating: 193
Five Mile Bridge: 17, 87, 201
Fort LaJonquiere: 46-47, 49-50
Fraser, Norman: 113-114
Frontier Lodge: 192, 204
Galloway, John: 197
Geographic Board of Canada: 48, 212
Geological Survey of Canada: 36, 72-73, 75-76, 82, 90, 93, 217
German Development Company Ltd.: 72-73, 75-77, 81-84, 93-94, 117, 119-123, 125, 151, 214, 217
Gheur, Ernest: 80, 95, 102-103, 109, 113-114, 141, 144
Goldeye Centre: 191-192, 204
Goodstoney, Chief Jacob: 33
Grand Cache (town): 91
Grand Trunk Railway: 77, 81, 84, 120
Grosso, Clayton: 195
Grouch Camp: 25, 90, 135, 142-143, 192
Hanna, D.B.: 120, 220
Haven brothers: 18
Haydon, Andrew: 72, 75, 117-120, 122-123, 214
Hector, Dr. James: 15, 64-65, 67
Hencley, Steve: 137-138
Henday, Anthony: 46, 50, 216
Henry, Alexander (the Younger): 15, 24, 27-28, 48, 59-62, 97
Henry, William: 60
Hill, Jim: 69
Hinton (town): 77

Hobbema Reserve: 40
Home Oil (Brazeau) Ltd.: 87
Horburg (town): 85
Hower, Charles: 80, 89-93
Howse, Joseph: 57
Hudson's Bay Company: 18, 31, 46, 48-49, 53, 55, 57, 63-65, 68, 70, 85, 212, 216, 219
Hughes, James: 54-55, 69
Hughes, Sam: 117
Innisfail (town0: 35, 85
Ives, W.C.: 161
Jasper (town): 16, 65, 75, 77, 79, 81, 84, 115, 126, 137, 182
Johnson, Bella: 18
Kadonna Ranch: 35-36, 40-41, 43, 57, 206, 211
Kananaskis Exploration and Development Co.: 165, 168
Kananaskis (mine): x, 75, 81, 83, 92-93, 121, 123-124, 164-169, 217
Kane, Paul: 30
Kemp, Rev. E.W.: 156
Kidd, Fred: x, 74, 215
Kidd, Stuart: x, 37, 73-74, 83, 92, 97, 108, 113-114, 120, 122, 126, 128, 189, 215
Killick, Harold: 182, 193
King, William Lyon Mackenzie: 122
Kootenae House: 57
Kostuck, Dr. Martha: 193
Kovach (town): 165, 168
Kovach, Joe: 165
Krause, George: 184
Ktunaxa: 20, 27-28, 43, 53-55, 209
Kutenais (see Ktunaxa)
Lacombe (town): 70, 87, 206
Lacombe, Father: 30
Laurier, Sir Wilfred: 71-73, 76
LaVerendrye, Jean Baptiste de: 46, 48
LaVerendrye, Pierre Gaultier de Varennes et de: 46-49
Lazard Brothers and Co.: 75, 77, 81, 83, 89, 119, 122, 125
Leduc (town): 167
Leslieville (town): 85, 87
Lethbridge: 16
Lewis and Clark: 55
L'Heureux, Guy: 42
Lost Lemon Gold Mine: 17
Lucarelli, Arturo: 57
MacDonald, Sir John A.: 68

Mackenzie, William: v, 77, 79, 81-84, 86, 94-95, 100, 104, 108, 113, 117-120, 141, 150, 169, 216
MacKenzie, Rev. Father Neil: 156, 182
Mah-Min, Chief: 30
Mann, Donald: v, 77, 79, 81-84, 86, 95, 100, 104, 113, 117, 119-120, 141, 150
Mannix Construction Company: 163, 192
Marcelle, Sonia (Nordegg): 125-126
McAndrew, John: 158
McDonald, Finan: 56
McDonald, John (of Garth): 53-55
McDonald, Norman: 107, 219
McDougall, George: 31-32
McDougall, John: 31-32, 35-37, 97
McEvoy, James: 76-77, 214
McGillivray, Duncan: 54
McGiverin, Harold B.: 72, 214
McKenzie, Alan: vii, 105, 195, 219
McKenzie, Ed: x, 194, 217
McKenzie, Gilbert: vii, 104, 114, 142, 194, 219
McKenzie, Tom: 95, 195, 217, 219
McKenzie, Vic: 195
McMullen, Arthur "Mac": iii, vii, 115, 141-142, 152, 161, 163, 170, 172, 182, 218
McMullen, Martha (Fallow): iii, vii, 107, 181, 219
Millar, Andrew: 113, 115, 161
Moberly, Walter: 68
Moore, Doug: 141
Morin Brothers: 186
Morley (reserve): 31-37, 40, 73-75, 83, 166
Morley, Dennis: x, 197
Mount Allan: 75, 81, 121, 164-165, 168-169
Mount Royal (suburb of Montreal): x, 100-101, 218
Murphy, Charles: 75
Niverville, Joseph-Claude Boucher Chevalier de: 45, 47
Nordegg (town): v, vii-xi, xiii-xiv, 16, 18-20, 22-25, 28, 33, 37-40, 42-43, 54-58, 64, 81-82, 85, 87, 90, 94-95, 97, 99-102, 104-106, 108-111, 113, 115-118, 120-122, 124-125, 127-133, 135-136, 138-139, 142-143, 145-146, 148-150, 153, 156, 159, 163, 165-170, 174, 178-189, 191, 193-196, 198-202, 204, 213, 216-222, 225-226
Nordegg Dramatic Society: 129
Nordegg Historical Society: ix, x, 109, 124, 145, 162, 186, 196-198, 202-203, 224,
Nordegg Historic Heritage Interest Group (see Nordegg Historical Society)
Nordegg Italian Society: 128
Nordegg Literary and Athletic Association: 132-134, 137
Nordegg Recreation Association: 191, 200, 221
Nordegg Slavic Society: 129
Nordegg, Berthe-Marie: 71, 118-119, 125
Nordegg, Marcelle: 71, 118-119, 122, 125-126
Nordegg, Martin (Cohn): v, vii, ix, xi, 36-37, 70-77, 79, 81-84, 86, 89-96, 99-101, 104-111, 113-123, 125-127, 141, 143, 150-151, 159, 162, 169, 181, 194, 196, 204, 214-220
Northwest Company: 48, 53-55, 59, 61-63, 212-213
North West Mounted Police: 31, 68
Nylund, Arnold: 133
Nylund, Gary: 133
O'Chiese band: 40
Odlum, Nelson: 163
Ojibwa: 40
Oliver, Frank: 73, 76, 103
Pacific Fur Company: 59, 61-62, 213
Palliser Expedition: 15, 33, 63-65, 68-69
Peigans: 28, 53, 55, 57, 60, 62
Peterson, Harley: 42
Peterson, Stan: 42
Pipestone Developments: 199
Potonie, Prof.: 75
Prohibition: 107, 109, 219
Red Deer: xiii, 18, 41, 65, 85, 87, 95, 97, 102, 105, 111, 113-115, 161, 183, 194, 200, 206
Ribbon Creek (town): 165-166, 168-169
Richardson, Jock: 97
Riverside Ironworks: viii, 170, 176, 178
Roan, Lazarus: 42
Roberts and Schaefer: 103, 108, 117, 143
Robbie Burns Night: 129
Rocky Mountain Collieries: 82-83, 86, 121, 169
Rocky Mountain House (fort & town): ix, 15, 17-19, 22-23, 30, 33, 40, 42-43, 48-50, 53-55, 57, 59-60, 63-65, 67, 69-70, 84-85, 87, 89, 95, 104, 109, 111, 113, 120, 129, 132-133, 135-136, 151, 180, 182-183, 185, 191, 193, 195, 209, 212, 216, 218, 224
Rogers, Major: 69
Ross, Ernie: 136-137
Rowbotham, Alan: 85
Royal Canadian Mounted Police: 184
Rundle, Rev. Robert: 30
Russell, Thomas: 79, 81

Sackrider: 19
Saint Pierre, Jacques Repentigny Legardeur de: 45, 47-50
Sarcee: 28
Saunders (town): 49, 130, 136, 193, 221
Seebe (town): 166, 168,
Shanks, Dave: 115, 160, 167-168
Shanks, Johnny: 115, 119, 122, 127, 129, 141-142, 152, 159-163, 182, 218, 220
Shanks, Kate: 129
Shaw, Brian: 132, 221
Sifton, Clifford: 79
Sioux: 46
Slavic Society: x
Smallboy, Chief: 40, 42
Snow, Chief John: 43
Socialists: 149
Southesk, Earl of: 65-67
Sports Days: 38, 133-134, 137, 195, 200, 221
Stauffer (town): 85
Stettler (town): 87
Stevens, Fred: 69
Stevenson, William: 113, 141
Stewart, Duncan: vii, 114
Stewart, Jimmy: 115, 158-160
Stewart, Mary: 181
Stoneys: x, 19, 20, 23-25, 27-43, 50, 53, 67, 69, 73, 89, 97, 133-134, 166, 179-180, 193, 195, 204, 206
Sturrock, Archie: 115, 159, 163, 176
Sunchild band: 40
Sundre (town): 18, 74, 194
Sylvan Lake (town): 87
Talbot, Onesiphore-Ernest: 71-72
Tchatka, Chief: 30
Thompson, Colin: 18
Thompson, David: 20, 23, 25, 28, 40, 48, 53-57, 59-62, 68-69, 137, 203, 212-213
Tollerton (town): 84
TransAlta Utilities (Calgary Power): 15, 41-42, 111, 152, 165, 193, 211
Treaty 6: 33
Treaty 7: 32-35, 40, 69
Treaty 8: 33
United Mine Workers of America: 132, 145, 149, 156-157
VanSant, Vern: 196, 226
Vaughan, Charles: 123
Vissac, Gustave: 151-152, 163-164, 171-173, 176, 223
Washburn, Stanley: 69-70, 214

Wassermann, Eugene de: 83
Wayne (town): 110
Weatherbee, Cory: 113, 220
Wesley band (Stoneys): xiv, 28, 34, 37, 39, 40-41, 43, 179
Wesley, Peter: 33-35, 38, 195, 210
West Bush Camp: 130, 141-142
Whitehall Mining: 196
Whitehaven Collieries: viii, 115, 141
Wilson, Tom: 35-36, 38, 40-41, 69, 97, 206, 211
Wolf Creek: 84

PRINTED AND BOUND
IN BOUCHERVILLE, QUÉBEC, CANADA
BY MARC VEILLEUX IMPRIMEUR INC.
IN MARCH, 1999